Rethinking Islam and Human Rights

RELIGION AND GLOBAL POLITICS

Series Editor
John L. Esposito
University Professor and Director
Prince Alwaleed Bin Talal Center for Muslim-Christian Understanding
Georgetown University

ISLAMIC LEVIATHAN
Islam and the Making of State Power
Seyyed Vali Reza Nasr

RACHID GHANNOUCHI
A Democrat Within Islamism
Azzam S. Tamimi

BALKAN IDOLS
Religion and Nationalism in Yugoslav States
Vjekoslav Perica

ISLAMIC POLITICAL IDENTITY IN TURKEY
M. Hakan Yavuz

RELIGION AND POLITICS IN POST-COMMUNIST ROMANIA
Lavinia Stan and Lucian Turcescu

PIETY AND POLITICS
Islamism in Contemporary Malaysia
Joseph Chinyong Liow

TERROR IN THE LAND OF THE HOLY SPIRIT
Guatemala under General Efrain Rios Montt, 1982–1983
Virginia Garrard-Burnett

IN THE HOUSE OF WAR
Dutch Islam Observed
Sam Cherribi

BEING YOUNG AND MUSLIM
New Cultural Politics in the Global South and North
Asef Bayat and Linda Herrera

CHURCH, STATE, AND DEMOCRACY IN EXPANDING EUROPE
Lavinia Stan and Lucian Turcescu

THE HEADSCARF CONTROVERSY
Secularism and Freedom of Religion
Hilal Elver

THE HOUSE OF SERVICE
The Gülen Movement and Islam's Third Way
David Tittensor

ANSWERING THE CALL
Popular Islamic Activism in Sadat's Egypt
Abdullah Al-Arian

MAPPING THE LEGAL BOUNDARIES OF BELONGING
Religion and Multiculturalism from Israel to Canada
Edited by René Provost

RELIGIOUS SECULARITY
A Theological Challenge to the Islamic State
Naser Ghobadzadeh

THE MIDDLE PATH OF MODERATION IN ISLAM
The Qur'ānic Principle of Wasaṭiyyah
Mohammad Hashim Kamali

ONE ISLAM, MANY MUSLIM WORLDS
Spirituality, Identity, and Resistance Across Islamic Lands
Raymond William Baker

CONTAINING BALKAN NATIONALISM
Imperial Russia and Ottoman Christians (1856–1914)
Denis Vovchenko

INSIDE THE MUSLIM BROTHERHOOD
Religion, Identity, and Politics
Khalil al-Anani

POLITICIZING ISLAM
The Islamic Revival in France and India
Z. Fareen Parvez

SOVIET AND MUSLIM
The Institutionalization of Islam in Central Asia
Eren Tasar

ISLAM IN MALAYISA
An Entwined History
Khairudin Aljunied

SALAFISM GOES GLOBAL
From the Gulf to the French Banlieues
Mohamed-Ali Adraoui

UNDER THE BANNER OF ISLAM
Turks, Kurds, and the Limits of Religious Unity
Gülay Türkmen

JIHADISM IN EUROPE
European Youth and the New Caliphate
Farhad Khosrokhavar

ISLAM AND NATIONHOOD IN MODERN GREECE, 1821–1940
Stefanos Katsikas

WAHHABISM AND THE WORLD
Understanding Saudi Arabia's Global Influence on Islam
Peter Mandaville

UMMAH YET PROLETARIAT
Islam, Marxism, and the Making of the Indonesian Republic
Lin Hongxuan

RETHINKING ISLAM AND HUMAN RIGHTS
Practice and Knowledge Production in the Case of Hizmet
Ozcan Keles

Rethinking Islam and Human Rights

Practice and Knowledge Production in the Case of Hizmet

OZCAN KELES

OXFORD
UNIVERSITY PRESS

Oxford University Press is a department of the University of Oxford. It furthers
the University's objective of excellence in research, scholarship, and education
by publishing worldwide. Oxford is a registered trade mark of Oxford University
Press in the UK and certain other countries.

Published in the United States of America by Oxford University Press
198 Madison Avenue, New York, NY 10016, United States of America.

© Oxford University Press 2023

All rights reserved. No part of this publication may be reproduced, stored in
a retrieval system, or transmitted, in any form or by any means, without the
prior permission in writing of Oxford University Press, or as expressly permitted
by law, by license, or under terms agreed with the appropriate reproduction
rights organization. Inquiries concerning reproduction outside the scope of the
above should be sent to the Rights Department, Oxford University Press, at the
address above.

You must not circulate this work in any other form
and you must impose this same condition on any acquirer.

Library of Congress Cataloging-in-Publication Data
Names: Keleş, Özcan, author.
Title: Rethinking Islam and human rights : practice and
knowledge production in the case of hizmet / Ozcan Keles.
Description: 1. | New York : Oxford University Press, 2023. |
Series: Religion and global politics series |
Includes bibliographical references and index.
Identifiers: LCCN 2023004884 (print) | LCCN 2023004885 (ebook) |
ISBN 9780197662489 (hardback) | ISBN 9780197662502 (epub)
Subjects: LCSH: Human rights—Religious aspects—Islam. |
Civil rights—Religious aspects—Islam. | Civil rights (Islamic law)
Classification: LCC BP173.44.K45 2023 (print) | LCC BP173.44 (ebook) |
DDC 297.2/723—dc23/eng/20230206
LC record available at https://lccn.loc.gov/2023004884
LC ebook record available at https://lccn.loc.gov/2023004885

DOI: 10.1093/oso/9780197662489.001.0001

Printed by Integrated Books International, United States of America

For my boys . . .

Contents

Foreword ix
Acknowledgements xiii

    Introduction: Rethinking Islam and Human Rights   1

1. Problematising the Islamic Responses to Human Rights: Turning to Practice   25

2. Operationalising a Practice Approach: Exploring the Epistemic Outcomes of Practice   64

3. Apostasy in Islam: From 'Off with His Head' to Humanising the Apostate   99

4. Women in Islam: From *Unseen Consumer* to *Active Producer*   135

5. Conclusion: The Symbiotic Interplay between the Formalised and the Experiential   183

Bibliography 199
Index 229

Foreword

John L. Esposito

Since the late nineteenth century, Islamic reformers have grappled with the relationship of Islam to the changing realities of modern life. A major challenge for many Muslim reformers has been the importance of linking, of showing continuity, between proposed changes and long-held Islamic beliefs and traditions. Therefore, the 'how' has been as important as the 'what'; the process of change (methodology) is often as important as the actual reforms themselves.

The fact that Islamic tradition, law, and theology are based on the Qur'an and Prophetic traditions led more conservative and traditionalist reformers to embrace a methodology that sacralises tradition or classical/medieval Islam as authoritative sources that cannot be substantially questioned or altered. In contrast, many recent reformers emphasise rereading the scriptural sources themselves with a new mind, influenced by the new historical, social, political, and scientific environment in which they live.

In contrast to the above, Ozcan Keles's *Rethinking Islam and Human Rights* provides us with a third alternative: it focuses on the unstated organic epistemic outcomes (i.e., changes in relation to Islamic law) to ensue from social *practice* rather than on the claims and theoretical reforms of any one *reformer* (i.e., person). To that end, Keles examines the Hizmet movement (also known as the Gülen movement after its founder M. Fethullah Gülen), which, beginning in the late 1960s, represents a Turkish cosmopolitan transnational Islamic movement that not only has operated in Turkey but has also expanded to over 160 countries with members and volunteers from many ethnic backgrounds. While Keles describes Hizmet within these pages as 'one of the most dynamic transnational Islamic movements in the world today' (Keles 2023, 5) I would enhance and expand Hizmet's importance and significance by describing it as *the* most dynamic transnational Islamic educational and cultural movements in the world today.

Using his distinctive methodological approach, Keles systematically traces and analyses the causal relationship between Hizmet's practices and its production of Islamic knowledge on human rights that represents and explains the changing of both Muslim sensibilities (lived religion) as well as scriptural interpretations (formalised Islam), through the interplay between the two, on two of the most intransigent issues in the context of Islam and human rights—apostasy and women's rights. Weaving together theoretical insights from a wide range of disciplines, Keles explains how and why knowledge arises from the *doing*-body (of the movement) to the *thinking*-mind (of any one practitioner) as opposed to vice versa, in the context of substantive Islamic knowledge.

Keles maintains that changes in Hizmet's approach to the premodern Islamic doctrine on apostasy and issues dealing with women's rights and the role of women within Hizmet and society at large, including the wearing of the headscarf, resulted over time not so much from religious counsel (in fact, he shows how, at times, these practice-based changes ensued in spite of Gülen's counsel to the contrary), but from the developments that ensued from Hizmet's practices. These developments produced, among other things, sustained social interaction with the other and cognitive dissonance, which in turn led to changes in attitude, judgements, and eventually an explicit reinterpretation of the respective Islamic teachings, doctrines, and scripture to justify the said changes. This is the heart of Keles's distinctive contribution.

While the issues he discusses are necessarily complex, Keles uses a range of diagrams to reflect the interplay within and between Hizmet's *doings* and *sayings* to illustrate and synthesise his points regarding how these changes came about. Keles's timeline in relation to Hizmet and the evolution of women's rights (Figure 4.1) is indeed astonishing in its ability to map development and reform on that particular front.

Keles's presentation of Hizmet's journey from a strong traditionalist to a more progressive position is nuanced, accurate, and where needed critical. He is especially strong in his discussion of the extent to which Gülen was very conservative in his teachings and life regarding gender issues and the extent to which his and Hizmet's new practice-led experiences in the globalisation of their schools, universities, and other activities influenced his considerable departure from ingrained traditions. Thus, as Keles notes, the effort to make a difference in other people's lives ultimately produced unanticipated changes among Hizmet's practitioners in and through their participation in Hizmet at not just the cultural level in terms of their attitude towards, for example, Western dress, music, or the shaking of hands between men and women but also on issues pertaining to 'democracy, secularism, pluralism, human rights, apostasy from Islam, women's rights, gender equality, the wearing of the headscarf.' (Keles 2023, 18).

Ozcan Keles has produced a major study, drawing on a range of theories and disciplines, to explain how Fethullah Gülen and Hizmet's religious worldview changed as well as to demonstrate how and why Hizmet evolved from a conservative Turkish movement to a globalised progressive movement spanning some 160 countries in the context of his focus on the production of Islamic knowledge on human rights. He demonstrates an impressive command of the major scholars and publications dealing with premodern and modern Islam (history, society, and law) and its impact on social and political change in general. His focus on the issues of apostasy and women in traditional societies and premodern Islamic law and the evolution in Hizmet's development and Gülen's thought on women's status, education, and rights is masterful.

Acknowledgements

If knowledge ensues through social practice, then this book owes a gratitude to the carriers of that practice. Consequently, I'd like to begin by acknowledging the nameless participants of Hizmet's practices in education, dialogue, and women's activities and those that have extended these practices to other parts of the world by partaking in another, *hicret* (migration)—that is, those practices whose epistemic outcomes are the focus of this study.

While the basic idea for this book originated from my theorisation about the relationship between knowledge and practice, *in* practice, over an extensive period of time, it first came into written fruition as a doctoral thesis from 2015 to 2021. I would therefore like to take this opportunity to state how grateful and indebted I am to my wonderful supervisors Fabio Petito and Louiza Odysseos. To this day, I remain in awe of their support. Many a time, I would submit a chapter in the early hours of the morning of the day after the deadline only to find that they had already provided me with initial feedback by the time I awakened later on in the day. That would be followed by further written feedback and a supervisory meeting where progress had already been made on the submission that had prompted the meeting. Complementing each other in their respective approaches to my thesis, both Fabio and Louiza pushed me to excel in ways that I could not have done on my own. I learned a great deal from their insights, questions, feedback, and approach. While I am of course grateful for this assistance, I am also grateful for their friendship, support, and care throughout our time together, which was often interrupted by unexpected 'extra-curricular' challenges such as my arrest in 2019 by the London Metropolitan Police at the request of the Turkish government to face the prospect of being extradited to Turkey on spurious terrorism charges. I cannot thank them enough.

I'd also like to thank Paul Weller, Şerafettin Pektaş, Erkan Toğuşlu, and two others who wish to remain anonymous for reading and commenting on earlier drafts of my thesis. I spent many hours discussing my thesis with each of them, which helped me to refine my arguments and to further develop my thoughts.

I wish to thank Mustafa Başarı for providing me with his 'draft memoir notes' that was very useful in illuminating the historical events leading up to, and immediately following, the founding of Hizmet's first all-girls' school in the early 1990s. I'd like to thank Ahmet Kurucan for sharing with me his notes of Gülen's unpublished ad hoc talks on dialogue and for being there as a sounding board for my comments and questions on Islamic law. I'd like to thank and acknowledge Halide Çelebi and Zeliha Doğan with whom I discussed *bayanlar hizmeti* (Hizmet's activities run by and for women) and who corroborated my findings on this topic. I'd like to offer my gratitude to those with whom I discussed my thesis over the years and who, knowingly or otherwise, contributed to the ideas developed therein through their questions, responses, challenges, and, at times, befuddled silence.

I would also like to thank my doctoral examiners, John L. Esposito and David Karp, for their valuable feedback and comments on my thesis, which was conducted under the somewhat peculiar 'Covid conditions.' I am grateful to John for encouraging me to submit my thesis as a book proposal to Oxford University Press, as well as for his support and encouragement throughout this process, which eventually culminated in the publication of this book for which he has graciously written the Foreword. I'd also like to thank the two anonymous readers for reviewing my manuscript for the publishers and for their suggestions and strong endorsement for publication. I'd like to thank the series editor Theo Calderara, the project editor Rada Radojicic, the project manager Dharuman Bheeman, and the copyeditor Betty Pessagno for all of their input and for seeing the manuscript through to publication.

Finally, I'd like to thank my beloved wife and children (the latter of whom multiplied in the course of my research) for supporting me throughout these years and for tolerating my absence as I agonised over questions that appeared to have little bearing on their lives at the time or since. I love you all very much.

Introduction

Rethinking Islam and Human Rights

The relationship between Islam and human rights has been debated for many decades.[1] The question of compatibility arose during the drafting process of the Universal Declaration of Human Rights formulated from 1944 to 1948 and continued during the drafting processes of the subsequent United Nations human rights instruments, where the 'right to change religion' and gender equality were among the main issues of concern for Muslim state delegates (Waltz 2004, 813–37; Morsink 1999, 24–26; P. M. Taylor 2005, 29–31, 35–36). The scholarly discussion on Islam and human rights, on the other hand, picked up from the 1970s and 1980s onwards. A basic, if early, example is Abul A'la Mawdudi's (d. 1979) *Human Rights in Islam* booklet published in 1977. This discussion proceeded under the influence of the growing Islamisation of state and society in the Muslim world, which in turn was precipitated by events such as the 1967 Arab-Israeli War, the Iranian revolution of 1979, the growing wealth of Arab states by the 1980s, and the Gulf War of 1991 (Haddad 2011, 80–84). Furthermore, the Western origin of human rights and the colonial past and contemporary instrumentalisation of human rights by Western powers to meddle in Muslim affairs also influenced (and continues to influence) the Muslim response to human rights during this period (Humphrey 1983, 29; Mayer 1995, 5; Falk 2000a, 87–89; Baderin 2003, 10–11; Dunn 2015, 19; Haddad 2011, 82). Thus, as discussed in Chapter 1, the reactionary impulse to either reject or neutralise human rights by Islamizing it ensued through the prism of these contextual forces.

The human rights idea, as expressed in international human rights standards, makes a bold and fundamental claim when it affirms that 'all

---

[1] As discussed in Chapter 1, some argue that Islam and human rights are intrinsically incompatible; others claim that they are indeed compatible, subject to change. The first claim is often referred to as the incompatibility thesis in the literature, whereas the second is known as the compatibility thesis. I will also use these shorthand labels throughout this book. Moreover, I use the question of compatibility and the compatibility challenge interchangeably throughout this book to refer to the discussion on the question/challenge of compatibility between Islam and human rights as well.

peoples and all nations' are entitled to a set of fundamental human rights 'without distinction of any kind, such as race, colour, sex, language, religion, political or other opinion, national or social origin, property, birth or other status' to recognise 'the inherent dignity and the equal and inalienable rights of all members of the human family' (Universal Declaration of Human Rights 1948). That fundamental claim amounts to a fundamental challenge when it is pitted against other worldviews, as found in Islam, that is interpreted as offering an alternative outlook that impinges upon the question of rights (Brems 2004, 6). Furthermore, the encounter between Islam and human rights raises a series of foundational questions about Islam in the modern age. That includes, '[w]hat will Islam stand for and represent in the contemporary age?' (Abou El Fadl 2009, 114). What does Islam say about the self, the other, and the relationship between the two in the interconnected world? (An-Na'im 1995, 230). What is the 'relationship between modern Islam and its own humanistic tradition'? (Abou El Fadl 2009, 114). Can the case for human rights be made from within Islam, and if so, what does that look like? How does Islam respond to the changing social, cultural, and political landscape in which it finds itself? How do we determine the immutable and changing aspects of Islam? How do we know what is and is not Islamic? Who speaks for Islam? In other words, the question of compatibility raises a broader set of questions about religion and the role of religion in modern society.

In addition to raising the aforementioned questions, the compatibility challenge also relates to the ideal of finding common ground in an increasingly polarised world. That pursuit is made all the more urgent by a number of interrelated factors, including the worldwide regression of democracy as authoritarianism, populism, identity politics, and misinformation in political discourse appear to be on the rise, pulling communities apart in an ever-shrinking world (Klaas 2016; Diamond 2021; Giusti and Piras 2020). Furthermore, while Islam continues to have been hijacked by the violent extremism of puritanical Islamists, far right extremism and Islamophobia is on the rise in the West (Abou El Fadl 2007; Grierson and Sabbagh 2020; Elahi and Khan 2017; Esposito 2019, 20; Warsi 2017, 138–39). Both extremes converge to mutually reinforce one another, to poison the political discourse and social relations, and to essentialise Islam as being fixed, absolutist, and alien to the modern world (Keles et al. 2019, 266, 268). Those trends are aided by the manner in which news and information are consumed and reproduced in the age of digitalisation, social media, targeted marketing, astroturfing, and the echo chambers of 'alternative facts'. Meanwhile, Muslims in the West are often made to feel unwelcome, under siege, and, at times, the 'enemy within' (Awan and Zempi 2017; Warsi 2017, 134–58). A number of cumulative factors feed into this sentiment. These include the interpretation of the war on terror as a war on Islam; the securitisation of the Muslim diaspora (knowingly or otherwise) through counter-extremism policies (Kundnani 2014; Kundnani and Hayes 2018, 14; Esposito 2010, 160–64); the reproduction of disparaging stereotypes about Muslims and Islam in the Western media (W. Ali et al. 2011, 5); the problematisation and qualified banning of the Muslim attire (notably, the *burka*, face veil, and headscarf), the minaret of mosques, and halal meat by certain Western European states (Bowen 2007; Scott 2007; Cherti 2010; Neslen 2020); and the repeated failure of the European Court of Human Rights to uphold the right to religious manifestation under article 9 when the religion in question happens to be Islam (Mayer 2003; Kayaoglu 2014). Thus, the efforts to bring about rapprochement between Islam and human rights become all the more important in the face of these factors, which are pulling in the opposite direction. It is with that view in mind that we now turn to the literature that aims to bring about, or explore the conditions of, that rapprochement.

The Problem and the Animating Question

As I will discuss in Chapter 1, there are numerous Islamic responses to the human rights challenge. Some are reactionary, as alluded to above, whereas others are more conciliatory, claiming that Islam can be made to be compatible with human rights. Scholars who subscribe to this view, however, are torn between two approaches. The first aims to reinterpret religious scripture through theoretical scholarly expositions, asking itself what does the scripture say? How can it be reinterpreted from within an Islamic framework? The second approach, on the other hand, advocates for reconfiguring the sensibilities of the faithful by focusing on the social conditions that hegemonise a particular religious reading, asking itself, what do Muslims believe? How can one scriptural interpretation be popularised over another? In other words, the first approach is focused on formalised religious knowledge, whereas the second approach is focused on experiential or lived religious knowing.[2]

As a result, these two approaches differ in substance (semiotic versus social), style (rhetorical versus practical), and disciplinary basis (theological/juridical versus sociological/anthropological). In Chapter 1, I demonstrate that a narrow focus on one or the other facet of religious knowledge impacts our ability to account for the symbiotic relationship between the two and therefore change within either. Consequently, the first approach fails to popularise its theoretical expositions among the faithful, whereas the second fails to, at the very least, account for religious legitimacy by, for example, locating itself within the inherited tradition of religious epistemology. In other words, the epistemological duality at the heart of religious knowledge produces, what I refer to as, the diametrical drawback of the two scholarly approaches noted above in the context of Islam and human rights. Given the foregoing, the animating question of this book can be stated as follows: how does social movement practice produce Islamic knowledge on, or as it relates to, human rights (hereafter, on human rights) in a manner that brings together the formalised and experiential facets of religious knowledge in the process of doing so? This form of knowledge production allows us to explain change in relation to both facets of religious knowledge by drawing our attention to the organic interaction between the two. That, in return, allows us to call into question the assumed incompatibility between Islam and human rights in a manner that the prevailing set of rapprochement literature that focuses on one or the other facet of religious knowledge does not.

It is at this juncture that I propose adopting 'practice' as an alternative theoretical paradigm for understanding the relationship between practice and knowledge production. To do so, I bring together theoretical insights from practice-based epistemology, practical theology, lived religion, social movement studies, social psychology, and organisational studies to centre social movement practice as the locus of Islamic knowledge production on human rights wherein the formalised and experiential facets of religious knowledge are relationally present in the performance of practice. This allows us to see the changing of Islamic knowledge on human rights through the prism of an interactive loop that organically connects the evolution of *knowing* and *doing* or formalised and experiential religious knowledge, in a single process.

---

[2] As we will see in Chapter 1, the literature on lived religion refers to this epistemological dichotomy as the distinction between formalised/lived, official/experiential, semiotic/social, and proper/popular facets of religious knowledge.

According to this view, as put forward in this book, the epistemic outcome (in this case, Islamic knowledge) ensues naturally, gradually, securely, and often unintentionally, in and through practice, passing through the level of intuitive, implicit, and pre-reflexive tacit knowledge before being articulated into universal, accessible, and formalised explicit knowledge, which then feeds back into the loop that produced it. In this way, an internalised appreciation for the epistemic position is achieved in the process of developing and delivering it, where knowledge *arises* from the doing-body to the reflexive mind as opposed to vice versa. As a result, this form of practice-based knowledge production eschews the 'duality problem' as discussed above.

I focus on a single case study analysis of the Hizmet movement (also known as the Gülen movement, as introduced further below) to explore this process. Hizmet, which originated in Turkey in the late 1960s, is one of the most dynamic transnational Islamic movements in the world today, active in over 140 countries worldwide. In particular, I focus on Hizmet's practices that pertain primarily to education, dialogue, migration, and women's activities since the 1970s as the site of Islamic knowledge production on human rights, through the practice-based knowledge production process described above, which accounts for the changes in Hizmet's doings and sayings on the issues under consideration. It is interesting to note that none of these practices were aimed at promoting or advancing human rights considerations and/or the production of Islamic knowledge on human rights whatsoever, but that is the unintended outcome that ensued nonetheless. I will describe the significance of this further below.

Reworking process tracing methodology, combined with a single case study analysis of Hizmet and its practices, I illustrate how and why these practices have enabled greater alignment along the axes of two of the most contested issues at the intersection of Islam and human rights: apostasy and women's rights. More specifically, I show how Hizmet's position has evolved from outright support for the premodern Islamic doctrine on apostasy that condemns ex-Muslims to capital punishment to an outright rejection of any temporal punishment for renouncing the Islamic faith whatsoever. As for women's rights, I show how Hizmet's position and practice have evolved from being deeply patriarchal, wherein women were considered to be ontologically inferior to men, towards one that increasingly considers women's equality and empowerment to be aligned with Islamic principles. Thus, centring practice-based knowledge production in this manner offers us an original and important pathway for reexploring age-old challenges at the cross-sectional 'impasse' of change, stability, and religious knowledge production, which extends beyond those challenges that relate solely to Islam and human rights.

Scope of the Study

The routes taken and not taken in this book were determined by the animating research question of this study. Elaborating on this calls for dissecting that question's focus at three points or intervals: where it focuses on Islam as opposed to Islam and/or human rights, where it centres on Islamic knowledge as opposed to Islam by any other delineation, and where it emphasises one set of Hizmet practices and outcomes as opposed to another. I will discuss these in turn.

The first point relates to the focus on Islam as opposed to Islam and/or human rights. This singular focus on Islam is not predicated on an idealisation of modern human rights. My research (both academic and legal) and personal and collective experience of state persecution since 2015 (discussed below) have alerted me to the discursive and practical shortcomings of modern human rights frameworks. Neither am I operating under the misguided assumption that we can account for the rapprochement between the two by merely accounting for the conditions of change within one or the other. After all, human rights' actors and instruments are not blameless bystanders in their interactions with the Muslim world and have, one way or another, contributed to the compatibility challenge as it is presently found.[3] Furthermore, my focus on Islam is not to deny 'that religion constitutes merely one component within a whole range of political, economic, social, and cultural factors that inhibit or foster the implementation of human rights' (Bielefeldt 2000, 102).[4] Nor am I claiming that Islam is a single monolithic entity. Rather, I acknowledge that it is a broad 'mosque' that includes numerous sects, schools of thought, competing interpretations, and manifestations (Hallaq 1997, vii; Nasr 2003, xviii; Esposito 2010, 11, 79).

That said, Islam is instrumentalised to legitimise human rights violations in the Muslim world (Mayer 2018, x). Furthermore, it is useful to explore the conditions of change from within an Islamic framework for those

---

[3] While my focus is on Islam, I will tease out relevant points of human rights criticisms when organising and reviewing the literature on Islam and human rights in Chapter 1.
[4] See also Abou El Fadl 2009, 113; An-Na'im 1995, 240–41.

who continue to value that framework. After all, the Muslim population continues to grow worldwide, while Muslim religiosity continues to hold strong according to recent polls (Pew 2016, 2017a, and 2017b). Finally, the coming together of Islam and human rights raises the question of change in relation to both. However, the conditions of change in relation to Islam are different from those in relation to human rights, which justifies a particular focus on one or the other within the confines of a single study. Altogether, these considerations justify my singular focus on Islam in the context of the present discussion. That said, and as pointed out in Chapter 5, it would be useful to apply the theoretical-methodological framework of this study to the production of human rights knowledge (response) on, or as it relates to, Islam in subsequent research as well.

The second point relates to the focus on Islamic knowledge as opposed to Islam by any other delineation. This position is justified by at least three considerations. First, given Islam's emphasis on practice (on actualising faith through worship and 'correct action'), the primary science in Islam is not theology, as it is in Christianity, but *fiqh* (Islamic law), which governs all aspects of a Muslim's life as it aims to address the question, 'what is God's will/law' in all instances (Esposito 1998, 68–69, 74–75). Thus, we cannot discuss Islam, without discussing *fiqh*, and we cannot discuss *fiqh* without noting its epistemic nature and construct, which Wael B. Hallaq describes in the following terms:

> [T]he embryonic formation of the schools [of law, which established the parameters of *fiqh*] started sometime during the last decades of the seventh century, taking the form of study circles in which pious scholars debated religious issues and taught interested students. The knowledge and production of legal doctrine began in these circles—nowhere else. Legal authority, therefore, became epistemic (i.e., knowledge-based) rather than political, social or even religious. That epistemic authority is the defining feature of Islamic law need not be doubted, although piety and morality played important supporting roles. A masterly knowledge of the law was the sole criterion in deciding where legal authority resided; and it resided with the scholars, not with the political rulers or any other source. (Hallaq 2009, 35)

Second, the primary points of friction between Islam and human rights arise in the context of *fiqh* and its position on a range of issues as discussed in Chapter 1, that is, change of religion, religious discrimination, equal rights of men and women, and corporal punishment (An-Na'im 1996, 8–9; Waltz 2004, 813–37; Brems 2004, 5; Shah 2006b, 869; Sachedina 2009; Haddad 2011, 73; Abou El Fadl 2009, 117). That raises the question of change, which in turn brings us to the fundamental distinction 'between those Islamic injunctions that are eternal and immutable and those that clearly are bound by time and space' (Hunter 2009, 291–92). This steers the conversation from identifying the points of conflict to the underlying epistemologies that produce and sustain them, which in the context of Islamic law leads to a discussion about *usul al-fiqh* (the methodology by which *fiqh* is produced). While the discussion progresses in this manner, it is still one that is centred on the nature of Islamic knowledge and how it is produced, sustained, and consumed.

Third, a focus on Islamic knowledge, however, is not to be misunderstood as a focus on simply formalised religious knowledge. To the contrary, and as shown in the discussions about lived religion, everyday Islam, and practical theology in Chapter 1, this study interprets Islamic knowledge as being both formalised/experiential, social/semiotic, explicit/tacit, reflexive/pre-reflexive, and produced by *faqih* (Islamic jurist) and folk alike on account of conceptualising knowledge as being provisional, processual, malleable, and organic as opposed to static and fixed. According to this approach, both facets of religious knowledge are in an interactive relationship with one another. Thus, in focusing on Islamic knowledge, as understood in the aforementioned terms, we can trace the effects of that interaction as manifested within both facets of religious knowledge, that is the changing practices of lived religion and the changing interpretations (to justify the changing practices) of formalised religious knowledge.

The third and final point touching on the study's research question relates to the focus on one set of Hizmet practices and outcomes (issues) as opposed to another. It is important to clarify how this determination was made. The first point to make is that I did not choose my issues of concern on the basis of the practices under consideration. To the contrary, I determined which practices to trace on the basis of which issues to explore. I determined which issues to explore by reviewing the literature on Islam and human rights as discussed in Chapter 1. This demonstrated that the right to change religion and women's rights were the two most controversial points of conflict in the context of Islam and human rights. I determined my practices on the basis of their causal relation with how those issues developed in the context of Hizmet in accordance with the methodological framework set out in Chapter 2, which combines process tracing methodology, single-case study analysis, and aspects of David Nicolini's practice theory toolkit. In other words, I determined my issues and practices systematically, not arbitrarily, nor did I determine them selectively for the purposes of proving a preconceived notion.

This had three consequences in terms of the practices and outcomes traced in this book (which in turn had implications for one of the routes not taken, as discussed below). First, I found that I was tracing Hizmet's practices that were not aimed at, nor related to, human rights.[5] This was unsurprising because Hizmet has only recently begun to engage in what could typically be defined as human rights practices.[6] Second, the epistemic outcomes (i.e., the production of Islamic knowledge on human rights) of these non-human rights practices were unforeseen, unintended, and in some instances, contrary to what was explicitly intended. Third, and as an extension of the first two points; the epistemic outcomes represented changes *within* Hizmet rather than those changes that Hizmet sought to produce *without* (i.e., changes within wider society). In that sense, I was exploring *unintended-internal* rather than *intended-external* movement outcomes. Put together, in tracing Hizmet's practice-based knowledge production on these issues of concern, I was in fact exploring Hizmet's unintended internal epistemic outcomes on human rights as a result of its non-human rights practices.

As I will show in Chapters 1 and 5, there are multiple upsides to this approach, the most significant of which is that it allows me to draw attention to an understudied aspect of the literature on Islam and human rights, which is the unintended impact of non-human rights practices on the compatibility of Islam and human rights.

This focus on the unintended outcomes of non-human rights practices also happens to explain why I have not directly engaged with the nascent body of literature on human rights practices (Preis 1996; Risse and Sikkink 1997; Goodale 2007; Goodale and Merry 2007; Stammers 2009; Beitz 2009; Miller 2010; Navin 2011; Karp 2013; Pruce 2015a, 2015b). After all, I am focused on the production of Islamic knowledge (on human rights) as a result of Hizmet's *non*-human rights practices. The literature on human rights practice, on the other hand, is concerned with the human rights implications

---

[5] In fact, some of these practices were designed to perpetuate, not reform or change, patriarchal Islamic orthopraxy (i.e., *bayanlar hizmeti* or women's hizmet in the 1980s and early 1990s).

[6] For example, Human Rights Solidarity in the UK (www.hrsolidarity.org), Solidarity with Others in Belgium (www.solidaritywithothers.com), and Huddled Masses (www.huddledm.org), and Silenced Turkey (www.silencedturkey.org) in the United States.

of *human rights* practices, which the literature refers to as 'the conduct of a community engaged in ordered, habituated action *with the stated objective* of safeguarding human dignity' (my emphasis) (Pruce 2015a, 5). What unites the various forms of human rights practices is the 'magnetism and centripetal force of human rights discourse,' which 'revolves around a central set of guiding principles or norms that reside in the Universal Declaration and elsewhere' (Pruce 2015a, 10). This refers to activities and practices such as 'fact-finding, monitoring, litigation, lobbying, direct assistance, and protest—as well as human rights education' (Dudai 2019, 277). The Hizmet practices traced in this study cannot be characterised in these terms, be it in aim, substance, or style. Even if we use alternative methods to broaden and complexify our notion of human rights practices (see, e.g., Karp 2013), they cannot be used, it seems to me, to encapsulate the practices discussed herein (e.g., running private schools, organising interfaith events, migrating abroad to expand Hizmet's reach, or organising religious activities for women) without 'blurring together practices that, in practice, are notably distinct' (Karp 2013, 983) and thereby defeating the very purpose of delineating 'what's in and what's out?' of human rights practice (Karp 2013, 975).[7]

Hizmet as a Case Study

Hizmet literally means 'service' in Turkish. The Hizmet movement (hereafter, Hizmet) is a transnational Islamic movement founded by the teachings and practice of Muhammed Fethullah Gülen, a prominent Islamic scholar (*'alim*), a formerly state-licensed Imam and preacher (*vaiz*), and a public

---

[7] Similarly, my focus on the production of Islamic knowledge, on the one hand, and non-human rights practices, on the other, also explains why I have not attempted to offer an exact definition of human rights, especially since it is a deeply contested term philosophically, legally, politically, historically, and sociologically (Hinchman 1984, 7–8; T. Evans 1996, 3; Lorenzen 2000, 50; Baxi 2002, 5–13; Waltz 2004, 800; Dembour 2006, 10–11; Tasioulas 2012; Goodale 2007, 5–8). According to Griffin, '[t]he term "human right" is nearly criterionless. There are unusually few criteria for determining when the term is used correctly and when incorrectly—and not just among politicians, but among philosophers, political theorists, and jurisprudents as well. The language of human rights has, in this way, become debased' (2008, 14–15). The above notwithstanding, my general conceptualisation of human rights can be summarised in the following form: '[h]uman rights are rights held by individuals simply because they are part of the human species. They are rights shared equally by everyone regardless of sex, race, [religion], nationality, and economic background' (Ishay 2004, 3). For all its imperfections (and it has many pertaining to the drafting process, in terms of what it includes and excludes, as a form of text and its non-binding status), I consider the Universal Declaration of Human Rights of 1948 to comprise a useful first attempt to articulate those rights at the international stage (Morsink 1999).

intellectual born in 1941 in Erzurum, eastern Turkey (H. Yavuz 2013, 23–67; Pahl 2019; Mercan 2017; Erdoğan 2006). Hizmet began as a religious congregation in the 1960s and 1970s centred around Gülen's sermons in the Aegean province of Turkey. By the 1990s, it had evolved into a nationwide education community. By the 2000s, Hizmet had founded a thousand highly successful fee-paying schools (that followed the national secular curriculum), over a thousand *dershanes* (university preparatory centres), fifteen universities, a best-selling newspaper (*Zaman*), fifteen TV stations, scores of radio stations, a nationwide bank (*Bank Asya*), regional and national business federations, hospitals as well as publishing houses, and book stores in Turkey as well as approximately a thousand (fee-paying and part-state funded) schools, dialogue organisations, relief charities, and media outlets in 160 countries worldwide (Resmi Gazete 2016; House of Commons 2017, paras. 81–91; Sunier and Landman 2015, 89; H. Yavuz 2013, 69–129; Ebaugh 2010, 23–32, 42–46; Park 2012, 188–201; Turam 2007, 11–12, 19–21; Özdalga 2005, 435–36; Oda TV 2013).[8]

While outsiders often identify the movement with Gülen's persona, referring to it as the 'Gülen movement,' insiders simply use the term 'Hizmet' (noun, 'Service') to identify themselves on the basis of what they claim to be doing, 'hizmet' (verb, 'providing service') (Weller 2015, 239). Given my focus, I too will use this name to underscore my emphasis on Hizmet's doings (practices).

Hizmet was born out of Gülen's efforts to reinvigorate religious consciousness through an emphasis on social responsibility (*mesuliyet duygusu*) and social action or practice, often referred to within Hizmet as *aksiyon* (literally, 'action') and *hizmet* (verb). According to Gülen, submission to Islam necessitates active effort (*cehd*) to attain the pleasure of God (*rida*) through dynamic social practice (Gulay 2007, 47–48). To prioritise social practice, Gülen repeatedly explains that we must allow practice to 'come before thought because thought is based on practice' (my translation) (Gülen 2006e). This statement is both descriptive (i.e., thought *is* based on practice) and prescriptive (i.e., thought *ought* to be based on practice). In other words, Gülen calls on Hizmet participants to embark upon practice (*aksiyon*) after brief deliberation (*istişare*) without, however, aiming to flesh out all details in advance (Gülen 2010b). This is what he means by 'practice leading thought' (my translation) (Gülen 2010c).[9] In that sense, Gülen discourages

---

[8] I will discuss Hizmet's sociohistorical development in Chapter 3.
[9] See also Can 1996, 14.

the overintellectualisation of practice as it can lead to overdetermination, which in turn can stifle practice. For example, when talking about Hizmet's dialogue, Gülen says, '[y]ou cannot pre-determine everything in your dialogue efforts. There are some things that are only determined by needs and necessities [as and when they arise]. Therefore, dialogue is not a static system; it is in constant motion and is a self-renewing dynamic system' (Gülen 2006d). Elsewhere, he warns against being 'bogged down in secondary matters. Jurists have narrowed down religion by attempting to say something about everything. Instead, we should make it easier not harder' (my translation) (Gülen 2010a). Thus, Hizmet's prioritisation of practice has allowed it to remain dynamic and nimble, which in turn has allowed it to grow across many countries and into many sectors, as noted above.

Gülen refers to this commitment to religious activism as a state of *metafizik gerilim* that is pent-up metaphysical tension or motivation, which he redirects toward inclusive civil society projects, such as the founding of secular schools or the running of interfaith and intercultural dialogue activities. In doing so, Gülen has also steered Hizmet's social and religious capital away from political Islam[10] which he has explicitly shunned from the outset (Gülen 2000a, 147–92). This is not to suggest that Gülen had no political considerations or, in time, ambitions in relation to the Turkish state. Rather, he was of the view that the movement's aims more generally and its considerations/ambitions in relation to politics more specifically could not be achieved through participation in the political process and far less so through founding or supporting an Islamist party. Instead, with Hizmet's emphasis on social action and predominantly civil society projects on the one hand and Gülen's discursive support for democracy, dialogue, passive secularism, pluralism, and positive relations with the West and Turkey's accession to the European Union on the other, both Gülen and Hizmet positioned themselves from within the framework of 'civil Islam' (Gülen 2000a, 189–90; Mercan 2017; Yilmaz 2005c, 399; Kuru 2007; Esposito and Yilmaz 2010, 94). Thus, while Hizmet is faith-based in its motivation, it is (so far as possible) faith-neutral and faith-inclusive in its practical manifestation, demonstrating a form of religiosecularity (Yilmaz 2012; Sunier and Landman 2015, 93; Keles 2016a, para. 6).

Organisationally, Hizmet comprises an overlapping matrix of formal and informal practices, entities, and networks. The formal includes

---

[10] I use the term *political Islam* to mean the pursuit of Islamist goals (or even religious goals, such as religious morality) 'through participation in political processes' (House of Commons 2016, para. 10).

Hizmet's schools, charities, hospitals, and social enterprise businesses (such as bookstores) as well as its consortiums (e.g., Voices in Britain)[11] and federations (e.g., Fedactio).[12] The informal includes Hizmet's *bölgecilik* (literally, regionalism): the entity that is responsible for raising religious sensibility among the grassroots of society through religious discussion forums (*sohbets*), religious retreats (*kamps*), student houses (*ışık evleri*), as well as mobilising financial support for Hizmet's projects by organising annual fundraising events (*himmets*); and *rehberlik* (literally, mentoring): the entity that is responsible for religious mentoring among the youth through its own set of *sohbets*, *kamps*, and related activities (Park 2012, 190; Voices in Britain 2018, para. 7, 20). Hizmet mobilises its informal entities and networks to support its formal activities and organisations (Keles 2016a, para. 7).

Hizmet is a modern Islamic movement with a traditional underpinning (Keskin 2009, 17; Sunier 2014, 2194, 2196; Yilmaz 2008, 897; Kuru 2005, 261). It aims to constructively engage with the modern world through modern tools in order to revitalise faith and religion by recalibrating its relationship with science, reason, state, and society (Turam 2004, 261, 2007, 19; Leaman 2007, 509). In its effort to do so, Gülen takes care to operate within the traditional boundaries of Sunni Hanafi Maturidi orthodoxy (Uğur 2004; Leaman 2007; Bruckmayr 2008, 175–76), conditioned by two fundamental sources: Anatolian Sufi Muslimness, which accounts for the emphasis on love, compassion, and forgiveness in Gülen's teachings (Keles 2013, 197–200; Saritoprak 2003; H. C. Kim 2008); and Said Nursi's (d. 1960) religious discourse, as found in his magnus opus *Risale-i Nur* (*the Epistles of Light*),[13] on religious proactivism (*musbet hareket*), social responsibility, religion in the modern age, and the relationship between religion and science (H. Yavuz 2013, 30–33; Tee 2016, 15, 35–50; Saritoprak 2011, 91; Tittensor 2015, 165; Balcı 2003, 151–53; T. Michel 2002). The fundamental difference between Nursi and Gülen is that Gülen places far more emphasis on social action/practice than Nursi, which Gülen interprets expansively and creatively (H. Yavuz 2013, 32–33; Tee 2016, 49). This has

[11] https://www.voicesinbritain.org/
[12] https://en.fedactio.be/
[13] Said Nursi is arguably the most influential Islamic scholar in modern Turkish history. Nursi's *Epistles of Light* is a fourteen-volume thematic Qur'anic exegesis on the fundamentals of Islamic religious belief, with a focus on 'nature and causality, belief and unbelief, righteous action, sincerity and brotherhood, love and politics' (Eickelman 2013, xi). The *Epistles* aimed to revitalise religious belief (*iman*) through robust rational argument in response to the challenges posed by the rising tide of atheism, modernism, and the scientism of the modern age.

allowed Gülen to redirect religious capital and fervor toward faith-neutral (secular) modern social projects (e.g., the running of schools that follow a secular curricula). This has permitted Hizmet to produce the inwardly religious/outwardly secular phenomena referred to above (Sunier 2014) and, in turn, has allowed Hizmet to maximise its range of activities as well as diversify its support base.

In so doing, Hizmet first became 'one of the most influential revivalist movements in modern Turkey' (Özdalga 2005, 430) before emerging 'over the course of the [next] four decades to become one of the largest and most powerful religious movements in the world' (Tee 2016, 34).[14] It has affected major shifts in attitudes among committed Muslims on a range of issues (Keles 2013, 196). For example, 'Gülen's pro-Western attitude has played a key role in the domestication and softening of other Islamic groups' anti-Europe and anti-U.S. positions' (Kösebalaban 2003, 176). According to M. Hakan Yavuz and John L. Esposito, Gülen's discourse is 'definitely' transformative in the Turkish public sphere, 'with the potential to influence the whole Muslim world' (2003, xxxii). A similar view is echoed by John O. Voll, who says, 'Fethullah Gülen is a force in the development of the Islamic discourse of globalized multicultural pluralism. . . . his vision bridges modern and postmodern, global and local, and has a significant influence in the contemporary debates that shape the visions of the future of Muslims and non-Muslims alike' (2003, 247). However, it is fair to say that much of that influence has dissipated in Turkey on account of the Turkish government's relentless demonisation and proscription of Hizmet in recent years. It is more difficult to gauge the effect of the Turkish government's campaign against Hizmet outside of Turkey.

This brings me to the question of the nature of Hizmet's organisational structure. There is a significant amount of literature that treats Hizmet as a social movement (H. Yavuz 2013, 15, 200; Bilici 2006, 15, 17; West II 2006; Turam 2007, 12; Ebaugh 2010; Çetin 2010; Gürbüz and Bernstein 2012; Park 2012, 190). However, other literature claims that it is 'not quite' a social movement when compared against the basic criteria of classical social movement theory (Hendrick 2013, 19). Both Joshua D. Hendrik and David Tittensor claim that the lack of 'conflict' in Hizmet's methods poses a point of challenge in this respect. On this issue, Hendrik points out that Hizmet's 'method of engagement is . . . only *passively* confrontational' (2013, 19). Similarly, Tittensor

---

[14] See also Sunier 2014, 2194.

notes that while conflict applied to Hizmet's formative years, it does not apply to Hizmet since the 1990s (2014, 5). As Bill Park puts it, the movement 'fuses faith with practical activity in a way that empirical and material analyses of it struggle to grasp' (2012, 190).

The above notwithstanding, we need to consider at least two points here. First, Hizmet is in flux; if it wasn't engaged in overt forms of confrontation yesterday (e.g., protests, marches, social media campaigns), it certainly is today as it faces an existential threat from the Turkish government's ongoing onslaught in recent years (Woolf et al. 2015; House of Commons 2017, para. 118, 121–122; Schenkkan 2018; U.S. Department of State 2019; Amnesty International 2019; Human Rights Watch 2017; Home Office 2017, para. 3.1.4). Thus, the criteria are a better fit today than they were yesterday. Second, numerous studies have pointed out that social movement theories have often overlooked the role of religion (C. Smith 1996, 2), religious altruism, volunteerism, philanthropy (Çetin 2010, 165), and Islamic activism (Wiktorowicz 2004, 3; Sutton and Vertigans 2006), which can be traced back to the 'core democracy bias' in social movement studies that 'may have limited the scope conditions of the theory, since so few studies were conducted on movements outside of North America and Western Europe' (Kurzman 2004, 294). Thus, an argument can be made about revising the basic definition and criteria of social movements altogether. This book contributes to that argument by suggesting that we should judge social actors, not so much by what they claim to be doing, but by their unintended fruits, which demonstrates their ability to bring about social and epistemic change with or without overt forms of 'conflict'. This reinforces the view that we should not be too concerned about categorising Hizmet, especially if the categories themselves are being called into question, as we have shown above. In any case, the argument about the exact nature of Hizmet is a tangential point. My focus on Hizmet's practices hold whether it is an organised religious community, a web of social and religious networks, or a loosely/tightly knit social movement.

Before moving on, I should point out that I do not address recent political controversies surrounding Hizmet in the Turkey context (e.g., the Turkish government's allegations that Hizmet operated a parallel state within the Turkish state, that it orchestrated the events of July 15, 2016 in Turkey (commonly described, and hereafter referred to as, 'Turkey's failed coup'), and that it assassinated key figures in Turkey such as the Russian ambassador in 2016) for a number of reasons. First, this book does not aim to provide a comprehensive examination of Hizmet. Rather, it focuses on a primary question, which it explores through an examination of the apostasy doctrine and women's rights. Thus, these allegations are not related to the qualified claims and issues discussed within these pages. Second, Gülen and Hizmet vehemently deny these criminal allegations of the tallest order. Third, if true, these practices would have been performed in secret and in a clandestine manner, making them impossible to reconstruct in the methodological manner I describe in Chapter 2. That said, I do concede that some of the Hizmet practices not traced in this book (albeit not the ones alleged above) may have impinged upon the epistemic outcomes of the practices under consideration by, for example, delaying them. (Here, I am thinking of Hizmet's practices pertaining to the movement's informal grassroots religious activism or *bölgecilik*.) While my methodological framework, as set out in Chapter 2, does not require me to account for these practices, I will nonetheless discuss this matter in the context of conflict between practices in Chapter 5. Finally, the fact that I do not address the recent political controversies surrounding Hizmet in Turkey is not because (as an 'insider') I want to shield the movement from criticism. Far from it; I have both called for Hizmet to engage in a process of public self-criticism and publicly criticised Gülen and Hizmet on a number of fronts and on numerous occasions. While I summarise some of these criticisms below, I will only pursue those in this book that are directly relevant to the primary concern herein.

This brings me to my numerous reasons for choosing Hizmet as my case study for the present research. First, Hizmet aims to work from within an Islamic framework, which (as noted above) is important for those who continue to value that framework, including this study, which aims to contribute to our understanding of change in the context of contemporary Islam as it relates to human rights.

Second, Hizmet contrasts at a number of levels with the prevailing voices that aim to reconcile Islam with human rights, which I describe as the conciliatorist approach in Chapter 1. This conciliatorist approach is distinguished by its efforts to make the case for human rights from within Islam by putting forward sophisticated theoretical expositions in academic books and articles that often explicitly critique and call for the reform of Islamic tradition and premodern *fiqh* by, among other things, using or calling for the use of *ijtihad* (religious reinterpretation) to achieve that outcome. Hizmet, on the other hand, does not explicitly engage with the present discussion, which explains why it is often absent in the context of those conversations that do.¹⁵ Furthermore, the scholarly nature of the conciliatorist approach values single original authorship, whereas Hizmet, as a social movement, values recursive collective social practice with practical implications as opposed to theoretical contributions. Moreover, unlike the conciliatorist approach, both Gülen and Hizmet organisations take care not to call Islamic tradition, history, *fiqh,* and even historic political figures (as recent as the Ottoman sultans) into question. What's more, Gülen denies that he is performing, or that he has called upon others to perform, *ijtihad* as well (Gülen 2012a; Weller 2008, 758). Thus, a focus on Hizmet in the context of the present discussion allows me to reexamine this longstanding challenge from a contrasting perspective.

Third, the gap in the literature on Gülen and Hizmet, as discussed in Chapter 1, was another reason for choosing Hizmet as my case study. Fundamentally, the literature on Gülen and Hizmet, including those authored by scholars professing critical independence from the movement, treat Gülen as the thinker and producer and the movement as the consumer and disseminator of the knowledge, *ijtihad,* theology, vision, and ideals under consideration (Atay 2007; H. Yavuz and Esposito 2003b; Yilmaz 2003, 2005a, 2018; Bakar 2005; Beşer 2006; Leaman 2007; H. Yavuz 2013; Bruckmayr 2008; Ergene 2008; Tee 2016; Albayrak 2011; Hendrick 2013; Tittensor 2014; Valkenberg 2015). This view, which is also common among Hizmet participants (Hendrick 2013, 70–88), perpetuates the Cartesian divide between the knowing-mind (Gülen) and the enacting-body (movement) where knowledge is treated as a mentalistic, rationalistic, and cognitivistic product. In so doing, this approach overlooks the role of Hizmet's collective practice in producing the epistemic outcomes on the issues under consideration— that is, the premodern Islamic doctrine on apostasy and women's rights as discussed in Chapters 3 and 4, respectively.

Finally, this choice embodies a personal dimension as well. As discussed further below, I have been a Hizmet participant for over twenty years. During this period, I slowly came to realise how my co-participants and I had changed, both in disposition and in our views, as a result of our continued participation in Hizmet's practices. Our aim in performing these practices was to make a difference in other people's lives, but in doing so, I came to

---

¹⁵ As noted above, Gülen has offered discursive support for human rights, democracy, and a passive form of secularism but this is usually expressed in an ad hoc fashion and couched in general terms without systematically grappling with the thorny issues discussed in Chapter 1.

appreciate how we were in fact changing ourselves in ways that we had not anticipated. In time, and upon critical self-reflection, I came to the realisation that our position had gradually and unknowingly evolved in step with our evolving practice on a number of issues, ranging from the more mundane (e.g., listening to music, wearing jeans, drinking Coca-Cola,[16] shaking hands with the opposite sex) to the more substantive (e.g., our position on democracy, secularism, pluralism, human rights, apostasy from Islam, women's rights, gender equality, wearing the headscarf).

I found that our practices had changed our sensibilities, reflexes, and behaviours on certain issues, which in turn had changed the epistemic Islamic justifications that we had used to underpin our previous positions. The changing of the epistemic justification then provided the original practice with further room and flexibility to grow and develop, which in turn prompted further dispositional change on our part, as the carriers of that practice. The result was a continuous spiral of change comprising practice, disposition, and explicit epistemic justification in one relational process. My subsequent research on practice further complexified my theorisation of practice-based epistemologies along these lines. My research on Islam and human rights, on the other hand, alerted me to the value of reexamining the issue of compatibility through the prism of this unifying epistemological perspective. Thus, this study applies an *inductively theorised* notion of practice to a *deductively problematised* challenge of compatibility. Therefore, given the foregoing, it made sense to use Hizmet as a case study, since it was my experience within Hizmet that had unknowingly set me off on a journey that has culminated in this research. This discussion raises questions about researcher positionality and insider bias, which I will turn to next.

Researcher Positionality

In the interest of transparency, I have often described myself as an 'insider' when addressing issues involving Hizmet in the public domain. This raises the issue of insider research, which occurs 'when researchers conduct research with populations of which they are also members so that the researcher shares an identity, language, and experiential base with the study

---

[16] The drinking of Coca-Cola was shunned and strongly discouraged within Hizmet during the 1980s and 1990s because of the miniscule amounts of alcohol it was rumoured to contain.

participants' (Dwyer and Buckle 2009, 58). Insider research, in return, raises the question of insider bias, which I will address below.

Before doing so, however, it is important to share some preliminary observations. First, the terms *insider/outsider* suggest a dichotomous fixed state of positionality in relation to the group under consideration, when in fact it should be conceptualised as a complex, relative, and fluid continuum (Chavez 2008, 476; Greene 2014, 2). Additionally, 'positionality bias' is often conflated with insider bias which overlooks the fact that all research is conducted from somewhere, including 'outsider research,' which inevitably comes with its own set of ontological, ideological, philosophical, and experiential presuppositions (Chavez 2008, 474). Moreover, qualitative research often requires an outsider to achieve some level of *insiderness* in order to conduct their research, which in turn raises the issue of positionality bias, whether or not the researcher was an insider to begin with (Balsiger and Lambelet 2014, 158). Finally, the potential for insider bias is often associated with insider research focused on a minority group. The same question is seldom raised when an insider of a majority group researches the group in question (Nzinga et al. 2018, 11435).

The above call for a more nuanced and complexified notion of positionality notwithstanding, I recognise that I am an insider relative to most and that I must therefore take stock of both the advantages and potential complications my position entails (Balsiger and Lambelet 2014, 159). In the present case, the advantages include intimate knowledge of Hizmet's inner workings, practices, sensibilities, and reflexes as they pertain to the issues discussed in this book, whereas the potential complications relate to overfamiliarity and the implicit bias for romanticising the case study by shielding it from criticism (Chavez 2008, 485). I have employed a number of tools and methods to mitigate against these biases, including reflexivity, making the familiar *unfamiliar*, alternating perspectives, triangulation, and the use of challenges and alternative explanations.

Reflexivity, or maintaining 'vigilant critical reflection on the effects of insiderness' (Chavez 2008, 490), starts with recognising one's positionality. In my case, that includes recognising that I am an insider on account of having participated in Hizmet in the UK for over twenty years.[17] During this time, I volunteered as a teacher, tutor, mentor (*rehber*), warden, and

---

[17] That said, these reflections are of course relative (as noted above, I am an insider compared to most) and provide a dated representation of my positionality in relation to Hizmet as it was when I theorised and began to research the relationship between practice and knowledge. My evolving position in relation to Hizmet today is more accurately described as 'critical friend/sympathiser' rather than participant.

project manager in Hizmet. I became the Executive Chairperson (Executive Director and Chair of the board of trustees) of the Dialogue Society (a registered charity in England and Wales) in 2008, which aims to 'advanc[e] social cohesion by connecting communities, empowering people to engage and contributing to the development of ideas on dialogue and community building [through] discussion forums, courses, capacity building publications and outreach' (Dialogue Society 2019). I resigned my executive role (day-to-day running of the organisation) in late 2014 and my role as Chairperson in 2022. Furthermore, following Turkey's failed coup, the British press and the Foreign Affairs Select Committee of the House of Commons called upon me to talk about recent political developments in Turkey and to address the Turkish government's allegations about Hizmet, including the unsubstantiated claim that Gülen had masterminded Turkey's failed coup (Keles 2016a, 2017; Keles and Aslandoğan 2016).

Cognizant of this insiderness, I have attempted to challenge any biases and preconceptions (in particular, cognitive dissonance and confirmation bias) that I may hold about Hizmet by making the 'familiar unfamiliar'. In the present case, that involved disrupting the cognitive schemata and linkages that are triggered when discussing Hizmet by making 'unconventional linkages between representations and things in order to reveal unseen aspects' (Wagoner 2008, 470). I achieved this objective by two means. First, I posed questions and lines of enquiry that removed Hizmet from its conventional setting, which allowed me to represent it in a new incongruity context (Wagoner 2008, 470). Focusing on practice, on unintended outcomes, and the adoption of a practice-based epistemological view, which reverses the conventional notion of top-down knowledge production in Hizmet, allowed me to do just that. Second, I alternated between an insider and outsider perspective throughout my research (Chavez 2008, 490), which was aided by the fact that I was no longer actively participating in the day-to-day running of Hizmet projects from late 2014 onward.

Furthermore, I used a number of methods and tools to further support my endeavour to challenge my biases and assumptions. For example, the multiplication of the number of issues and practices under consideration and the expansion of the temporospatial axis upon which they were traced helped me to avoid misattribution and false generalisation. Triangulating my theories in Chapter 1 and methodologies in Chapter 2 allowed me to develop a theoretical-methodological framework that was sensitive to the biases of researching the object of study. Triangulating my primary and secondary sources helped me to determine the issues under consideration and to reconstruct Hizmet's practices in a manner that made confirmation bias and cognitive dissonance less likely. Finally, scrutinising my analyses and findings with challenges and alternative explanations helped me to minimise the risk of misattribution and false generalisation of the causal explanations of the epistemic outcomes under consideration.

This brings me to the potential risk of insider research romanticising the object of study to the point of shielding it from criticism (Chavez 2008, 475; Balsiger and Lambelet 2014, 159). This risk appears to be an ever-present one for insider researchers, and one that can (inadvertently) prompt outsider researchers to adopt an opposite impulse (i.e., bias) to *balance the scales*, potentially skewing the research in the opposite direction (Eyerman and Jamison 1991, 40, 42). That said, my repeated public calls for Hizmet participants to engage in a process of public self-criticism in order for the movement to learn from its past mistakes going forward renders this less of a challenge in the present case. In my interview to *Ahval* (an English-language daily focused on Turkey), I argued that '[i]t's good that there is this internal and external criticism.... A number of us have said, ... "Let's embrace this." But the criticism should go further up the chain.... "It's not enough.... We need to do more of that soul-searching, and it needs to be more public"' (Ashdown 2018a). Moreover, I have not just called upon others to engage in this process of critical self-reflection, but I have done so myself on a wide range of crucial issues such as the lack of transparency, accountability, and diversity (e.g., gender) in Hizmet's decision-making processes; Hizmet's politicisation in the Turkey context; 'Hizmet's inability to offer public self-criticism for its support of Turkey's Justice and Development Party and its uncritical support of the Ergenekon and Sledgehammer trials' (Keles et al. 2019, 277); Hizmet's lack of empathy (until recently) for the persecution of Kurds in Turkey and its denial of the Armenian genocide; Gülen's failure to provide effective leadership of Hizmet from 2010 onward; how Hizmet participants and sympathisers employed by the Turkish state (as, e.g., civil servants) inadvertently internalised and reproduced (or were, at the very least, at the risk of reproducing) the Turkish state's problematic habitus and practice on nationalism, statism, securitisation, favouritism, and xenophobia, etc. (Keles 2016b, 2018d, 2018b, 2018a, 2018c, 2019, 2021; Keles et al. 2019, 276–78; Ashdown 2018a, 2018b; Robinson 2018).[18]

---

[18] In addition to the above, I have also posted many critical Tweets and Twitter-threads about Hizmet and Gülen from as early as 2015 onward. The Turkish government included some of these

I have not shied from contradicting or criticising Gülen and Hizmet in the body of this book either. Among other things, in Chapter 3, I argue that Gülen's present-day characterisation of his 1980 response on the apostasy doctrine is factually incorrect. In addition, I unearth and critically engage with the substance of Gülen's 1977 'Women and Family in Islam' sermon series (which Hizmet appears to have wanted to keep out of the public domain) on women, the role of women in society, and women's rights in Chapter 4. Thus, while insider researchers must avoid the impulse to shield their object of study from criticism, I do not believe that this applies in the present case. Nonetheless, I have also demonstrated how I have remained vigilant against the risk of doing so through the tools and methods discussed so far.

This brings me to another form of bias, which relates to both insider and outsider research, that is normative bias. As Jillian Schwedler puts it, albeit in the context of another field of research, 'normative bias undergirds much of the inclusion-moderation literature: we want Islamists to become more moderate, and so we prioritize causal arguments about which mechanisms produce [such] moderation, and in what sequences those mechanisms interact' (2011, 371). Schwedler goes on to add that she does not 'find it problematic that analytic perspectives are shaped by normative commitments, but those commitments ought to be acknowledged head on and examined for the ways in which they structure our analyses' (2011, 371).

In response, I should point out that my research is rooted in a theorisation that was not motivated by a normative bias that *wanted* Hizmet to become this or that (i.e., 'more moderate'). Nor was it motivated by an impulse to *prove* one particular explanation for the outcomes under consideration over another. Rather, and as discussed above, I naturally began to theorise about the relationship between knowledge production (i.e., change) and practice, *in practice*, over a number of years, to make sense of what I was experiencing within Hizmet for my own benefit. In other words, I was not theorising to prove the epistemic outcomes under consideration (i.e., Gülen's statements

---

Tweets in the extradition request against me as 'evidence' of my 'membership' of Hizmet (Bowcott 2019). I have not cited these Tweets here because I have since closed my said Twitter account (I opened a new Twitter account in 2021 from which I continue to share my views and comments on a range of issues, including Hizmet and Gülen). I have also uploaded a number of YouTube videos in recent years in which I provide critical insight and commentary on Hizmet in Turkish (see youtube.com/ozcankeles). Finally, for a collection of my critical articles and blogs on Gülen and Hizmet, see https://www.ozcankeles.org/topic/hamteli/.

on apostasy and women's rights as the fact of those statements were never in dispute), nor was I theorising about practice and knowledge production with the expectation of demonstrating this to others. At the time, the easiest explanation would have been to attribute Hizmet's socially transformative knowledge production to Gülen, as so many within and without Hizmet had done, and continue to do so, to date. Arriving at an alternative explanation was neither easy nor comfortable for me. Furthermore, this theorised relationship between practice and knowledge holds whether it produces change (say, moderation) or reproduces the status quo (say, conservatism) on the issue of Islam and human rights. After all, in both scenarios, it directs our attention to the understudied notion of practice as a form of knowledge production (and perpetuation) in the context of Islam and human rights.

Finally, I began this section by discussing reflexivity and have come full circle with Schwedler's call for 'head-on' acknowledgement and examination of 'normative commitments' (2011, 371). That form of critical self-reflection presumably includes an acknowledgement of those factors that stand in the way of achieving it. In the present context, that manifests itself in the form of the Turkish government's relentless persecution of all things Hizmet related, myself included. I have been targeted by the Turkish government since 2015 for my public association with Hizmet and my public criticism of the Turkish government, as noted above. That persecution reached new heights in 2016 when our family home in Turkey was raided by twenty anti-terror police accompanied by a news agency (Keles 2016c). Within hours, I was branded as a 'terrorist' and as 'Gülen's right-hand man' in Turkey's mainstream print, online, and broadcast media (Keles 2016c). I stand charged (and remain on trial) in Turkey since late 2017 on two grounds: (1) membership and (2) propaganda of an 'armed terrorist organization' (i.e., Hizmet) (my translation) (İddianame No: 2017/325 2017, 3). I was arrested in May 2019 by the London Metropolitan Police as a result of an extradition request issued by the Turkish government. My case was heard at the Westminster Magistrates' Court where the central issue hinged on whether or not I was a 'member' of Hizmet (Bowcott 2019). The request was eventually dismissed at a preliminary stage after seven months and two preliminary hearings when the District Judge finally ruled that 'I am not satisfied that the request, as supplemented by further information, has sufficiently identified—to the requisite standard—any criminal offense said to have been committed by Mr. Keles' (Keles 2020). Thus, *demonstrating* reflexivity is not without its risks in the present context. Nonetheless, I have explicitly discussed how I have

Overview of Chapters

In this chapter, I summarised the animating question and the practice-based theoretical perspective of this book, predicated on the analyses and discussions I develop in Chapter 1. Thus, in Chapter 1, I will unpack the propositions put forward here. To do so, I will first review, organise, and problematise the Islamic responses to, and literature on, human rights. I will then bring a number of theoretical insights together to justify the centring of 'practice' as an alternative theoretical paradigm for understanding the relationship between social movement practice and religious knowledge production that addresses the animating question of this book. I will operationalise that theoretical paradigm into a methodological framework in Chapter 2 by combining single-case study analysis, process tracing methodology, and aspects of David Nicolini's (practice theory) toolkit. In doing so, I will reimagine and adapt the organisational studies' notion of knowledge conversion for my own purposes, which I will then contextualise within the epistemic framework in which it will be explored—that is, *fiqh*, the most prominent Islamic discipline within the body of Islamic knowledge. I will apply that theoretical-methodological framework in Chapters 3 and 4 to trace the interplay within and between Hizmet's doings and Gülen's sayings over an extended period of time and terrain to explore how and why Hizmet's emergent *ijtihads* ensued on the two topics under consideration—that is, apostasy and women's rights, respectively. In doing so, I will continually circle back to what was problematised, theorised, and operationalised in Chapters 1 and 2 to ensure theoretical and methodological consistency throughout this book. In Chapter 5, I will appraise my findings from Chapters 3 and 4 together to offer a more abstracted way of visualising what I have explained in the preceding chapters as the symbiotic relationship between the formalised and experiential facets of religious knowledge in the context of practice-based knowledge production. In doing so, I will show how my research contributes to the literature on Islam and human rights, social movement studies, (Islamic) knowledge production, and Hizmet, and I will also discuss the limitations of my study and further avenues of research.

1
Problematising the Islamic Responses to Human Rights

Turning to Practice

I summarised the animating question and the practice-based theoretical perspective of this book in the Introduction, which was predicated on the analyses and discussions developed in this chapter. As a result, this chapter will unpack the propositions put forward in my Introduction. To achieve this, I will first organise and critically review the Islamic responses to, and the literature on, human rights. I will then narrow my attention to the ('rapprochement') literature that focuses on *making* Islam compatible with human rights. In doing so, I will problematise the epistemological duality (or the duality problem) that is inherent in the scholarly approaches that focus on either *Islamic scripture* (conciliatorists) or *Muslim sensibility* (e.g., Asef Bayat) by appraising the challenges associated with each, together. Ultimately, my aim in the first and second part of this chapter is to understand the nature of the compatibility challenge, how it is said to manifest, from where it is shown to draw its strength, and what the efforts to make Islam compatible with human rights tells us about the challenges of doing so. I will explain how and why a practice-based epistemology, as theorised below, allows us to account for the production of Islamic knowledge on human rights while overcoming the limitations associated with the aforementioned scholarly approaches as problematised in this chapter. I will then contextualise this practice-based perspective and knowledge production within social movement studies and the literature on Hizmet.

As will be shown below, most scholars agree that there are many points of conflict between Islam and human rights. Malcolm Evans rightly notes that the literature on Islam and human rights is biased in its critical focus on Islam (2011, 113). Thus, an appraisal of this lopsided literature inevitably leads to a focus on Islam and its response to the human rights challenge. Furthermore, I too, will focus on Islam and the Islamic response to human rights for reasons already explained in the previous chapter. However, when doing so, I will highlight relevant points of criticism of human rights as and when they relate to this focus.

The Islamic Responses

Numerous scholarly pieces have organised the literature on Islam and human rights (Bielefeldt 1995, 2000; Abou El Fadl 2009; Cesari et al. 2004; Brems 2004; Akbarzadeh and MacQueen 2008b; Johnston 2015; Hellyer 2018; Shah 2006b). In an extensive report commissioned by the European Commission on Islam and Fundamental Rights in Europe, Jocelyne Césari, Alexandre Caeiro, and Dilwar Hussain organised the Islamic literature on human rights as either rejectionist, embracive, or conciliatory (2004, 61–64). Shannon Dunn, on the other hand, identifies four basic paradigms in the scholarship on Islam and human rights: (1) a secular paradigm for rights, (2) a Muslim apologist paradigm of rights, (3) a Marxist/postcolonial critique of rights, and (4) 'a Muslim reformist paradigm of rights that highlights points of continuity between western legal and Muslim legal traditions' (2015, 2). Heiner Bielefeldt provides a similar categorisation, when he refers to the 'Islamisation' of human rights, pragmatic approaches, liberal reconceptualisation of (traditional) *fiqh* (Islamic law), and secular positions (2000, 103). Niaz Shah, on the other hand, organises the Islamic response as being secular, non-compatible, and reconciliatory (2006b).

While these four reviews broadly overlap with one another, there are some differences between them. For example, Dunn, Bielefeldt, and Shah categorise the secular response separately, whereas Césari et al. do not. On the flip side, Césari et al. categorise the rejectionist position separately, whereas Dunn, Bielefeldt, and Shah do not. Dunn and Bielefeldt address criticisms levelled at human rights, whereas Césari et al. and Shah do not.

None of these categorisations are exhaustive, and there is always a risk of over-generalisation. What's more, some responses will fit more than one category. Nonetheless, these categories describe the persistent trends in the Islamic response to human rights. Having explored the literature, as well as the aforementioned reviews, I will broadly follow the Césari et al. categorisation, which discusses the rejectionist (but not the secular) position as a separate approach. Given the present and future trajectory of Muslim demographic growth and religiosity, both of which remain strong and stable, the secular position, unless justified from within Islam, is unlikely to garner widespread appeal among conservative Muslims (Pew 2016, 2017a, and 2017b). Furthermore, where the case for a secular position is made from within Islam, the style and substance of that justification are not markedly different from the conciliatorist approach to necessitate a separate categorisation. As for the rejectionist position, which rejects human rights altogether, this *is* markedly different from the more popular apologist approach,[1] and therefore deserves to be discussed separately—hence my preference for the Césari et al. categorisation. That said, I will adapt and nuance this categorisation in the process of reviewing the literature for the purposes of the present study.

Between Categorical Rejection and Uncritical Appropriation

The rejectionist approach is an amalgamation of fundamentalism, puritanism, conservatism, isolationism, and extremism (Abou El Fadl 2007, 95–110; Keles et al. 2019, 265). This attitude is prevalent among violent Jihadi groups such as Al Qaida and Daesh on the one hand and non-violent Salafis and Wahhabis and political Islamists such as Hizbu Tahrir on the other (Césari et al. 2004, 61). While marginal among Muslims worldwide, this strand of Islamic exceptionalism has resonated among Muslim youth and is backed by Saudi petrodollars (Eligür 2010, 114; Tibi 2014, 16).

The rationale for this approach is that the Qur'an and Sunna (Prophetic tradition)[2] express the divine, infallible, and immutable will of God, which must not be replaced by the profane, fallible, and whimsical will of humankind. To achieve this, Muslims must inoculate Islam from human interpretation and foreign cultural innovation through robust literalism of scripture that suppresses human agency and epistemic uncertainty (Abou El Fadl 2007, 98–99). Thus, this approach opposes anything that is not explicitly stated in the Qur'an and Sunna, including a recognition of the *madhhabs* (legal schools of law; Abou El Fadl 2007, 47). Modern-day laws, norms, standards (including human rights), and forms of governance (such as the modern nation state,

---

[1] Césari et al. refers to this as the 'embracive' approach while noting its apologetic undertones (Césari et al. 2004, 63). I prefer to refer to it as the apologist approach to distinguish it from the conciliatorist approach, which could also be described as being 'embracive'.
[2] Sunna refers to the Prophetic tradition comprising Prophet Muhammad's words and actions (or his sayings and doings) in relation to his Prophetic mission.

secularism, democracy, and free market economy) are not explicitly found in either of these two sources and must therefore be rejected as *bida*, that is, outright innovation. According to Khaled Abou El Fadl, the rejectionists project their 'sociopolitical frustrations and insecurities upon the [religious] text' from which they then derive their disdain for the West (2007, 96). Thus, their primary objective is to 'react to Western supremacy in the modern world by, effectively, constructing Islam into the antithesis of the West' (Abou El Fadl 2009, 123). According to this view, human rights is not just alien to Islam but is 'part of the Western cultural invasion of Muslim lands' (Abou El Fadl 2009, 118). Some even suggest that the human rights project is the West's hidden agenda to replace all godly religions with a form of godless humanism (Baderin 2003, 16). Consequently, the rejectionist approach is reactionary, categorical, and uncompromising in substance, style, and purpose.

Ironically, Muslim rejectionists and Western secular liberal scholars are united in their common view that Islam and human rights are intrinsically incompatible (Akbarzadeh and MacQueen 2008a, 2; Shah 2006b, 871). For example, Samuel Huntington claims that the incompatibility is rooted in the inescapable cultural conflict between Western and non-Western civilisations, such as Islam. Thus, efforts towards rapprochement are futile (Huntington 1993; Mayer 1994, 308–9). Michael Ignatieff claims that the core of human rights is 'moral individualism' and that it is wrong to tamper with this by placing 'greater emphasis on social duties and responsibilities to the community' to respond to the Islamic and Asian challenge to human rights (2001, 108). Jack Donnelly, on the other hand, argues against tampering with human rights for a different reason (2007). He claims that 'properly understood', the universality of human rights, leaves 'considerable space for national, regional, cultural particularity and other forms of diversity and relativity' (2007, 281). So much so, that this relativity or 'tolerance for deviation' (2007, 301) should extend, for example, to 'Islamic countries' to 'impose modest disabilities on apostates,' as long as they do not 'violate the human rights of apostates' (2007, 302) because the prohibition of apostasy in Islam 'has a deeply rooted doctrinal basis, supported by a long tradition of practice' (2007, 301).[3] Donnelly does not provide a satisfactory explanation as to how a state can impose 'modest disabilities' upon ex-Muslims without violating their right against religious discrimination in the process of doing so.[4]

---

[3] See also Oh 2008, 417–18; Hollenbach 2010, 581.
[4] See also Saeed 2018, 63–78.

Furthermore, there are parallels between the rejectionist critique of human rights and the extensive body of the classical, liberal, and non-liberal critique of human rights (Dembour 2006, 4–8). For example, following in the footsteps of postcolonial critics, a number of scholars such as Tony Evans (2005) and Richard A. Falk (2000b, 87–93), claim that human rights is defined and enforced in the interest of Western hegemony (Dunn 2015, 19). Human rights scholars have echoed similar critiques in the context of the present discussion, where human rights is criticised for being far too Western and far too Christian (Humphrey 1983, 29; Bielefeldt 2000, 91; Baderin 2003, 10–11). Césari et al. claims that human rights is tainted with Western political interests and failed nationalist secular projects in the Middle East propped up by Western governments, causing a Muslim aversion to human rights (2004, 8, 68). Ann Elizabeth Mayer draws attention to the criticism of Western hypocrisy (or double standards) on account of its past and present human rights violations (1995, 5).[5] Falk argues that Muslim states have been geopolitically excluded from the authority structures of international human rights such as the UN (Falk 2000a, 153, 163).

This brings us to the apologist approach, which appears to be the 'most widespread' among Muslims (Césari et al. 2004, 63; Brems 2004, 5). The popularity of this approach can be explained by its reliance on a traditionalist religious perspective, which 'continues to hold sway as the most authentic Islamic scholarship in the Muslim world' (Sachedina 2009, 20). Notable apologists include Abul A'la Mawdudi (d. 1979) (1977), Sayyid Qutb (d. 1966) (Oh 2007), Yusuf Qaradawi (Césari et al. 2004, 68), and Ayatollah Tashkiri (Bielefeldt 2000, 104). If the rejectionist reflex is to *reject* human rights to declare the supremacy of Islam, the apologist attitude is to *appropriate* it on the basis that everything that is 'good' (including human rights) originates from Islam. In doing so, it uncritically redefines human rights in an exclusively Islamic frame. This apologist attitude allows it to ignore any conflict between Islam and human rights or to simply reduce the 'offending' human rights norm down to size (Brems 2004, 6). At times, this uncritical appropriation is achieved by adding a hopelessly vague caveat to (Islamized) human rights articles and provisions, which restricts them in accordance with Islamic law, as found in the Universal Islamic Declaration of Human Rights of 1981 and the Cairo Declaration of Human Rights of 1990. The first document is the product of the London-based Islamic council whose signatory

---

[5] See also Santos 2009, 4.

members were largely Islamist groups engaged in political opposition to repressive Muslim regimes, whereas the second document is the product of the Organization of the Islamic Conference (OIC), which represents fifty-seven Muslim majority states (Dunn 2015, 5–6). Both documents are apologetic in nature, deferring to Islamic law as the ultimate source and interpreter of, and arbiter on, human rights, which limits the rights expressed therein (Dunn 2015, 6–7). According to Bielefeldt, this is a superficial, one-sided, uncritical 'Islamization' of the human rights language (2000, 104, 106). For Mayer, this approach represents 'strained attempts' at 'retroactively Islamizing [modern intellectual developments] by inventing supposed Islamic antecedents' for them (1995, 171).

The fundamental challenge with the rejectionist and apologist approach on human rights is that it is guided by a sense of religious absolutism. This is both *inhibitive*, as it denies us the opportunity of insight to be gained from an open and critical engagement on the issue, and *indicative*, as it alerts us to the challenge of exploring compatibility in the face of such absolutism.

Reconciliation through Theoretical Expositions

The conciliatorist approach is scholarly, critical, analytical, and methodical. It is common among Muslim scholars specialising in Islamic studies and human rights law with a background in Western academia (Taha 1987; Mernissi 1991; An-Na'im 1992, 1995, 1996; An-Na'im and Henkin 2015; Tibi 1994, 2009, 130–46; Wadud 1999; Abou El Fadl 2001, 2004, 2009; Ramadan 2001, 97–108, 2009; Soroush 2002; Baderin 2003; Shah 2006a, 8–13; Sachedina 2009).

The proponents of this approach acknowledge that there are significant points of conflict between Islamic law (i.e., *fiqh*, which is sometimes confusingly referred to as *Sharia*, as discussed a little further below and more extensively in Chapter 2) and international human rights standards (i.e., the 'manifestly discordant') (Césari et al. 2004, 79; Brems 2004, 6).[6] While

---

[6] I am not suggesting that conciliatorist scholars *only* frame the compatibility challenge in these terms. For example, Sachedina points to the foundational disconnect between the metaphysically rooted Islam and the secularised nature of modern human rights instruments, as an impediment towards the dialogue between the two. According to Sachedina, the Declaration and subsequent UN human rights instruments have been rendered 'foundationless' by their drafters on account of being secularised to the point that these documents have been severed from their metaphysical, moral, and philosophical foundations, that is, the Christian experience, Enlightenment thought, and natural rights philosophies (2009, 7–16). Thorwald Lorenzen makes a similarly forceful point about the

those who belong to this group are also critical of human rights politics (as discussed below), they consider the premodern nature of *fiqh* to be responsible for those legalistic points of conflict (An-Na'im 1996, xiv; Brems 2004, 6; Césari et al. 2004, 63). Others, including the Grand Chamber of the European Court of Human Rights have also framed the compatibility challenge in these terms and have arrived at the same conclusion:

> The Court concurs in the Chamber's view that sharia is incompatible with the fundamental principles of democracy, as set forth in the Convention: '72.... It is difficult to declare one's respect for democracy and human rights while at the same time supporting a regime based on sharia, which clearly diverges from Convention values, particularly with regard to its *criminal law and criminal procedure, its rules on the legal status of women and the way it intervenes in all spheres of private and public life in accordance with religious precepts* (my emphasis). (Refah Partisi v. Turkey 2003, para. 123)

A closer examination of the literature demonstrates what those points of conflict are and how they have remained largely unchanged over the years, which (insofar as Islam is concerned) all pertain to the Islamic discipline of *fiqh*. For example, according to Suzan Waltz, the Muslim state delegates took 'special interest' in the following 'five main issues' during the twenty-year period it took to draft the Universal Declaration of Human Rights of 1948 and the two covenants that followed it—that is, freedom of religion or belief ('FoRB') and the right to change religion, gender equality in marriage, social justice and the indivisibility of rights, the right to self-determination, and measures of implementation (2004, 813–37). Others have listed the thorny issues (beyond those that persistently arose in the context of the drafting of the UN instruments) as relating broadly to the same issues: change of religion, religious discrimination, equal rights of men and women, and corporal punishment (An-Na'im 1996, 8–9; Waltz 2004, 813–37; Brems 2004, 5; Césari et al. 2004, 3; Shah 2006b, 869; Akbarzadeh and MacQueen 2008a, 1; Sachedina 2009; Abou El Fadl 2009, 117). Among these various accounts of the issues of contention, apostasy from Islam and women's rights are the

---

'moral foundation' (or lack thereof) of human rights instruments (2000, 55). That said, conciliatorist scholars agree that the incompatibility between Islam and human rights is most evidently manifest at this legalistic level of analysis and that any attempt to make the case for human rights from within Islam needs to address that in doing so.

two most commonly cited as being the most intransigent and controversial (Akbarzadeh and MacQueen 2008a, 1). Hence, my reason for choosing to examine Hizmet's practice in the context of these two topics in Chapters 3 and 4, respectively.

While conciliatorist scholars acknowledge 'that religion constitutes merely one component within a whole range of political, economic, social, and cultural factors that inhibit or foster the implementation of human rights' (Bielefeldt 2000, 102),[7] that religious component often serves to justify the position of the other said factors. Moreover, while the challenge is multidimensional, it is nonetheless rooted, insofar as it pertains to Islam, in the fundamental distinction 'between those Islamic injunctions that are eternal and immutable and those that clearly are bound by time and space' (Hunter 2009, 291–92). This, according to conciliatorist scholars, is the crux of the matter (Soroush 2002, 27–29; Ramadan 2009, 1). To differentiate between the immutable and changing aspects of Islamic law depends on our ability to differentiate between those aspects of Islam considered to be sacred and profane.

Here, numerous scholars draw attention to the distinction between the religion of Islam (or the *Sharia*, i.e., God's law in abstract form as found in the Qur'an and Sunna) and *fiqh* (i.e., the human interpretation of the *Sharia*, that is, the Qur'an and Sunna) (Baderin 2003, 33–34; Shah 2006a, 69; Abou El Fadl 2001, 75–76; 2009, 136; Ramadan 2009, 17–22, 91–100). Abdolkarim Soroush, on the other hand, proposes a much more fundamental distinction by claiming that the divide is between religion and religious knowledge. Religion is regarded as divine, infallible, and unchanging, whereas religious knowledge (i.e., everything we know about religion) is limited, flawed, and subject to change on account of our limitedness. According to this, everything we know about religion (including but not restricted to *fiqh*) is in fact religious knowledge and is therefore no more sacred or immutable than any other branch of human knowledge (Soroush 2002, 29–37). Accordingly, Soroush desacralises not just *fiqh* but all forms of human cognition of religion as being human interpretation.

This steers the discussion away from a narrow focus on the manifestly discordant dictums of *fiqh* to the underlying traditional epistemologies that produce them. That, in the context of Islamic law, is *usul al-fiqh* (the methodology by which *fiqh* is produced) (An-Na'im 1996, 52–68; Soroush 2002, 29–37; Abou El Fadl 2009, 127; Sachedina 2009; Ramadan 2009; Vahdat

---

[7] See also An-Na'im 1995, 240–41; Abou El Fadl 2009, 113.

2000a, b; Sadri 2001, 261). Some conciliatorist scholars claim that the thorny issues can be reinterpreted by remaining within the conventional boundaries of *usul al-fiqh* by, for example, employing classical legal devices such as *maslahah* (public interest) (Baderin 2003, 42–43, 222). Others claim that the conventional boundaries of *usul al-fiqh* are too restrictive and that we need to construct new epistemologies to overcome the problematic aspects of *fiqh* to make the case for human rights from within Islam in a more robust manner. However, this effort must be rooted in the spirit of the Qur'an and Sunna and can be guided or supported by traditional Islamic teachings and concepts on, for example, *fitra* (human nature), *haqq* (right or entitlement), *adl* (justice), *sirat al-mustaqeem* (the right way), and *maqasid al-Sharia* (overall objective of the *Sharia*) (An-Na'im 1996, xiv, 28, 34; Abou El Fadl 2009, 142–158; Soroush 2002; Sachedina 2009; Ramadan 2009; Johnston 2015, 124–44).

Furthermore, if religion (or at the very least, *fiqh*) is in fact a form of human knowledge, then our efforts to produce new religious epistemologies can be aided by bringing Islam into conversation with other branches of human knowledge, such as the social sciences and humanities. This, for example, is the position adopted by conciliatorist scholars such as Mohammad Mojtahed Shabestari (Sadri 2001, 261; Vahdat 2000a, 38), Tariq Ramadan (2009, 130–33), and Mohsen Kadivar (Vahdat 2000b, 143).

If the fossilised nature of premodern *fiqh* is criticised for its inability to converse with other branches of human knowledge, human rights has also been criticised for its unilateralism and inability to engage in dialogue with Muslims (Brems 2004, 14; Ven 2006, 423, 429; Abou El Fadl 2007, 201; Ghanea-Hercock et al. 2007, 16; Petito 2009). There appears to be a number of factors that inhibit this dialogue: the Muslim world's aversion to the West's role in promoting human rights given its colonial past (Baderin 2003, 10–11); the Western and Christian origin of modern-day human rights instruments (Nurser 2003, 2005; Humphrey 1983, 29; Baderin 2003, 10–11; Bielefeldt 2000, 91); the West's control of human rights knowledge in a manner that excludes Muslim actors (Oh 2008, 409); and the 'foundationless' (i.e., secularised) nature of modern human rights instruments (Sachedina 2009, 7–16).[8] To overcome this, Eva Brems calls for an inclusive universality, which brings both Muslim societies and human rights doctrines closer to one another through an intercivilisational dialogue on human rights, a human rights debate within Islamic societies, as well as on the commitment

---

[8] For a brief explanation of the 'foundationless' disconnect, see footnote 6 above.

to diversity within the international human rights community by allowing for a progressive realisation of human rights (2004, 15).

The advantage of the conciliatorist approach is that it engages with the challenge of compatibility in a critical manner. As a result, it allows us to go beyond rejectionism on the one hand and uncritical appropriation on the other. This approach not only deconstructs Islamic orthodoxy, but also erects in its place internally consistent interpretive paradigms that are founded on the essential teachings, ethics, and ethos of Islam. This provides us with a far more promising platform from which to make the theoretical case for human rights from within Islam. That said, there is a drawback to this approach, which helps to further illuminate the nature of the compatibility challenge, which I will examine below.

Torn between Two Foci: Text and Reader

In this section, I will focus on the drawbacks associated with two approaches that aim to *make* Islam, or *account* for how it might be made to be, compatible with human rights. I will first examine the drawback associated with the conciliatorist approach we just discussed, which aims to make *religious text* compatible with human rights through theoretical reinterpretations of the primary sources and methodologies of Islam. I will contrast that with the drawback associated with a more recent approach that instead calls for a focus on making *Muslim sensibility* about religion compatible with democracy and human rights (e.g., in the example of Asef Bayat's approach). By appraising them together, I will problematise the reciprocal epistemological drawback associated with each, which will allow me to justify my alternative theoretical paradigm for the purposes of this study, as discussed further below.

Missing the Reader for the Text

The conciliatorist approach is dominated by highly intellectualised theoretical expositions produced through conventional means of knowledge production in the West, that is, scholarly exposition and debate, made publicly accessible through the publication of books and articles. In other words, this approach focuses on reexamining *religious texts* by producing *texts on religion* in an academic context that inevitably excludes a broader 'readership' on account of its style and format. Cheryl Benard expands on the drawback of this approach with the following:

> They [i.e., modernist conciliatorists] tend to be well educated and well integrated. They do not hold sensationalist views that provide interesting sound bites, and they do not proselytize. They tend to write academic texts or editorials, not mass-market propaganda. This makes their work relatively inaccessible to the bulk of the population, especially the restless young. One of the authors cited above, Khaled Abou El-Fadl, writes long, complicated volumes critiquing the different schools and philosophies of Islamic jurisprudence. His analysis of the Saudi religious establishment's more absurd religious fatwas is highly readable and entertaining, but it is buried in an expensive, 361-page-long theoretical volume about the significance and evolution of religious authority in Islam....
>
> Modernists become professors at universities, not teachers in madrassas or at mosque Sunday school. They dress like everyone else, which reduces their attractiveness to journalists who are writing a piece about 'Muslims in America,' and they do not segregate themselves socially, which makes them harder to find—you cannot just call an Islamic cultural center and find them there. Since Islam is not their overriding personal identity, they are not prone to establishing Islamic organizations or clubs. This gives them poor visibility. (2003, 40)[9]

Many conciliatorist scholars concede this drawback explicitly or implicitly. Abdullahi Ahmed An-Na'im suggests that since the vast majority of Muslims are traditionalist, it is important to build on Islamic tradition so as to cause them to rethink their approach to the *'constructed' fiqh* (1996, xiv, 11–2; Johnston 2015, 143). Abdulaziz Sachedina however suggests that '[a]s it stands, I do not believe that Na'im's proposed alternative can carry any implications beyond the Western academic interest in it' (1993, 156). If Sachedina doubts the reach of An-Na'im's work, David L. Johnston wonders how 'effective Sachedina's arguments are among the traditionalist scholars who worry that human rights norms are simply the Trojan Horse of secular fundamentalism come to silence the voice of Islam in the public sphere' (2015, 140). According to Johnston, 'it will take a good deal more advocacy at

---

[9] See also The Netherlands Scientific Council 2006, 51–52.

the grassroots to advance more reformist conceptions of Shari'a' (2015, 145). According to Sachedina, however, it is not a matter of time but the participation of the traditional scholars, without whose support 'it is doubtful if the modernists can advance anything beyond formal academic expositions,' which presumably includes himself (2009, 142). Conversely, Abou El Fadl claims that traditional scholars and jurists cannot play the historic role of marginalizing puritans (2007, 105) but that moderate Muslims can through 'unrelenting intellectual activism' (2007, 286). According to Abou El Fadl, this effort must include the production of 'beautifully printed but cheaply priced' literature that is accessible to the masses (2007, 285), which according to Benard would exclude Abou El Fadl's publications (2003, 40), including the one in which he makes this suggestion. According to Jamie Schillinger, '[t]he goal, therefore, of influencing and guiding the social-epistemological discourse concerning rights and their abuses is a critical one,' which requires more effort to 'advance this goal beyond offering another "formal academic exposition"' (2011, 577).

Thus, the challenge of this approach is popularising highly sophisticated theoretical arguments within wider society—that is, producing change within *religion popular*, through efforts focused solely on *religion proper* (these terms will be unpacked a little further below). As we will see below, Bayat arrives at the same conclusion in relation to the efforts of these scholars, whom he refers to as 'religious intellectuals' (2007, 86–88). This approach appeals far more to an educated Western audience than it does to socially conservative Muslims and traditional Islamic clerics.[10]

Why does popularisation matter? It matters because these are not just 'theological disputes without practical effects as to the way Islam is lived and experienced today' (Abou El Fadl 2007, 278). To the contrary, the question as to whether or not Islam and human rights are compatible has real-life implications for both the universality of human rights and the welfare of Muslims and non-Muslims alike in Muslim majority countries. However, as discussed in the Introduction, the question of compatibility goes beyond that. It raises a series of foundational questions about how Muslims conceive the nature, role, and purpose of Islam in the modern age and Islam's ability to respond to the challenges of modernity. That in return, has implications for our ability to seek out common ground in an increasingly polarised world.

---

[10] Notable exceptions to this include Mohsen Kadivar and Mohammad Mojtahed Shabestari who have received classical Islamic training but have nonetheless adopted the type of conciliatorist approach as discussed here.

Missing the Text for the Reader

Asef Bayat espouses an approach in counter-distinction to the one just discussed. He explains that those who advocate the incompatibility thesis (i.e., secular Western intellectual circles on the one hand and Islamists on the other) and those who advocate the opposite (i.e., conciliatorist scholars, whom he refers to as religious intellectuals) 'share an exclusive commitment to texts, drawing their arguments from the literal reading of sacred scriptures (the Qur'an and *hadith*), and pay astonishingly little attention to what these texts mean to the fragmented Muslim citizenry in their day-to-day lives' (2007, 4). Bayat later discusses some of these conciliatorist scholars in greater detail in the context of the post-Islamist reform in Iran. While he acknowledges that these 'religious intellectuals' brought about a 'major discursive shift' by navigating through theology and jurisprudence (Bayat 2007, 84), he adds that, as noted above, the 'power of the word' failed to develop a social base and reach the grassroots (Bayat 2007, 133–35).[11]

Given the foregoing, Bayat claims that we should not be concerned with what the sacred texts says on this or that issue (e.g., democracy) because '[n]othing intrinsic to Islam—or, for that matter, to any other religion—makes it inherently democratic or undemocratic' (2007, 4). This is because 'religious injunctions are nothing but our understanding of them; they are what we make them to be' (Bayat 2007, 5). Simply put, 'we humans define the truth of sacred texts' (Bayat 2007, 188). As a result, '[r]ather than resorting to the Qur'an or *Sharia* to make sense of Osama bin Laden, or of Islamist radicalism in general, we need to examine the conditions that allow social forces to make a particular reading of the sacred texts hegemonic' (Bayat 2007, 5–6). This extends to the question of compatibility: '[t]he question is not whether Islam is or is not compatible with democracy or, by extension, modernity, but rather under what conditions Muslims can make them compatible' (Bayat 2007, 4). According to Bayat, *that* question 'inevitably leads us into the realm of social movement theory and practice' (2007, 6). Bayat explains that social movements are best placed to undertake this task as they can popularise a particular interpretation of Islam through their sustained activism, mobilisation, cultural production, and what he calls the 'art of presence,' that is, active citizenry in the form of sustained presence of individuals and groups in every available social space, whether institutional or informal,

---

[11] See also Esposito 2010, 93.

where they assert their rights and fulfil their responsibilities (2007, 14, 187–205). By doing so, social movements can make Islam compatible with democracy (and human rights).

Bayat is not alone in emphasising the social over the semiotic. Jillian Schwedler locates Bayat's argument within the broader 'scholarship on political Islam [that] has moved away from abstract debates [i.e., the conciliatorists' approach] about the compatibility of Islam and democracy and toward *empirical studies of the practices* and commitments of Islamist groups' (my emphasis) (2011, 347)—the 'inclusion-moderation hypothesis,' which Schwedler defines as 'the idea that political groups and individuals may become more moderate as a result of their inclusion in pluralist political processes' (2011, 348). Similarly, following the September 11, 2001 attacks, a number of think tanks in Western capitals published policy recommendations suggesting that Western governments should support 'moderate' Muslim networks and groups in the Muslim world to help them popularise an 'enlightened' and 'moderate' interpretation of Islam among their fellow believers (e.g., Benard 2003; Benard and Schwartz 2007; The Netherlands Scientific Council 2006).

Bayat accurately identifies the challenge with the conciliatorist approach: they narrowly focus on 'sacred texts,' while failing to account for the 'social forces [that] make a particular reading of the sacred texts hegemonic' among the faithful (2007, 5–6). Proverbially put, they miss the forest (the social forces that shape the interpretation of religious texts) for the trees (the religious texts themselves). However, in attempting to correct this myopia, Bayat commits the same mistake, only this time in reverse: he narrowly focuses on the social forces that appear to be relevant to the popularisation of any particular religious reading of the 'sacred texts,' without accounting for the role of the inherited tradition of religious knowledge and epistemology (which includes theoretical discussions about the meaning of sacred texts) in the process of doing so. This is a natural consequence of claiming that 'religious injunctions are nothing but our understanding of them' (Bayat 2007, 5). Forough Jahanbakhsh expands upon this oversight in the following excerpt:

> [Bayat] tends to underestimate the role of theoretical discussions that challenge centuries-old political traditions, social ethos, and religio-ideological convictions of a society in the process of democratization. As for religion, it is, after all, through theoretical re-examinations of inherited traditions that new understandings develop, including those that can provide a plausible

structure for the faithful to participate in the process of the democratization of their societies without the fear of violating the precepts of their religion. In general, overemphasizing the role of social groups in changing the political ethos of an Islamic society could be as misleading and narrow an analysis as overemphasizing the merely theoretical and intellectual debates over the compatibility of Islam and democracy, for there is a symbiotic relationship between interpretations of the "sacred" and dispositions of the society of the faithful. No interpretation happens in a vacuum. Any interpretation of religion (radical or democratic) reflects the principal conditions of its time and context. Equally, no social movement that heralds new values and ideals can develop roots in a religious society without the endorsement of an authoritative reinterpretation of religion that could harmonize its new ideals with society's spiritual and religious sensibilities, let alone the inspiration that social groups receive from intellectuals who, by virtue of their role, sow the seeds of such ideals. (2010, 152)

To underestimate the inherited tradition of religious knowledge and epistemology (and the theoretical discussions surrounding it) has, at least, two consequences. First, it overlooks the role that it plays in *legitimising* new religious interpretations and practices as being authentic in the eyes of the faithful. Here, the inherited tradition of religious knowledge and epistemology matters because it is considered a legitimising point of reference for the faithful. The theoretical discussion matters insofar as it demonstrates that the new religious interpretation is anchored in the inherited tradition of religious knowledge for the purposes of legitimising it as being an authentic expression of the religion itself (An-Na'im 1995, 237). Second, it overlooks the symbiotic relationship between the religious text and the religious reader or, to put it another way, between (that which is considered to be) the *text of revelation* and the *text of human experience* in the *production* of religious interpretation (Graham 2009, 151). This brings to mind what An-Na'im refers to as the 'organic, dynamic relationship between the Qur'an and Islam on the one hand, and the nature of human beings (that is, their comprehension, imagination, judgement, behaviour, experience, and so forth) on the other' (An-Na'im 1995, 236).

In other words, while religious texts rely on human interpretation to generate meaning and knowledge, human interpretation relies on religious text (or the established meaning of it) to anchor itself within a certain framework, even if that framework is a socially constructed orthodoxy. By overlooking the role of the inherited tradition of religious knowledge, Bayat fails to appreciate the role of formalised, traditional, semiotic, and theoretical religious knowledge in the production, legitimisation, and popularisation of religious knowing within the lived, experiential, social, and contemporary dimension of religious life.

What we are discussing here, according to lived religion, is the difference between two types of religious knowledge: 'religion proper,' that is, the formalised, scriptural, official, institutional, orthodoxical, and explicit facet of religious knowledge, and 'religion popular,' that is, the everyday practice of religion that is experiential, lived, public, vernacular, and tacit (Orsi 1985; Certeau 1988; Lambek 1997, 136; D. D. Hall 1997; Ammerman 2007; McGuire 2008; Schielke and Debevec 2012, 1; Neitz 2012, 47; Ammerman 2016, 7). As a relatively new field, lived religion emerged from the recognition that religion proper is not the same as religion popular. This generated an 'important epistemological and methodological shift' in the study of religion (Sunier 2015, 13), with 'attention to laity, not clergy or elites; to practices rather than beliefs; to practices outside religious institutions rather than inside; and to individual agency and autonomy rather than collectivities or traditions' (Ammerman 2016, 1). Thus, this suggests that our conciliatorist scholars hoped to reshape *religion popular* (lived religion) through their efforts within *religion proper* (formalised religion). Bayat on the other hand calls for reshaping *religion proper* (formalised religion) by accounting for how a religious reading can be hegemonised among *religion popular* (lived religion).

With that in mind, let us return to unpacking the aforementioned symbiotic relationship between the two facets of religious knowledge further. Here, I will make use of Stanley Hauerwas's *King Lear* analogy (2005), which John Swinton and Harriet Mowat use to introduce practical theology (2006, 4).[12] According to this analogy, there is a difference between the *play* (i.e., text) and the *performance* (i.e., lived experience) of *Lear*. Hauerwas says that the Christian faith is the *performance*, rather than the *play*, of *Lear*, which appears to support Bayat's position. Similarly, lived religion challenges the implicit hierarchy between official (textual) and lived (performative) religion and 'emphasizes that individuals do not simply "copy" institutional religious prescriptions; instead, it posits that people have an active and reflexive role in

---

[12] I will introduce and discuss practical theology a little further below.

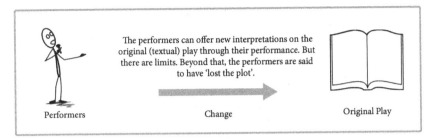

Figure 1.1 The limits to a performance changing the original play[a]

shaping, negotiating and changing their own beliefs and practices' (Nyhagen 2017, 495).[13]

While *Lear* lends itself to many interpretations, 'there remains a fundamental plot, structure, storyline, and outcome without which it would be unrecognizable. Lack of adherence to these key aspects of *Lear* indicates that the performer has "lost the plot"' (Swinton and Mowat 2006, 4). Performers (i.e., the faithful or believers) can innovate and improvise but within reason. To go beyond 'the recognizable and accepted' scripts, boundaries and narratives would 'require the creation of another play' (Swinton and Mowat 2006, 5). Thus, one cannot change the performance without consideration for the play as it is embodied in the established meaning of the text (see Figure 1.1). Therefore, the established meaning of the text *does* bear upon how the play is interpreted and how that interpretation is legitimised as it is performed and enacted.

A symbiotic relationship works both ways. That means that a theoretical reinterpretation of the play (i.e., a theoretical reinterpretation of the established meaning of the text), which fails to account for how its performers (i.e., the faithful) perceive that reinterpretation, also runs the risk of failure. After all, and continuing the analogy, the performers are there to perform what they believe to be *King Lear*. The ability to convince them to perform the reinterpreted version of *Lear* is closely related to the *way* in which the play is reinterpreted and how it can be *shown* to be (as distinguished from *actually* being) an honest and authentic rereading of it. This 'reverse failure' is demonstrated in the experience of the conciliatorist approach as discussed

[a] The clipart of the 'performer' and 'scroll' was downloaded from http://clipart-library.com/, which allows the free use of clipart for non-commercial purposes. The website did not provide the name of the artist for the two images used for Figures 1.1 and 1.2.

[13] See also Neitz 2012, 47–48; Schielke and Debevec 2012, 2.

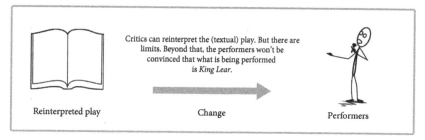

Figure 1.2 The limits to a reinterpreted play being accepted by the performers

earlier. The conciliatorists operated, by and large, within the theoretical/intellectual realm (they reinterpreted the textual play, so to speak, through textual expositions) conveying their message in an idiom and style that was not necessarily accessible and distinguished as being Islamic (Benard 2003, 40). Thus, they found that however robust their textual expositions were, they had limited traction with the 'performers' (i.e., observant lay Muslims) (see Figure 1.2).

Thus, the foregoing discussion demonstrates that while the conciliatorist approach aims to reinterpret religious scripture through theoretical expositions operating within the formalised, propositional, explicit facet of religious knowledge (asking itself, what does the scripture say? How can it be reinterpreted from within an Islamic framework?), Bayat's approach advocates for reconfiguring the sensibilities of the faithful by focusing on the social conditions that hegemonise a particular religious reading within the experiential, lived, tacit facet of religious knowledge (asking itself, what do Muslims believe? How can one scriptural interpretation be popularised over another?).

Hence, these two approaches differ in substance (semiotic versus social), style (rhetorical versus practical), and disciplinary basis (theological/juridical versus sociological/anthropological). Consequently, each approach overlooks the epistemological role of the other and the symbiotic relationship between the two in the production of either (i.e., formalised and experiential) facet of religious knowledge. As a result, the first approach fails to penetrate the depths of Muslim grassroots sensibility, whereas the second, at the very least, fails to account for religious legitimacy by, for example, locating itself within the inherited tradition of religious epistemology. The failure in one direction impacts the potential to effectuate and explain change, respectively, in the other. This, therefore, clarifies the problem of this study: that is, to explore an interdisciplinary approach that allows us to account for the production, legitimisation, and popularisation of Islamic knowledge on, or as it relates to, human rights in a manner that connects the fragmented epistemological dualisms of religious knowledge, interchangeably referred to as proper/popular, formalised/experiential, official/lived, explicit/tacit, propositional/pre-propositional, and systematic/vernacular.

That can be achieved by adopting a theoretical framework that recognises the symbiotic relationship between the formalised and experiential facets of religious knowledge in the production of Islamic knowledge on human rights. This would allow me to examine both sides of the symbiotic relationship, on its own (relatively speaking) and in its interaction with the other, while explaining how that interaction accounts for the change and stability of the dispositions of the faithful and their interpretations of the sacred. Having problematised the literature in this respect, I suggest that adopting social movement practice as our basic unit of analysis will allow us to do just that. I will now turn to unpacking that further.

Turning to Practice

It is at this point that a growing awareness and appreciation in a number of disparate fields and disciplines for practice and its multidirectional and multirelational implication comes to our aid.[14] Davide Nicolini suggests that this trend began in the 1970s in part due to the Marxist, Heideggerian. and Wittgenstein traditions, which cleared the way in social theory to eventually allow for practice to be rescued from its 'historical demotion' (2013, 41). Furthermore, the works of Pierre Bourdieu (1977, 1990), Anthony Giddens (1979), Michel Foucault (1980), Charles Taylor (1995), and Harold Garfinkel (1967) were early contributors in this regard. This resulted in what has now been dubbed, the 'practice turn' in social theory (Schatzki et al. 2001). This orbital shift is marked by 'a return of the practice concept in studies of organizing, learning and knowing' (Corradi et al. 2010, 265), which are interchangeably referred to as 'practice-based studies,' 'practice-based approach(es),' and 'practice theories'. These approaches have not produced a

---

[14] These include philosophy, cultural theory, history, sociology, anthropology, organisational studies, sociology of knowledge, knowledge management, adult education, cognitive psychology, and neurolinguistics (Schatzki 2001a).

unified grand theory in the form of a series of interconnected premises that dictate a predictive or explanatory outcome (Corradi et al. 2010, 267), which is unsurprising given the 'multiplicity of impulses, issues, and oppositions' they entail and comprise (Schatzki 2001a, 11). Nicolini argues that attempting to produce a grand unified theory would in fact 'run against the spirit of most practice approaches which strive to provide a thicker, not thinner, description of everyday life' (2013, 9). Rather, practice accounts are joined in the ontological belief that 'phenomena as knowledge, meaning, human activity, science, power, language, social institutions, and historical transformation occur within and are aspects or components of the *field of practices*' (Schatzki 2001a, 11) or that 'many social and organizational phenomena occur within, and are aspects or components of, the field of practices' (Nicolini 2013, 13).

That, in return, means that we must adopt practice (as opposed to structures, institutions, and authority) as our basic unit of analysis for the purposes of the present study (Nicolini 2013, 3). That includes a focus on practice as opposed to the practitioner (Nicolini 2013, 7). After all, and as Bourdieu puts it, 'practice has a logic which is not that of the logician' (1990, 86), which suggests that 'practices tend toward their own elaboration regardless of our explicit intentions' (Spinosa 2001, 210).[15] This has implications for how we theorise about the relationship between practice and knowledge production, to which I turn to next.

Practice and Knowledge

Practice approaches 'depict the world in relational terms as being composed by, and transpiring through, a bundle of practices' (Nicolini 2013, 8), which helps us to overcome 'problematic dualisms like mind/body, actor/structure, human/non-human' (Gherardi 2006, 39).[16] Instead, all of these elements are simply present in the performance of practice. This approach, coupled with an interest in understanding the link between work (practice) and knowledge production/learning in organisational studies, has resulted in the recognition of a practice-based epistemology (Gherardi 2000, 2003, 2006, 2009; Orlikowski 2002; Sole and Edmondson 2002; Gherardi and Nicolini 2003; Corradi et al. 2010; Cook and Wagenaar 2012). This epistemology rejects

---

[15] This encourages us to explore the unintended (epistemic) outcomes of practice, which I will pick up a little later on.
[16] See also Schatzki 2001a, 10.

rationalistic, cognitivistic, and functionalistic notions of knowledge wherein knowledge is treated as a fixed, objective, standalone tangible commodity (Gherardi 2000, 211; Corradi et al. 2010, 270; Souto 2013, 51–61) that resides (only) in people's heads (Gherardi 2000, 212, 2003, 352), 'detached from human action and disconnected from users' sense-making' (Souto 2013, 55).

The modern mind is founded upon this rationalistic notion of knowledge, which in turn, is rooted in Cartesianism (Tarnas 2010, 275). According to this philosophical tradition, the physical world is 'entirely objective' and 'solidly and unambiguously material' and therefore 'inherently measurable' (Tarnas 2010, 278). As a result, we can attain definitive, explicit, objective, universal, and dispassionate (formalised) knowledge through critical rationality, mathematical logic, and systematic skepticism. This outcome is achieved by dividing the world into the 'thinking substance' (*res cogitans*) and the 'extended substance' (*res extensa*) where the knowing, observing, and measuring human mind is separated from the knowable, objective, and mechanistic natural world (Tarnas 2010, 277–80). This produces and perpetuates the problematic dichotomies that pertain to knowledge such as mind/body, subjective/objective, and knowing/known, which in turn underpins the conventional view that practice is no more than the application of knowledge as held in people's heads (Cook and Wagenaar 2012, 4).

Conversely, according to a practice-based epistemology, to know is to be 'capable of participating [i.e., doing] with the requisite competence in the complex web of relationships among people, material artefacts and activities' (Gherardi 2006, 2). After all, it is 'through action and interaction within practices that mind, rationality and knowledge are constituted and social life is organized, reproduced and transformed' (Schatzki et al. 2001, i). Furthermore, '[p]ractice . . . involves awareness and application of both *explicit* (language, tools, concepts, roles, procedures) and *tacit* (rules of thumb, embodied capabilities, shared worldviews) elements' (my emphasis) (Sole and Edmondson 2002, 18) and 'affords understanding of the everyday interactions between the "expert" [explicit] and "local" [tacit] dimensions of people's knowledge' (Corradi et al. 2010, 276).

This suggests that 'knowing is not a static embedded capability . . . but rather an ongoing social accomplishment, constituted and reconstituted as actors engage the world of practice' (Orlikowski 2002, 249) and that 'practice itself is not passive but active, and that among its active traits is that it gives shape to knowledge and context, that the contents of knowledge and context are accepted, sustained, and modified or rejected through practice'

(Cook and Wagenaar 2012, 27). This notion of knowledge and practice, in return, supports 'a relational conception of practice, knowledge, and context in which practice is distinct and primary' and 'knowledge and context can be explained in terms of—and are evoked within—practice, and not the other way round' (Cook and Wagenaar 2012, 5). Thus, a practice-based epistemology connects knowledge (knowing) with doing through practice (Gherardi 2000, 215). As a result, 'knowledge' (noun) is in fact 'knowing' (verb) because knowledge, like practice, is never complete, static, fixed, or finalised but is in fact dynamic, provisional, constructed, emergent, relational, processual, situational, interactive, and continually reproduced (Gherardi 2000, 2003, 356–57, 2006, 38–39; Gherardi and Nicolini 2003, 204–8; Corradi et al. 2010, 274–75; Souto 2013, 55, 62, 64, 68).

This practice-based epistemological perspective of knowledge extends to all 'lay, practical and theoretical knowledge' (Gherardi 2006, 2). Consequently, knowledge 'does not arise from scientific "discoveries"; rather, it is fabricated by situated practices of knowledge production and reproduction, using the technologies of representation and mobilization employed by scientists' (Gherardi 2000, 218–19). Similarly, 'formal knowledge emerges out of, and cannot be seen apart from, an often unacknowledged and largely tacit context of hunches, cues, bodily predispositions, expectations, appreciations, values, affects, and so on' (Cook and Wagenaar 2012, 8). As a result, 'all knowledge, including formal knowledge, is embedded in ordinary experience, and, in an essential sense, gets its meaning, its life, from it' (Cook and Wagenaar 2012, 8).[17]

Therefore, practice-based epistemology does not deny different forms of knowledge and knowing (Souto 2013, 63). After all, knowledge, 'as the collected, solidified, and systematized remnants of earlier experiences, *does play an important role* in how we grasp the world' (my emphasis) (Cook and Wagenaar 2012, 14). Rather, and as explained above, a practice-based epistemology takes all forms of knowledge (e.g., explicit and tacit) and faculties of consciousness and connects them together in practice. In doing so, it claims that while,

> [w]hat we know indeed plays a role in how we act . . . it is not something that comes before or underlies what we do. We may use a hammer in building a bookcase—it helps us interact with wood and nails, and it helps us give

---

[17] See Corrardi et al. on 'science as practice' (2010, 271–72).

shape to the bookcase. But the hammer does not give rise to what we do. It may be necessary in deploying our skills, but it alone does not produce those skills. It can be a valuable and, in some ways, necessary tool in the practice of building a bookcase. But it is the hammer that is an artefact of the practice of building a bookcase, not the practice that is a product of the artefact. Likewise, with knowledge: it is a valuable and necessary part of practice. But it is something that is evoked and deployed within and by way of what we do, not something that underlies and enables what we do. It is in this way that we see knowledge as an artefact of practice. (Cook and Wagenaar 2012, 24)

Thus, and in sum, a practice-based epistemology allows me to focus on practice as the locus of knowledge production, which ensues in a relational manner wherein the formalised and the experiential facets of knowledge and the dynamics that produce, sustain, and change them are symbiotically present in the performance of practice. Here, the focus is not solely on the formalised or on the experiential facet of knowledge but on both, including the interaction between the two.

The above notwithstanding, what about the relationship between practice and the production of *religious* knowledge? After all, that is the type of knowledge that we are concerned with. It is here that the underlying premise of practical theology, lived religion, and everyday Islam comes to our aid.

While practical theology was originally conceived as the 'Cinderella of theological studies, occupying itself with the pragmatic and relatively untaxing practicalities of "applied Christianity"' (Graham 2009, 135), today, it makes a different claim. According to this, practice is 'generative of theological insight' (Graham et al. 2005, 3), and 'proper theological understanding cannot be formed independently of practical engagement' (Graham et al. 2005, 170). After all, 'theological reflections [are] essentially a series of conversations between a contemporary situation and the sources and resources of faith' (Graham 2009, 180–81) or, put differently, between the *text of human experience* and the *text of revelation* as previously discussed (Graham 2009, 151). Interpreting one without the other leads to a disconnected theology (Farley 1987, chap. 1). It is that dimension that practical theology aims to fill (Swinton and Mowat 2006, 15).

Similarly, Stephen Pattison and James Woodhard claim that 'practical theology is a place where religious belief, tradition and practice meets contemporary experiences, questions and actions and conducts *a dialogue that is mutually enriching*, intellectually critical and practically transforming' (my emphasis) (2010, 7). Therefore, practical theology 'finds itself located within the uneasy but *critical tension* between the script of revelation ... and the continuing innovative performance [practice] of the gospel' (my emphasis) (Swinton and Mowat 2006, 5). This circles back to the discussion on the symbiotic relationship and the *King Lear* analogy, which demonstrates that theology is not *didactically linear* (in one direction or the other) but *dynamically circular*, oscillating between the scriptural/experiential, explicit/tacit, semiotic/social facets of religious knowledge.

Lived religion and studies on everyday Islam, on the other hand, support the premise that practice produces Islamic knowledge. Early studies in this respect include those by Reinhold Loefflller (1988), John R. Bowen (1993), and Michael Lambek (1993). According to Ingvild Flaskerud, these studies conceive of 'the production of knowledge to be relational, and the method for meaning production is expanded from being seen only as semiotic to one that is both performative and embodied' (Flaskerud 2018, 489). More recently, a number of publications have adopted the anthropological perspective of lived religion to explore the role of non-specialists in the production of Islamic knowledge (Jouili and Amir-moazami 2006; Bruinessen and Allievi 2011; Flaskerud and Leirvik 2018; Flaskerud 2018; Martensson and Vongraven Eriksen 2018, 465–83).

An edited volume by Martin Van Bruinessen and Stefano Allievi (2011) looks further into the processes by which Muslims in the West acquire and produce Islamic theology in an informal manner. Bruinessen cites two 'new practices' by European mosques as an example of the production of 'practical Islamic knowledge that developed quite naturally out of interaction with the environment' (2011, 13). The first is the organisation of 'social and cultural activities that are not strictly religious,' such as inviting non-Muslims to *iftar* (fast-breaking) meals organised within and by the mosque (2011, 10). The second is the practical changes made to the manner in which Muslims slaughter for *Eid al Adha* (the Feast of Sacrifice). That is, rather than Muslims slaughtering the animals themselves, today most mosques in Europe collect money from Muslims and slaughter (or organise for the slaughtering of) these animals on the donor's behalf in other parts of the world where the meat is most needed. According to Bruinessen, this practice began with the example of one mosque in the Netherlands (2011, 12). Thus, Bruinessen claims that these are examples of knowledge production in Islam that did not emerge as a result of a *fatwa* (religious edict) of an Islamic scholar but developed as a form of practice (2011, 13).

The above notwithstanding, lived religion suffers from a number of limitations, which is why I have reached beyond it to explore the relationship between practice and knowledge production. I will highlight only two examples for the present purposes. First, lived religion tends to skew the emphasis towards the social, experiential, and popular dimension of religion in its analysis. This is understandable since lived religion emerged to counterbalance the opposite emphasis. Nonetheless, this sustains 'the dichotomies we know as "official/popular", "normative/local", . . . "religious expert/laity", "institutional/non-institutional", [and] "orthodoxy/orthopraxis" . . . —thus creating "blind spots" in the study of religion, even in the study of "lived religion"' (Flaskerud and Leirvik 2018, 421).[18] Second, and connected to the first, lived religion claims that 'religion is not about the authority of traditions or institutions or clergy' but 'is what individuals choose on their own authority' (Ammerman 2016, 8).[19] This is similar to Bayat's position, which I have already challenged above. Moreover, some of the lived religion literature has also challenged this view. For example, Bruinessen claims that this assumption (based on earlier pieces published in the first decade of the twenty-first century that pinned great hopes on the growing sense of individuality, personal autonomy, and use of the Internet among the Muslim youth) has been shown to be misplaced and that traditional forms of religious authority continue to persist, in part, because they too have, for example, made use of the Internet and technological developments (2011, 18–19). Therefore, while lived religion has its uses for present purposes, I found it necessary to reach beyond it when conceptualising the relationship between practice and knowledge production for the reasons just stated.

Thus, the foregoing discussion demonstrates that practical theology, lived religion, and studies in everyday Islam allows me to extend the analysis of a practice-based epistemology to the relationship between practice and the production of religious knowledge. That, in return, allows me to overcome the epistemological challenge as problematised in the earlier part of this chapter. There are two particular implications of a practice-based epistemology, which we must discuss before moving on. They relate to the

---

[18] See also Ammerman 2016, 7; Neitz 2012, 52.
[19] See also McGuire 2008, 16; Sunier 2015, 13.

relationship among practice, knowledge, and context, on the one hand, and the unintended internal epistemic outcomes of practice, on the other.

Practice, Knowledge, and Context

The conventional view is that practice is the application of knowledge shaped (and sometimes inspired) by context (Cook and Wagenaar 2012, 9–10), which is also the underlying assumption found in the literature on Hizmet as discussed below. Therefore, it is important to reexamine this relationship according to a practice-based epistemology, which claims that 'knowledge and context can be explained in terms of—and are evoked within—practice, and not the other way round' (Cook and Wagenaar 2012, 5) and that the context of the epistemic outcomes under consideration are the practices that produced them (Cook and Wagenaar 2012, 15). This is not to deny that context (i.e., the sites of practice) influences practice. Neither is it to deny that practices are 'contextually embedded actions,' which means that we cannot interpret the meaning and effect of practice without paying particular attention to the context in which it was performed (Pouliot 2015, 238). After all, without context we cannot know whether the flickering of an eyelid is in fact a flirtatious wink or just an inadvertent twitch (Pouliot 2015, 243). However, the need to understand context to interpret the meaning and effect of practice does not necessarily mean that the former determines the latter. To argue otherwise would take us back to the dichotomy of structure/agency, which practice-based approaches aim to overcome.

Rather, a practice-based perspective suggests that the 'context of practice' only exists as and when the practice occurs. Thus, knowledge and context 'only have ontological status when and to the extent that we interact with them in practice' (Cook and Wagenaar 2012, 15). Accordingly, a sumo ring acts as the context for a sumo match, 'afford[ing] and constrain[ing] the practice of sumo,' as and when the sumo wrestling occurs. At other times, it is merely a circle on the floor (Cook and Wagenaar 2012, 24), which suggests that practice brings about the context of practice, rather than vice versa.

Furthermore, order, sense, meaning, and knowledge producing dynamics, which are often confused for immutable structures (e.g., laws, systems, and institutions), are in fact artefacts of other forms of practice that may or may not impinge upon the practice under consideration. Thus, unenforced laws have no practical bearing on account of being *unenforced* (i.e., not practiced), which suggests that in the case of legislation, the influence flows from the *implementation* (practice) of the law, not the mere *fact* of the law. Moreover, a change or modification of practice can change the 'context' and its resultant influence. Thus, in many instances, context is not an immutable force that determines the practice under consideration (Cook and Wagenaar 2012, 13).

Therefore, a practice-based perspective shifts our understanding of the relationship among practice, knowledge, and context, which is why Nicolini replaces the term 'context' for the 'wider picture' as he cautions:

> Studying 'context' from a practice perspective implies, in fact, studying analytically and processually how different practices are associated, and what are the practical implications of their relationships for the practice at hand. I use the terms 'analytically' and 'processually' because the reference to context as an explanatory factor is often a sign of bad or lazy social science. Too often, in fact, the notion of context (just like the ideas of system, structure and the like) is used as a shortcut and substitute for a more detailed analysis of how the conditions for actions came about. In this sense, the notion of context plays an eliminativist role, and as such it should be avoided or used extremely cautiously by those interested in a practice-based approach. (Nicolini 2013, 234)

I will return to this issue in Chapter 4 when challenging my findings with an alternative explanation that relies on 'context' as opposed to 'practice' to explain some of the epistemic outcomes under consideration.

Unintended Internal Epistemic Outcomes of Practice

The discussions so far point to the pre-reflexive nature of knowledge, practice, and practice-based knowledge production. This has implications going forward, which is why it is important to pause here and unpack this a little further.

Earlier, it was said that a practice-based epistemology describes knowledge as a living organism that is dynamic, provisional, relational, tacit, emergent, processual, interactive, and continually reproduced through practice (Gherardi 2000, 2003, 356–57, 2006, 38–39; Gherardi and Nicolini 2003, 204–8; Corradi et al., 2010, 274–75; Souto 2013, 55, 62, 64 and 68; Cook and Wagenaar 2012, 5). The tacit nature of knowledge is closely related to the 'hidden, tacit, and often linguistically inexpressible' nature of practice, which also happens to explain why 'practices are difficult to access, observe, measure or represent' (Gherardi 2009, 116). According to this practice-based epistemological perspective, even formal knowledge 'emerges out of, and cannot be seen apart from, an *often unacknowledged* and largely tacit context of hunches, cues, bodily predispositions, expectations, appreciations, values, affects, and so on' (my emphasis) (Cook and Wagenaar 2012, 8), which are produced and conditioned by practice. If knowledge is pre-reflexive, then it cannot be pre-determined and controlled in the manner foreseen by rationalistic notions of knowledge (Gherardi 2003, 352). Furthermore, the claim that 'practices tend toward their own elaboration regardless of our explicit intentions' (Spinosa 2001, 210), has the similar effect of decentering the practitioner's (explicitly stated) intent and comments as the basis of our analysis. The discussions to follow on habitus, cognitive praxis, and incidental learning in this chapter and the discussions on tacit/explicit knowledge that follow in Chapter 2 underscore the same point.

What does the foregoing discussion on the pre-reflexive, tacit and dynamic nature of knowledge and practice mean in practical terms? It means that we must be attuned to, and remain focused on, the unintended, unforeseen, unanticipated, and pre-reflexive (so far as the practitioner is concerned) epistemic aspects and outcomes of practice. This focus is not to deny the explicit aspects and outcomes of practice-based knowledge production but to suggest that in most instances, these explicit aspects and outcomes are rooted in tacit antecedents that need to be examined as part of the wider process. Having done that, we can then assess how the practice-based unintended epistemic outcomes under consideration fare against the practitioners' stated intent at the time and thereafter.

Overall, this attunement will allow me to shift my analytical focus onto two types of understudied movement outcomes: the *unintended* and the *internal*. According to Doowon Suh, 'most movement outcome research has focused on "external" and "intended" consequences' (2012, para. 2.4). On the latter, Suh says, '[s]ocial movements do not always succeed in accomplishing their goals. Moreover, the "unintended consequences" of social movements can create outcomes inconsistent with or even contrary to movement demands' and that these consequences produce 'no less significant socio-political and cultural impacts than intended ones do' (2012, para. 2.4).[20] Suh goes on to explain that 'another understudied area of movement outcome is "internal consequences". The consequences that social movements bring about not only affect society but also influence movements and organizational

---

[20] See also Merton 1936; Giugni 1999, xxi; Tilly 1999, 270; McAdam 1999; Meyer and Whittier 1994; Bosi et al., 2016, 7, 10.

members.' Suh adds that the effort to bring about external change can often lead to significant internal change (Suh 2012, para. 2.5). I will explain how I operationalise this focus on the unintended internal outcomes and consequences of Hizmet's practice in Chapter 2.

Social Movements, Knowledge, and Practice

This brings us onto practice-based knowledge production in social movement literature. That in turn raises three questions. First, what does social movement literature say about social movement practice and knowledge production? Second, have social movement studies utilised practice theories to conceptualise movement practice? And third, given the layered and interconnected nature of practice, at what level of manifestation and abstraction should Hizmet's practices be examined to explore the nature of its epistemic outcomes?

To address the first question; social movement literature discusses a number of topics on social movement activism and knowledge production. This literature includes contributions that acknowledge the challenge of recognising the epistemic value of social movement practice (Choudry 2009, 2010; Choudry and Kapoor 2010; Cox and Fominaya 2009); social movement theorisation about social movement practice (Bevington and Dixon 2005, 194; Howley 2008, 100); social movement knowledge production in the context of imperialism (Connell 2007; Santos, Nunes, and Meneses 2008; Choudry 2009); and concepts that pertain to the different epistemic aspects of social movement struggle, activism, and practice, such as 'cognitive praxis' (Eyerman and Jamison 1991); 'formal learning,' 'movement intellectuals,' and 'adult educators' (Holford 1995, 105–6; Crossley 1999b; Cox and Fominaya 2009, 2); and 'non-formal,' 'informal,' and 'incidental social learning' (Holst 2002, 87–88; Foley 2004; Haluza-DeLay 2008; Choudry 2009, 6; Austin 2009; Langdon 2009; B. L. Hall 2009, 46; Choudry and Kapoor 2010; Motta and Esteves 2014).

According to Aziz Choudry, 'thus far relatively few attempts have been made to theorize informal learning and knowledge production through involvement in social action' (2009, 8). While there appears to be a number of reasons for this, I will highlight only two. The first relates to the conceptualisation of social movement practice. Ordinarily speaking, 'our standards for evaluating social movements pivot around whether or not they "succeeded" in realizing their visions rather than on the merits or power of the visions themselves' (Kelley 2002, ix). In other words, the focus on social movements as vehicles for social and political change overshadows the latent epistemic dimension of social movement practice (Choudry and Kapoor 2010, 1–2). The second reason relates to the conceptualisation of knowledge production. As Choudry and Dip Kapoor point out, '[i]n the realm of academic knowledge production, original, single authorship is valued, which inadvertently contributes to a tendency to fail to acknowledge the intellectual contributions of activism, or to recognize the lineages of ideas and theories that have been forged outside of academe, often incrementally, collectively, and informally' (2010, 2). Hence, we are faced with the need to reconceptualise both *movement practice* and *knowledge production* to see the value of one within the other.

Of the various concepts noted above, 'cognitive praxis' (Eyerman and Jamison 1991) deserves particular mention because it sought to do just that from within the framework of social movement studies. Ron Eyerman and Andrew Jamison set out to 'read social movements as producers of knowledge, not as rational operators in a world of competing movement industries' (1991, 55). They claimed that knowledge production was inherent to social movement practice and that this knowledge comes in three types: cosmological (worldview), technical, and organisational (1991, 68–78). Eyerman and Jamison distinguished this epistemic dimension of movement practice from the movement message and teachings. Accordingly, this knowledge, 'must be found by someone looking for them' because it usually remains unknown even to its participants (1991, 62). After all, a 'movement is what it does and how it does it, not what its members *think* and *why they think* the ideas that they do' (my emphasis) (1991, 46). Thus, they were not necessarily in the 'heads of the activists,' but they had to be 'sifted out of movement documents and activist recollections, and their emergence and development had to be reconstructed' (1991, 62). This circles back to the discussion of practice-based epistemology above. While ahead of its time, this theory has been critiqued for being based on a superficial analysis of social movements, which hinders its ability to defend its conditions of generalizability (Oliver 1993; Rehin 1993).

The social movement literature published since then has primarily focused on informal learning in the context of adult education. The significance of this literature, for the present purposes, is that it connects social movement practice with social learning theory, which underscores the point that participation in social movement practice produces informal, incidental, and social learning, that is the non-deliberate pre-reflexive sharing of movement knowledge in the act of doing (Foley 2004, 3–4; Holford 1995; B. L. Hall 2009; Holst 2002, 87–88; Haluza-DeLay 2008).

The above notwithstanding, there are two points of challenge with this literature. The first challenge relates to the tendency of this literature to focus on organisational, operational, or instrumental knowledge when discussing movement knowledge and informal learning (Holford 1995; Foley 2004, 4; Haluza-DeLay 2008; Prasant and Kapoor 2010, 207; Ziadah and Hanieh 2010, 96; Cox and Fominaya 2009; Maddison and Scalmer 2006, 43–44 and 46; Yates 2015).[21] If organisational knowledge is defined as relating to 'how movements generate agreed analyses of society, strategies and tactics, understandings of internal practice, and so on' (Cox and Fominaya 2009, 4), then it is rather restrictive for the present purposes.[22] The second challenge with some of the literature that examines social movements as sites of informal learning is that it also credits conventional methods and movement intellectuals with sharing movement knowledge and knowledge production (see, for example, Holford 1995; Crossley 1999b). This approach focuses on people rather than practices, and it identifies 'adult *learning* with adult *education* as a field of professional practice' (my emphasis) (Foley 2004, 136), which tells us little about (informal and incidental) knowledge production that is unique to movement practice.

Thus, the social movement literature discussed so far validates the overall intuition of this research, namely, that social movement practice has an underlying pre-reflexive epistemic dimension, which can reach beyond organisational knowledge as understood in the narrow sense described above. It also underscores the challenge and therefore importance of examining this form of knowledge production.

As for the second question, there is a subset of literature that uses practice theories to expand and explore social movement theory and practice (Crossley 1999a, b, 2001, 2002; Haluza-DeLay 2008; Yates 2015; Ibrahim 2015). Most of this literature is based on habitus, the cornerstone concept of

---

[21] As also pointed out by Jihyun Kim: '[f]rom a review of the literature, it was found that the previous literature in adult education paid little attention to learning content in social movements' (2016, 48).

[22] That said some have ventured beyond this narrow definition of organisational knowledge in the context of social movements and informal learning. For example, J. Kim found that the learning content of social movements included knowledge about the background of the issue on which the movement was mobilised, which extends beyond strictly organisational matters (2016).

Bourdieu's practice theory (Bourdieu 1977, 72). The aim of habitus is to resolve the subjectivism/objectivism or agency/structure dichotomy in social theory (Ibrahim 2015, 12). According to Bourdieu, practice is the outcome of the interaction among habitus, capital, and field or formulaically put, (habitus x capital) + field = practice (1984, 101). *Capital* refers to the cultural, economic, social, and symbolic assets that a person acquires throughout their lifetime (Bourdieu 1977, 177, 187). *Fields* are spheres of life such as art, education, religion, economy, or politics where actors use their capital to take part in a game-like scenario to gain success (Bourdieu and Wacquant 1992, 16–7). *Habitus* refers to acquired dispositions, know-how, 'feel for the game' and second nature that formats tastes, preferences, mindsets, perceptions, actions, and practices (Bourdieu and Wacquant 1992, 16; Bourdieu 1990, 52–66). According to Bourdieu's notion of practice, an actor pre-reflexively internalises the habitus of any given field by merely taking part in it (Haluza-DeLay 2008, 211; Nicolini 2013, 55). Therefore, practice is the outcome of the pursuit of an interest through a game-like activity taking place within a field based on an actor's habitus (know-how) and capital (purchasing power).

The drawback of habitus is that it is mainly, albeit not exclusively, understood to operate at the pre-reflexive (tacit) level of consciousness (Bourdieu 1990, 73; Bourdieu and Wacquant 1992, 128), which is restrictive if your concern includes but extends beyond this level of consciousness.[23] Furthermore, habitus struggles to explain change. This is connected to how Bourdieu conceives of habitus reproducing the field in which it operates. As numerous critics have pointed out, if habitus and field are co-generating, they are a closed system, replicating each other in a circular fashion, which precludes change (Bourdieu 1990, 60–61; Bourdieu and Wacquant 1992, 132n. 85; King 2000, 427–28; Schindler and Wille 2015, 355).[24] Thus, on its own, habitus is not well suited to accounting for the production (i.e., change) of Islamic knowledge in a manner that connects the pre- and reflexive level of consciousness. Nonetheless, alongside social learning as discussed above, habitus is useful for present purposes in providing a convincing theory about how actors unknowingly internalise a durable set of embedded dispositions through practice or the 'internalisation of externality' (Bourdieu 1977, 72).

This brings us to the third question. Practices can be conceptualised as concentric circles comprising practices within, while being interconnected

---

[23] This is a contested view. For an alternative view, see Tittensor 2014, 39.
[24] This is also a contested issue, with others arguing otherwise. For example, see Crossley 1999b, 822, 2001, 130; Haluza-DeLay 2008, 208; Bourdieu and Wacquant 1992, 82 and 130.

with an array of practice bundles without. That being the case, at what level of empirical manifestation and theoretical abstraction should a practice be studied? Simply put, while I will zoom in and out of a Hizmet practice, can I conceptualise these practices at a higher level of generality (e.g., the running of schools) in order to capture the latent epistemic effect of multiple Hizmet practices across numerous issues over an extended period of time and terrain?

To answer this question, we must first confront the question of what constitutes a practice? Gessica Corradi, Silvia Gherardi, and Luca Verzelloni remind us that while practices are ever present in our day-to-day lives, they 'are not directly accessible, observable, measurable or definable; rather, they are hidden, tacit and often linguistically inexpressible in a propositional sense' (2010, 267), which makes it harder to capture and define. This explains why practice is a polysemic term, which has often been interpreted expansively (Schatzki 2001a; Corradi et al. 2010). For example, Giddens defines practice as regularised types of acts (Nicolini 2013, 46). Marx, on the other hand, defines practice as a 'relatively homogenous human activity which can take many forms and can range from bodily labour of the most humble sort to political revolutions' (Nicolini 2013, 31). According to Theodore R. Schatzki, a central core of practice theorists 'conceives of practices as embodied, materially mediated arrays of human activity centrally organized around shared practical understanding' (2001a, 11). Thus, 'moving a hand forward is ... not a practice but can become a component of the practice of "greeting by shaking hands"' (Nicolini 2013, 10). According to Elizabeth Shove, Mika Pantzar, and Matt Watson, practice is the active integration between three elements: material, competence, and meaning (2012, 22, 82), wherein driving is the integration of the vehicle (material), the know-how to drive (competence), and the reason for driving (meaning) (2012, 31). Therefore, practice can be understood as recursive meaningful action. These practice-comprising actions, on the other hand, are themselves constituted by a set of bodily doings and sayings[25] according to Schatzki (2001b, 56–58). Thus, among other things, we can conceptualise practice 'as a set of doings and sayings,' which spans those types of human activity that we might consider to be mundane (e.g., paying for goods) to the more complex (e.g., the running of an organisation) (Schatzki 2001b, 56, 61).

---

[25] A saying is 'a doing that says something about something' (Schatzki 2001b, 63, footnote 2).

While one practice comprises multiple elements within, it is also connected to multiple practices without. Thus, 'practices link, one to another, to form bundles and complexes. Bundles are loose-knit patterns based on the co-location and co-existence of practices. Complexes represent stickier and more integrated combinations, some so dense that they constitute new entities in their own right' (Shove et al. 2012, 81). For example, while flossing in the morning comprises the integration of the floss (material), know-how (competence to floss), and concern for dental hygiene (meaning), it is also interconnected within a wider mesh of practices centered around the morning bathroom routine. Furthermore, and as noted above, practices (like Matryoshka dolls) often comprise 'smaller' practices within. For example, running a classroom is a form of practice that embodies constitutive practices, such as the taking of the register or the quizzing of students within. Similarly, the running of a classroom is also a 'smaller' (constitutive) practice of the running of a school without. This brings us back to the question of how we determine our point of analysis. Do we analyze practice(s) at their smallest possible point, vice versa or somewhere in between?

I would suggest that this question is determined, at least in part, by the practice-based effect that is being pursued—in my case, practice-based knowledge production. To pursue this, I must trace multiple practices across numerous issues over an expansive temporospatial axis. I would not be able to achieve this if I aimed to reconstruct each practice at its 'smallest' possible point or to observe it in real time (Nicolini 2013, 217–18). While making a slightly different point, Nicolini appears to concede that the level of focus is in fact relative to the outcome being pursued, when he cautions against the use of contemporary conversational analysis in practice-based studies: '[t]he extreme level of granularity of the descriptions produced through the use of conversational analytical methods ... steer us away from the account of observable reportable practices' (Nicolini 2013, 222). My focus is on Hizmet's practice-based epistemic outcomes. As discussed further in Chapter 2, this ensues cumulatively through the interaction of multiple of practices. Thus, while zooming in and out of Hizmet's practices, I must be able to focus on Hizmet's practices and practice bundles at a certain level of generality in order to trace and evaluate their long-term epistemic effects. Thus, while my focus will be on practices (e.g., the opening of Hizmet schools in Turkey and abroad), at times, I will organise and group these practices as practice bundles (e.g., dialogue-based activities, educational efforts).

Hizmet and Knowledge Production

There is a large body of scholarly literature on Gülen and Hizmet, as cited in the Introduction, which focuses on Gülen's teachings, leadership, and theology and Hizmet's activities and socio-political influence and reach, including those authored by movement intellectuals. There is also a smaller subset of literature and scholarly commentary on Gülen and knowledge production. All of this literature, including those works that explicitly profess critical independence from the movement (H. Yavuz 2013; Hendrick 2013; Tittensor 2014; Tee 2016), treat Gülen as the thinker and producer and the movement as the consumer and disseminator of what they consider to be Gülen's knowledge, reinterpretation, theology, vision, and ideals (Leaman 2007; Yilmaz 2003, 2018; Bakar 2005; Atay 2007; Yilmaz 2005a; Bruckmayr 2008; Ergene 2008; Beşer 2006; Albayrak 2011; Valkenberg 2015).[26] It is fair to say that this view is also pervasive among the movement as well (Hendrik 2013, 70-88).[27] According to this widely-held view, Hizmet or 'the new Anatolian bourgeoisie' act as 'implementers of Gülen's ideas' (H. Yavuz 2013, 120) or, as Margaret J. Rausch puts it, 'affiliation with the Hizmet movement encompasses implementing the ideas . . . advanced by Gülen in pursuit of God's pleasure' (2015, 132). Yavuz's criticism in this context is that Gülen 'provides ready-made opinions for the use of his followers, who are thus relieved from the necessity of forming of (sic) their own opinions and not much involved in critical thinking' (2013, 65). In so doing, this literature perpetuates the Cartesian divide between the knowing-mind (Gülen) and enacting-body (movement).

---

[26] A welcome exception to this are two volumes (especially the one that focuses on the person and teachings of Gülen (2022a)) that were published in tandem by Paul Weller immediately prior to my submission of this manuscript, which emphasises the role of practice—alongside other factors, such as Gülen's biography, geographical and temporal context and historical and intellectual inheritance—in the development of Gülen's thought and how this feeds back into the movement's practice through a 'hermeneutical circle of engagement with Hizmet' (2022a, 239; 2022b). The fundamental difference between Weller's religious studies-based perspective and my interdisciplinary approach, however, is that Weller continues to consider this to be Gülen's 'constructed theology' to which, alongside other factors, the movement has 'contribut[ed]' through its practice (2022a, 241-2), whereas I take practice, as opposed to any one practitioner, as my basic unit of analysis for understanding the epistemic outcomes under consideration. Furthermore, while Weller's meticulously-researched volumes make an important and thoughtful contribution to how contextual dynamics have influenced Gülen's thought and teachings more generally, I provide a more specialist focus on the granular dynamic of the relationship between practice and the (unintended) production of Islamic knowledge on human rights.

[27] Joshua D. Hendrik provides a useful summary of both in-house produced material and examples from interviews with movement participants, which demonstrate this point (2013, 70-88). See also Gülen 2000a, 1-42, 2006c, 3-9; Albayrak 2011.

Of all the scholarly pieces on Gülen and Hizmet, Ihsan Yilmaz's deserves particular attention for its focus on knowledge production and dissemination (2003, 2005a). Yilmaz argues that '[h]aving almost replaced the ulema's doctrinal authority, faith-based movement leaders exercise or advocate ijtihad [religious reinterpretation] and, most importantly, have the means to implement their ideas in the civil realm' (2005a, 205). According to this view, 'it is *obvious* that [the movement's innovative practices and developments] are results of Gülen's ijtihads, even though he would neither claim nor admit that they were so' (my emphasis) (Yilmaz 2005a, 205). Thus, 'Gülen's discourse is not only meant on a rhetorical level; he encourages all his followers and sympathizers to realize his ideals and to put into practice his discourse' (Yilmaz 2005a, 202). Consequently, 'the transformative influences of Gülen's discourse can be observed initially and primarily in the movement he has inspired' (Yilmaz 2003, 209). Yilmaz goes on to explain how this occurs, '[a]s elaborated earlier, after espousing Gülen as a prominent intellectual and religious leader, many people may adapt themselves to his discourse and follow his ijtihads' (2003, 237). They do this by opening schools and establishing institutions to 'put into practice *his discourse* and realize *his ideals*' (my emphasis) (Yilmaz 2003, 237). According to Yilmaz, this overcomes the shortcoming that John L. Esposito identified with earlier reformists; that is, they 'were not succeeded by comparable charismatic figures, nor did they create effective organizations to continue and implement their ideas' (Yilmaz quotes Esposito in Yilmaz 2003, 218).[28] Therefore, according to this argument, the movement implements and disseminates the *ijtihads* that Gülen produces. Yilmaz refers to this production/implementation process as 'ijtihad and tajdid [religious renewal/revival] by conduct' (2003). The challenge with this prevailing perspective (as analysed more closely through the work of Yilmaz), however, is that it overlooks the role of Hizmet's practice in knowledge production.[29]

---

[28] For the original source, see Esposito 1998, 145.

[29] I criticised this perspective in an earlier piece, where I pointed out that 'Gülen's *tajdid*' was in fact co-constructed, and not just disseminated, through the movement's practice (2007, 688). I explained that the movement's practice amounted to a form of interpretation, reformulation, adaptation, indigenisation, contextualisation, feedback, and innovation, which I referred to as a 'collectively constructed *tajdid*' (2007, 688). I further elaborated on this 'continuous and interactive' loop and relationship between (Gülen's) teachings and (Hizmet's) practice in an edited publication of this piece (2013, 195–96).

In a more recent piece, Yilmaz concedes that movement participants are not just disseminators but that they also 'contribute to this process in different ways, such as by transferring knowledge to him from their own local contexts or by contextualizing and disseminating the knowledge produced by Gülen' (2018, 7). Nonetheless, this does not shift the Cartesian notion of knowledge production. According to Yilmaz, *people* and *mentalistic* processes are still responsible for knowledge production: 'Gülen is the main actor in the movement who has engaged with producing new Islamic knowledge in his constant responses to the socio-political affairs and challenges by reinterpreting Islamic sources in tune with contemporary time and space' (2018, 7). Furthermore, Yilmaz states that alternative forms of knowledge production in and on Hizmet, respectively, comprise, 'several expert participants in the movement who have been producing knowledge as theologians, social scientists and intellectuals in different parts of the world' (2018, 7) and two critical websites (*Mavi Yorum* and *Kıtalararası*) run by ex-Hizmet academics who publish critical pieces on Hizmet (2018, 16). Again, the focus here is on people and conventional forms of knowledge production, which is predicated on a rationalistic, mentalistic, and cognitivistic notion of knowledge production. Moreover, by treating knowledge production as a mentalistic process, this account also overlooks the creative role of Gülen's *practice* in this epistemic process and outcome.

It is interesting to note that this problematic dichotomy (mind/body, producer/consumer, producer/disseminator) persists when the comparison is shifted from Gülen and Hizmet to Said Nursi (d. 1960) and Gülen. However, in this instance, Nursi is seen as the original thinker and Gülen as the activist-implementer (T. Michel 2002), or as Yavuz puts it 'if Said Nursi was the architect of religious enlightenment in Turkey, Gülen is both the contractor and engineer of these ideas in terms of their actualization and implementation' (2013, 47). The reason for this, at least in some part, is that Nursi was more text-based; he authored a 6000-page fourteen-volume Qur'anic exegesis in conjunction with founding the Nur movement (thinker-activist), whereas Gülen is more social action-based; he founded Hizmet, which ran 2000 schools in 160 countries, while authoring numerous books (activist-thinker). However, a practice-based perspective eschews the distinction between the authoring of scholarly works and the running of social projects. Instead, it reduces both endeavors into one: practice. If both are practices, then one does not necessarily need to be the implementation of the other. Furthermore, both are equally capable of producing epistemic outcomes.

This mind/body dichotomy reinforces the leader/follower paradigm in the literature on Hizmet, wherein Gülen leads and Hizmet follows.[30] That paradigm, in return, is justified by recourse to the movement: '[t]o understand the inner motivating forces of the Gülen movement, it is important to examine how the movement itself sees its own mission. The followers of Fethullah Gülen compare themselves with the *sahaba* (the companions [i.e., first believers] of Muhammad)' (H. Yavuz 2013, 71). In other words, Yavuz says that we must see Hizmet participants as 'followers' because they see themselves as followers of their leader, Gülen. While we must factor the movement's self-perception into our analyses, we must also be cautious of taking it at face value. After all, is it not possible that the movement's relationship with Gülen vis-à-vis knowledge production is more complicated and nuanced than that which the leader/follower paradigm allows us to conceptualise? Furthermore, and as discussed above (e.g., cognitive praxis), movement participants are often unaware of their creative contribution to the movement's epistemic outcomes. Thus, by essentialising knowledge (production) as a mentalistic process and movement participants as followers, Yavuz and others overlook the creative role of practice in knowledge production.

By adopting a practice-based approach to knowledge production, I will take practice, and not practitioners, as my basic unit of analysis. 'Practice theories are thus an alternative to the (many) views which suggest that organizational phenomena stem from the more or less rational action of individual subjects. In other words, practice theories require a "Copernican revolution" in addressing many of the seemingly familiar phenomena' (Nicolini 2013, 7). This in return means focusing on 'managerial and entrepreneurial activities, not managers and entrepreneurs; strategy making and sale practices, not strategists and sales persons; leadership practices, not leaders' (Nicolini 2013, 7) or knowledge-producing practices and not knowledge-producing practitioners. This is not to deny Gülen's intellectual contribution or his leadership skills. Rather, it is to connect *knowing* with *doing* through a focus on Hizmet's collective practice (including Gülen's practice, which is an integral part of that whole), in order to appreciate the symbiotic relationship between the formalised and experiential facets of knowledge in the production of Islamic knowledge on human rights.

---

[30] See for example, Tee 2016, 13, 19 and 21.

Conclusion

By appraising the scholarly approaches that focus on making *either* Islamic scripture or Muslim sensibility compatible with human rights together, I problematised the epistemological duality that is inherent in both. In doing so, I demonstrated that we need a theoretical lens that allows us to account for the symbiotic relationship between the semiotic and social facets of religious knowledge in the production of Islamic knowledge on human rights. The discussion on practice-based approaches, practice-based epistemology, and practical theology provides us with an alternative theoretical paradigm that combines these elements as relationally present in the performance of practice. As a result, this breaks down the problematic dichotomies between knowing/doing and mind/body on the one hand and formalised/experiential and explicit/tacit facets of knowledge on the other. Moreover, practical theology, lived religion, and everyday Islam extends this analysis to the production of religious knowledge. Therefore, practice provides us with a unifying perspective that accounts for not just the two facets of religious knowledge but also the symbiotic interaction between the two. This allows us to account for the production of Islamic knowledge on human rights without narrowly focusing on one or the other. After all, 'practice is on the one hand a way to acquire knowledge in action and, on the other, a way to change/perpetuate such knowledge and to produce and reproduce' (Corradi et al. 2010, 274). However, before we can apply this theoretical perspective to the case study in hand, we must first operationalise it into a coherent methodological framework, which is what I will turn to next in the following chapter.

2
Operationalising a Practice Approach
Exploring the Epistemic Outcomes of Practice

In Chapter 1, I reviewed and problematised the Islamic literature and responses to the human rights challenge. I offered 'practice' as an alternative theoretical paradigm for understanding knowledge (production), which posits that practice produces knowledge. I demonstrated that this perspective circumvents the problematic epistemological dualisms, which overlooks the symbiotic relationship between the formalised and the experiential facets of religious knowledge. I will now operationalise that theoretical paradigm into a methodological framework. To that end, this chapter is divided into three sections. The first will explain the methodological approaches adopted and triangulated in this book, which are a single-case study analysis, process tracing methodology (PTM), and aspects of the practice theory toolkit associated with Davide Nicolini. The second will conceptualise and adapt 'causal mechanisms' as understood in PTM for the purposes of using it to trace practice-based epistemic outcomes. To do so, I will draw on a number of concepts to help me to capture, examine, and explain the various elements of a practice-based causal mechanism, which I refer to as the 'intervening process' between practice and knowledge production. The third will contextualise the conceptualised causal mechanism within the wider epistemic context in which I explore its effect, that is, *fiqh* (Islamic law), a significant branch of Islamic knowledge. This will help me determine the *emic* criteria for knowledge production for this particular discipline, against which I can assess the epistemic outcomes of practice in Chapters 3 and 4.

How to Explore the Epistemic Outcomes of Hizmet's Practices

The methodological approach of any scholarly piece must be consistent with the basic assumptions about the nature of the phenomenon under consideration, in this case, practice-based knowledge production. As discussed in Chapter 1, practice-based approaches theorise about practice and its effects. These studies commend a practice-based ontology, which informs the theoretical paradigm of this book, that is, 'the belief that many social and organizational phenomena occur within, and are aspects or components of, the field of practices' (Nicolini 2013, 13). According to this approach, we must adopt practice as the basic unit of analysis, which is what this book sets out to do. This ontological assumption has epistemological and methodological implications for how we conceptualise and research practice and its effects. One of the epistemological implications is to move beyond the meta-theoretical categorisations in social sciences. After all, practice has both a particular and general nature, which eschews the positivist-generalisation versus the interpretivist-contextualisation dichotomy (Pouliot 2015, 238). This also explains why practice-based approaches do not provide us with either a unified theory of practice or a unified methodological approach (Nicolini 2013, 8–9; Gherardi 2006, 37). Rather, the researcher is encouraged to tailor an eclectic approach that is best suited to capturing the type of practice under consideration (Nicolini 2013, 213). Thus, on the question of consistency, I will focus on achieving the above by designing my methodological lens in a manner and form that is sensitive to the general disposition of social movement practice.

In the context of the present study, being sensitive to the nature of practice and its artefacts has three methodological implications, which can be summarised as *interpretive, processual,* and *multiresolutional*. First, the social, relational, fluid, tacit, pre-reflexive, complex, and cumulative nature of practice commends an interpretive evaluation of practice. After all, practice cannot be studied through 'surveys and interviews alone' (Nicolini 2013, 217). Moreover, 'practice has a logic which is not that of the logician' (Bourdieu 1990, 86), which suggests that 'practices tend toward their own elaboration regardless of our explicit intentions' (Spinosa 2001, 210). As a result, the logic, meaning, trajectory, and outcome of practice must be interpreted from the 'wider picture' that is an 'understanding of the association between practices and how they are kept together' (Nicolini 2013, 234). Second, and as an extension of the above, the *processual* nature of practice commends a temporospatial examination of practice and its outcomes. After all, 'practices are performances, which unfold in time and over time' (Pouliot 2015, 241). The dynamic, cumulative, and latent nature of practice-based outcomes also supports such a methodological approach. Third, and as a result of the above, the interconnected and multidirectional nature of practice requires a multiresolutional (in and out, back and forth) lens that allows the researcher to trace the elemental evolution within and the interconnected nexus between practice(s) (Nicolini 2013, 219–37).

With the foregoing considerations in mind, I will combine three methodological approaches in this study: case study analysis, process tracing methodology (PTM), and Davide Nicolini's (practice theory) toolkit. An in-depth within-case study approach will allow me to pay close attention to Hizmet's multiple practices across numerous issues over an extensive temporospatial axis while accounting for the wider socio-political contexts. PTM will help me focus on the processual and unfolding nature of practice and practice-based outcomes by allowing me to conceptualise the causal relationship between practice and knowledge production as an intervening process comprising interconnected activities between cause and effect. With its multiresolutional lens, Nicolini's toolkit will allow me to augment the limitations of PTM by zooming in and out of Hizmet's practices to discern the evolution within and the connections between practices and practice-based outcomes (Nicolini 2013, 219–20).

By combining these three methodological approaches into one, I will produce three integrated layers of analysis of the intervening processes in Chapters 3 to 5: chronological, causal, and abstracted. The first will be a chronological overview of Hizmet's doings and sayings. Among other things, the focus here is on *what* is happening. A chronological overview will allow me to set the scene, to study the overall picture, and to determine the temporospatial span of any given practice (i.e., to determine where to begin and end). This will also allow me to explore the connections among practices and their effects as well as trace the points of change, breakage, and fusion between Hizmet's doings and sayings. That, in return, will help me to determine the points of interest for further exploration. This will help me to produce my second layer of analysis, which will conceptualise the intervening process as a causal mechanism comprising theoretical and empirical entities with interconnected activities. Thus, at this level of analysis, I will group the entities and their activities by causal relation. I will produce my third level of analysis by lifting the level of abstraction of the causal mechanism by reducing its case-specific details, which will help produce generalizable insights that may further illuminate the causal relationship between practice and knowledge production in other cases (Beach and Pedersen 2019, 74). The focus of my second and third layer of analysis will be on *how* and *why* the outcomes under consideration came about.

To reconstruct and analyse Hizmet's practices in the manner just described meant collecting empirical data that pertains to Hizmet's practices, their effects, and the wider socio-historic developments at play at the time in question. This involves the collation of historic accounts from primary and secondary material. According to process tracing studies, primary and secondary sources include archival materials, memoirs, oral histories, newspapers, and interviews. PTM does not require the researcher to uncover new facts. Rather, this methodology often reconfigures public information to 'urge the reader to see old problems in a new light' (Ritter 2014, 107). Accordingly, my primary sources include Gülen's spoken and written word, published interviews with Gülen and Hizmet participants, publications by Hizmet participants and Hizmet's organisations, organisational documents and materials, archival material, memoirs, oral histories, and observational insight.[1] My secondary sources include scholarly research and publications on Gülen and Hizmet, historic newspaper articles and columns, together with any historic account pertaining to the practices under consideration. In addition, as an insider for over twenty years, I am immersed in the movement's day-to-day practices as they relate to the practices discussed herein. I will triangulate and challenge my insider knowledge in the ways discussed in the Introduction but also against the primary and secondary sources noted above.

Case Study

Alexander L. George and Andrew Bennet define a case study approach as 'the detailed examination of an aspect of a historical episode to develop or test historical explanations that may be generalizable to other events' (George and Bennett 2005, 5). According to Donatella Della Porta and Michael Keating,

---

[1] It is important to note that the Turkish government has been engaged in a systematic campaign to eradicate Gülen and Hizmet from Turkey's public consciousness. To achieve this objective, it has set out to expunge all printed and online material authored by, and/or relating to Gülen or Hizmet from the public domain (Yilmaz 2015b; Flood 2019). That includes removing all online material on Gülen and Hizmet from Turkey-based servers, including the online archive of all Hizmet-related media outlets (e.g., *Zaman* newspaper) that have since been taken over by the Turkish government. Unfortunately, these actions have made it more difficult to research and document Hizmet's historical development and practices.

there are five forms of case study research: 'descriptive/configurative; interpretive, using theory to explain a case and then refining theory; hypothesis-generating, providing a basis for further work; deviant-case, to suggest new hypotheses and theories; and theory-evaluating' (Della Porta and Keating 2008a 13). Therefore, while case study research can be 'conducted within a more traditional positivistic framework,' it may also be 'conducted within a more interpretative framework in which the process is more concerned with a rich, complex description of the specific case' (Gherardi 2006, 55), which is the approach I will adopt for the present study.

As stated in the Introduction, the case study for this book is the Hizmet movement. One question that could be posed at this juncture is why I have chosen to focus on a single, as opposed to, multiple case studies? There are a number of reasons why. First, I am exploring the basic dynamics between practice and knowledge production, which requires an in-depth examination of multiple practices across numerous issues over a fifty-year period. To include more than one case study would have detracted from my ability to achieve that level of detailed research, analysis, and articulation. Furthermore, I am not exploring an exclusivist claim that would be discredited by an alternative explanation in the context of another movement. My study calls into question the assumed incompatibility between Islam and human rights by exploring Hizmet's practice in the context of knowledge production. The underlying theoretical assumption here is that practice produces knowledge through the symbiotic relationship between formalised and experiential knowledge. That assumption does not suggest, at least not in the present study, that such knowledge can *only* be produced through practice. Thus, a comparison with another movement that supports an alternative explanation would not necessarily discredit my research and analysis in relation to Hizmet's example. Moreover, comparative case studies are useful in isolating the conditions of generality, after the basic phenomena, process, or event have been sufficiently explained or taken as granted; that is not the case here. Thus, 'the decision to employ a single case study was mandated by the exploratory nature of this study' (Bell-Townsend 2007, 10–11).

On the other hand, it is important to point out that by tracing Hizmet's practices over an extended period of time, I will in fact be bringing Hizmet into comparison with itself, across its various socio-historic developments and typological evolutions (i.e., from a small religious congregation to a nationwide education-focused community to a transnational multisectoral social movement). Thus, this *is* a comparative analysis, albeit one between different versions of itself. In addition, I will challenge my tentative evaluations by comparing them with alternative explanations. In doing so, I will contextualise those alternative explanations to Hizmet's experience and ask if they are more or less useful in helping us make sense of the observed phenomenon. This 'comparison of explanations,' if not case studies, is also a comparative exercise. Finally, I will focus on multiple practices, not just one, over an extended temporospatial axis. This approach will reduce the risk of misattributions, which is one of the objectives in cross-case comparative analysis.

Process Tracing

George and Bennett explain that in PTM, 'the researcher examines histories, archival documents, interview transcripts, and other sources to see whether the causal process' of the theory he or she is using 'is in fact evident in the sequence and values of the intervening variables in that case' (2005, 206).[2] Della Porta and Keating describe the ultimate goal of process tracing as providing 'a narrative explanation of a causal path that leads to a specific outcome' (2008a, 235). According to Derek Beach and Rasmus Brun Pedersen, '[t]he essence of process-tracing case studies is that we shift the analytical focus from causes and outcomes to hypothesized causal mechanisms *in between*. That is, mechanisms are *not* causes but are causal processes that are triggered by causes and the link between them with outcomes in a productive relationship' (2019, 1). Pascal Vennesson claims that '[p]rocess tracing is an important, perhaps indispensable, element of case study research' and that '[p]rocess tracing can be fruitfully used in both positivist and interpretivist research designs' (2008, 224). An interpretivist process tracing 'leads to a detailed examination of the causal mechanism and explains how specific variables interact' (Vennesson 2008, 236).[3] Furthermore, PTM has been used in the context of social movement research as well (Meyer and Whittier 1994; Kuru 2005; Bell-Townsend 2007; Ritter 2014; Nassauer 2016; Mueller 2016; Stefanovski 2016).

---

[2] In a subsequent publication, Bennet replaces the term *intervening variable* with *causal mechanism* (Bennett and Checkel 2015, 7).

[3] See also the following on PTM: Mahoney 2010, 2015; Collier 2011; and Jacobs 2015.

PTM will help me focus on the processual and unfolding nature of practice and practice-based outcomes by expanding the space between cause and outcome as the intervening process between practice and knowledge production. I will now locate my own process tracing approach among the four variants of process tracing as discussed by Beach and Pedersen and I will discuss how I will conceptualise the notion of causal mechanisms in the context of PTM.

According to Beach and Pedersen, process tracing has at least four variants (2019, 9): theory-centric (theory-testing, -building, and -revision forms of process tracing) and case-centric (explaining-outcome process tracing) (2019, 9–12). Each variant has a different objective and a way in which it should be conducted. Theory-centric process tracing aims to produce general theory about the causal mechanism by testing, building, or revising a pre-given theory against the evidence pertaining to the causal mechanism of the case in hand. Case-centric process tracing aims to provide a 'minimally sufficient explanation' for the causal mechanism that produced the observed outcome (Beach and Pedersen 2019, 282), which is achieved when we arrive at the conclusion that 'all the relevant facets of the outcome have adequately been accounted for and whether the evidence is best explained by the developed explanation rather than plausible alternatives' (Beach and Pedersen 2019, 286). Beach and Pedersen claim that 'most case studies that use process-tracing employ a case-centric variant that we term the explaining-outcome process-tracing' (2013, 9).

My primary aim is to make sense of the causal relationship between Hizmet's practice and knowledge production by conducting an in-depth examination of Hizmet's unfolding practices over a fifty-year period (1966–2016). This suggests that my study is a case-centric one. While theory-centric process tracing is based on neopositivism or critical realism, which aims to produce law-like generalisations, case-centric process tracing builds on 'analyticism,' a variant of interpretivism, that is 'a set of different philosophical positions that have the common denominator that we as observers are part of the social world we are studying. In this view, knowledge cannot be separated from our place in the world' (Beach and Pedersen 2019, 281–82). This suggests that everything we know is contextually bound, which precludes the production of cross-case generalisations. Given its focus on crafting a case-specific explanation of the observed outcome, this type of process tracing is said to often include reference to non-systematic case-specific entities (e.g., unique events, developments, or interventions) within its causal mechanism

(Beach and Pedersen 2019, 283–84), which also precludes cross-case generalisations. This is why it is often argued 'that interpretivists are interested in singular events, while many [positivist] process tracers strive for the general' (Pouliot 2015, 258).

At this juncture, it is important to recall the theoretical discussions in Chapter 1 where I demonstrated that a practice-based ontology eschews the problematic epistemological dualisms of formal and informal knowledge (production). Similarly, practice in the context of process tracing avoids the duality between theory- and case-centric forms of process tracing as well. In his paper on practice tracing (i.e., the process tracing of practice), Vincent Pouliot posits that '[p]ractices are both particular (as contextually embedded actions) and general (as patterns of actions)' (2015, 258).[4] As a result, a successful account of practice tracing should accomplish two tenets: the demonstration of 'local causality' and the production of 'analytically general insights' (Pouliot 2015, 239).

According to Pouliot, the first tenet is 'drawn primarily from interpretivism [that] posits the singularity of causal accounts: it is meaningful contexts that give practices their social effectiveness and generative power in and on the world' (2015, 237). Thus, interpreting practice and its effects means 'embedding [them] in their social contexts' (Pouliot 2015, 240). As for the second tenet, it is 'in tune with process analytics, [that] holds that no social relationships and practices are so unique as to foreclose the possibility of theorization and categorization' (Pouliot 2015, 237). After all, 'practices have causal power' and are recursive and patterned by nature (Pouliot 2015, 240). As a result, 'one may heuristically abstract them away from context in the form of various social mechanisms' to produce 'analytically general insights' (Pouliot 2015, 240).

Thus, Pouliot argues that we must 'move beyond meta-theoretical divides—which are by nature irresolvable—and let social scientific practices guide our methodological debates' (2015, 240).[5] Therefore, while I am aware of them, I will not consider myself bound by the ontological (and by extension, the methodological) parameters of the variants of process tracing as described by Beach and Pedersen. In practical terms, this means that I will attempt to abstract the causal mechanism away from its local context to produce analytically general insights. According to Beach and Pedersen,

---

[4] See also Nicolini 2013, 48.
[5] See also Della Porta 2014, 9.

'theories of causal mechanisms can have varying levels of analytical abstraction. Theorized mechanisms can be made more abstract by dropping details (typically dropping parts or making them simpler) and can be made more specific by adding details' (2019, 73). As a result, once the (how and why) case for the causal mechanism is made, it should be possible to increase the scope of generalizable insights about the mechanism by 'lifting the level of abstraction by dropping case specifics' (Beach and Pedersen 2019, 74).

This brings us to the discussion of the causal mechanism in process tracing. According to Beach and Pedersen,

> [t]he essence of making a mechanism-based claim is that we shift the analytical focus from identifying causal effects to explaining how causes are linked to an outcome—that is, from causes —> outcomes to the process *in between*. Mechanisms are *not* causes but are causal processes that are *triggered* by causes and that *link* them with outcomes in a productive relationship. Viewing causation in mechanism-based terms means that we explain why something occurred by analysing the productive processes that link a cause (or a set of causes) with an outcome. (2019, 30)

Beach and Pedersen claim that all variants of process tracing share a common notion of causal mechanisms, which are described as a '[t]heorized system that produces outcomes through the interaction of a series of parts that transmit causal forces from X to Y. Each part of a mechanism is an individually insufficient but necessary factor in a whole mechanism, which together produces Y. The parts of causal mechanisms are composed of entities engaging in activities' (2013, 176).[6] This is illustrated in Figure 2.1 where the entity is expressed as a noun and the activity as a verb.

Causal mechanisms 'are more than just a series of events. A sequence of events tells us who did what but does not tell us why or how the events were linked together in a causal sense' (Beach and Pedersen 2019, 32). To move beyond such a 'descriptive narrative,' we must ask how and why the events were linked together. To answer the 'how does it work' question requires that the arrows in between the entities are 'elucidated in enough detail that the critical parts of the process are made clear' (Beach and Pedersen 2019, 80). As for addressing the *why* question, this involves translating the narrative 'into parts

---

[6] This definition is from the first edition of this book, which I have chosen owing to its succinct clarity. Beach and Pedersen stand by this notion of causal mechanisms in their second edition (2019, 37–41).

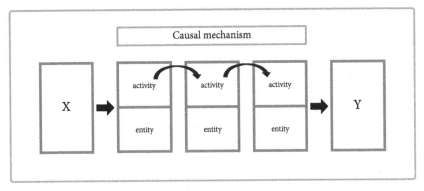

Figure 2.1 PTM causal mechanisms (adapted with permission of University of Michigan Press from Beach and Pedersen 2019, 71; permission conveyed through Copyright Clearance Center, Inc.)

that focus on the causal links in the process—that is, not just what happened but why.... this becomes the first stage of the theorization of a mechanism' (Beach and Pedersen 2019, 87–88). To answer the *how* and *why* question, we must make use of both empirical and theoretical elements. At the empirical level, this involves a focus on the activities of the entities, as opposed to the entities themselves, and how those activities are connected to produce the observed outcome. At the theoretical level, this involves elucidating, so far as possible, the activity-producing entities and the causal connections between those entities (i.e., the arrows as shown in Figure 2.1) (Beach and Pedersen 2019, 37–38). It is the 'interaction of theory and empirics [that] enables us to converge on the best explanation in the particular case' (Beach and Pedersen 2019, 286).

While I will utilise Beach and Pedersen's notion of causal mechanisms, there are limits to how far we can demonstrate this mechanical form of causality in the context of practice and its epistemic outcomes. For example, Beach and Pedersen ascribe a critical and irreplaceable value to each entity of the causal mechanism. Accordingly, 'explicit in a mechanismic ontology is a view that the parts that we include in our conceptualization of a given causal mechanism are absolutely vital (necessary) for the "machine" to work, and in the absence of one part, the mechanism itself cannot be said to exist' (Beach and Pedersen 2013, 30–31). Most practice-based outcomes are produced cumulatively, in conjunction with other practices. While it should be possible to make the case for which practices contributed to the observed outcome, it may not always be feasible to do so with such clinical categorical counterfactual certainty as is required here. I will elaborate upon the further limitations of this notion of causal mechanisms when they become relevant in Chapter 4.

Therefore, a degree of flexibility is required when conceptualising practice-based causality. To be fair, Beach and Pedersen note that not all causal mechanisms 'exhibit machine-like qualities' (2019, 29). Pouliot observes that 'because practices are by nature repeated and patterned, one may heuristically abstract them away from context in the form of various *social mechanisms*' (my emphasis) (2015, 240). Vennesson reminds us that 'the process that is uncovered does not have to be only causal, it can be constitutive as well—that is, accounting for the property of the phenomenon by reference to its structures and allowing the researcher to explain its conditions of possibility' and that '[i]n his original formulation, George talked not only about a causal mechanism, but also of an *intervening process*, a causal nexus' (my emphasis) (2008, 234). Thus, in recognition of the limits of Beach and Pedersen's idealised form of causal mechanisms and my adaptations of it, I will hereafter refer to the practice-based causal mechanism under consideration in this book as the 'intervening process'.

Zooming in and out

I will augment PTM with Nicolini's practice theory research toolkit. Although this toolkit was offered for the study and representation of practice at work, there is no reason it cannot be adapted for the study of social movement practice. Moreover, practice theory's processual, fluid, and performative notion of practice makes it an ideal fit for process tracing. After all, 'all practices are involved in a variety of relationships and associations that extend in both space and time' (Nicolini 2013, 229). Augmenting process tracing with Nicolini's toolkit will also help reinforce consistency between the ontological premise and methodological approach of this study.

Nicolini's toolkit comprises three basic movements. The first two are *zooming in* on the accomplishments of the practices and *zooming out* to discern the connections between practices and between practices and their products, accompanied by a corresponding set of 'sensitizing questions.' The third movement involves 'using the above devices to produce diffracting machinations that enrich our understanding through *thick textual renditions* of mundane practices' (my emphasis) (Nicolini 2013, 219). That is achieved when we can provide 'a convincing and defensible account of both the practice and its effects on the dynamics of organizing, showing how that which is local … contributes to the generation of broader effects' (Nicolini 2013, 219).

My first aim in zooming in and out will be to uncover which particular practices were associated with the evolution of Hizmet's position on the issues of concern. I will then zoom in to explore how those particular practices came about; how they have changed, and how that change was justified; how (the changing) practice influenced its own dynamics, its carriers (i.e., the practitioners), the movement's organisational position, and its associated epistemic outcomes on the issues of concern. In doing so, I will use Nicolini's sensitising questions to support the PTM employed in this research. I will integrate any insight I glean from these questions into the 'causal mechanism' of the PTM, as discussed in the next section, rather than list these insights separately. That said, not all of these sensitising questions will be relevant for all of the practices explored. Moreover, while I have a particular focus (practice-based knowledge production), the evasive nature of practice and its epistemic effects means that we cannot capture this phenomenon by merely asking direct questions. Rather, an indirect approach is required, which explores the nature of the practices, its links, and outcomes more generally.

With those caveats in mind, some of the adapted zooming in questions are as follows: what are Gülen, Hizmet participants, and organisations saying and doing? How are Hizmet's 'official' teachings produced? How do Hizmet's sayings (teachings) and doings (performances) interact over time and to what effect? How are Hizmet's sayings and doings temporally organised? What sort of things are done in the performance of practice? How do the practitioners define the objectives of their practices? How is the practice shaping itself and its practitioners? What are the formal and informal rules of practice? What are the areas of contention of practice? In which direction is the practice stretching and being stretched, and how is this change coming about? How has practice produced and/or responded to challenges and crises? How has practice changed? How have the associated teachings changed? What happened immediately before, during, and after a change occurred? How are these practices sustained and legitimised? (Nicolini 2013, 220).

As for zooming out, this means 'moving between practices' (Nicolini 2013, 229) by 'following them in space and time' (Nicolini 2013, 231). Another way to zoom out is to 'focus on the local and translocal effects produced by... practice networks' (Nicolini 2013, 232). My aim in zooming out will be to distil the connections between practices and the connections between practices and their effects. In doing so, I will pay particular attention to the link and logic between practices and practices and their associated effects, the evolution of practice, the evolution of the justification for practice, the retrospective justification for practice, and the macro effects of practice—with an overarching objective of exploring the epistemic effects of practice. I will probe these issues by using an amended version of Nicolini's zooming out questions, such as '[w]hat are the connections between the "here and now" of the practising and the "then and there" of other practices? Which other practices affect, enable, constrain, conflict, and interfere, etc., with the practice under consideration?' (Nicolini 2013, 230). How are these practice bundles kept together? 'How does the practice under consideration contribute to the "wider picture"? In which ways does the practice reproduce existing social arrangements or generate [change,] tension and conflict? How did we get to where we are? What are the interests, projects, hopes, and manoeuvres, etc., that led us to the current state of affairs?' (Nicolini 2013, 230). How does practice sustain, produce, evoke, and evolve knowledge? And 'who is empowered and disempowered' by this practice (Nicolini 2013, 239).

As noted above, the iterative zooming in and out stops when we can provide 'a convincing and defensible account of both the practice and its effects on the dynamics of organizing, showing how that which is local... contributes to the generation of broader effects' (Nicolini 2013, 219). According to Beach and Pedersen, case-centric process tracing stops when we have crafted a 'minimally sufficient explanation of an outcome' (2019, 282), which is achieved when we arrive at the conclusion that 'all the relevant facets of the outcome have adequately been accounted for and whether the evidence is best explained by the developed explanation rather than plausible alternatives' (Beach and Pedersen 2019, 286). Social movement outcome theory cautions against false attributions by encouraging researchers to subject their tentative conclusions to alternative explanations within a temporal context (Suh 2012, 1). Thus, I too will subject my tentative interpretations to alternative explanations, including challenges that do not of themselves amount to alternative explanations, in the course of formulating them.

Conceptualising the Intervening Process of Practice and Its Epistemic Outcomes

I will now turn to conceptualising the intervening process (causal mechanism) that connects practice to knowledge production. In doing so, I will operationalise the theoretical paradigm of this study as discussed in Chapter 1 into a more refined theoretical lens that will allow me to capture, examine, and explain the intervening process. My aim here is to lay the theoretical groundwork to help explore the *how* and *why* questions when examining Hizmet's practice in Chapters 3 and 4. This will permit me to reimagine the symbiotic relationship between the experiential and formalised facets of religious knowledge as discussed in Chapter 1 as the symbiotic relationship between tacit and explicit knowledge.[7] To achieve the foregoing, I will bring together a range of theoretical discussions from different fields and disciplines, including tacit and explicit knowledge, knowledge conversion, internalisation, cognitive compromise, and cognitive dissonance from practice-based approaches, practice-based epistemology, organisational studies, and social psychology. In doing so, I will show that it is possible to reimagine and reformulate the tacit-to-explicit knowledge conversion of organisational studies in a manner that is consistent with the pre-reflexive organic nature of both knowledge and practice as envisaged by practice-based epistemology.

Tacit and Explicit Knowledge

Michael Polanyi distinguishes between explicit and tacit knowledge (1962, 2009). Explicit (also referred to as formal, formalised, general, universal, codified, propositional) knowledge is a form of knowledge that can be easily articulated, shared, and transferred with others (Choo 2006, 8). For example, information found in a manual or textbook is explicit knowledge. Conversely, tacit (also referred to as intuitive, informal, practical, knowing-in-practice, know-how, pre-propositional, and pre-/non-reflexive) knowledge is 'personal knowledge that is hard to formalise or communicate to others. It

---

[7] A symbiotic relationship refers to a two-way interaction, whereas the tacit-to-explicit knowledge conversion referred to here implies a one-way relationship. I will address this objection a little later on in the chapter.

consists of subjective know-how, insights, and intuitions that comes to a person after having worked on an activity for a long period of time' (Choo 2006, 8)[8] or, as Ikujiro Nonaka puts it, '[t]acit knowledge is... deeply rooted in action and in an individual's commitment to a specific context—a craft or profession, a particular technology or product market, or the activities of a work group or team' (1991, 98).[9] According to Maurice Merleau-Ponty, tacit knowledge is inscribed in corporeal schema (1962), which 'operates below the level of reflexivity and are, in fact, inaccessible to discourse' (Nicolini 2013, 56).

Polanyi uses the well-known bicycle-riding example to explain the difference between tacit and explicit knowledge. Knowing how to ride and being able to verbalise how to ride a bicycle are two different types of knowing; the first is tacit, the second explicit. Most of those who know how to ride a bicycle will struggle to articulate the dynamics of doing so (Polanyi 1962, 51, 91). Similarly, most native speakers will instinctively know the correct form of expression without necessarily knowing why it is (Collins 2001, 116). Simply put, tacit knowledge is that which we know, without knowing (without thinking about what we know), which is why we often struggle to verbalise the substance of this knowledge (Polanyi 2009, 4–5).

Thus, according to this rationale and the preceding discussion on practice, tacit knowledge, and pre-reflexivity in Chapter 1, we can expect practice to precipitate, shape, and develop tacit knowledge in and through the *act of doing*. This raises the following questions: what is the link between tacit and explicit knowledge, and more specifically, can practice-based tacit knowledge evolve into explicit knowledge and if so, how can we conceptualise such a process? For this, I will turn to Nonaka's work on knowledge conversion (externalisation), which will help us to conceptualise this process.

Externalisation of Tacit Knowledge: Organisational Studies

While extensively cited and critiqued,[10] Nonaka's work on knowledge conversion provides us with a useful starting point. Nonaka credits the ability of

---

[8] See also Nicolini 2013, 57.
[9] See Chapter 1 for a discussion on the relationship between tacit knowledge and practice in the context of lived religion, practice-based epistemology, and habitus.
[10] For examples of this critique, see Zhu 2006; Gourlay 2006; Bratianu 2010; Souto 2013, 59; Nicolini et al. 2003, 6.

Japanese companies to tap into the tacit knowledge of its employees in order to *externalise* these 'often highly subjective insights, intuitions, and hunches' into explicit knowledge for the benefit of the organisation and company as a whole (1991, 97).[11] Nonaka identifies a 'spiral of knowledge' comprising four modes or 'patterns for creating knowledge in any given organization' (Nonaka 1991, 98). This involves *socialisation*, where tacit knowledge is transferred from one individual to another (tacit to tacit); *externalisation*, where tacit knowledge is converted into explicit knowledge (tacit to explicit); *combination*, where pre-existing explicit knowledge is brought together in meetings and discussion to produce new forms of explicit knowledge (explicit to explicit); and *internalisation*, where explicit knowledge is internalised by employees (explicit to tacit), which thereby connects the loop (Nonaka 1991, 98–99; Nonaka and Takeuchi 1995, 61–72).[12] Of these four patterns, externalisation is the 'quintessential knowledge-creation process' (Nonaka and Takeuchi 1995, 230), which is the 'process of articulating tacit knowledge into explicit concepts' (Nonaka and Takeuchi 1995, 64).

According to Nonaka, this is how the Osaka-based Matsushita Electric Company developed its own automatic home bread-making machine in 1985. After many failures, a company software developer suggested that she should train with the bread-maker of the Osaka International Hotel, one of the best bread-makers in the city. By doing so, this Matsushita employee was able to isolate the baker's distinctive way of stretching the dough in the process of kneading it. After a year of working with its engineers, the company succeeded in manufacturing a product that reproduced the baker's 'twist dough' stretching technique which proved a great success (Nonaka 1991, 98).

Nonaka's SECI model and his notion of externalisation are useful in conceptualising knowledge conversion in a workplace environment. However, while suited for its intended purposes, Nonaka's notion of externalisation is of limited use in the context of social movement practice for two reasons. First, Nonaka's model describes a process of externalisation

---

[11] Nonaka first discussed the notion of a 'spiral of knowledge' in his 1991 article in the *Harvard Business Review* (1991). Nonaka subsequently expanded on this article in a co-authored book that was published in 1995 (Nonaka and Takeuchi 1995). In 2007, the *Harvard Business Review* reprinted Nonaka's 1991 article without revision for its enduring relevance (2007). Thus, to avoid confusion, I will reference either Nonaka's original 1991 article or his 1995 co-authored book when representing his views on this subject but not the 2007 reprint of his 1991 article as both articles are identical.
[12] Abbreviated as the SECI model: socialisation, externalisation, combination, and internalisation.

that is external to, rather than a natural outcome of, practice. Put differently, the Matsushita Electric Company engineers *dropped in* (an external process) to observe, shadow, and analyse the baker's bread-making practice to extrapolate the relevant explicit knowledge; they were not a natural part of that bread-making process per se (the externality limitation). Second, this form of externalisation *deliberately aims* to extrapolate explicit knowledge from practice rather than account for an organic form of knowledge conversion that ensues from an 'unsuspecting' practice. After all, the Matsushita Electric Company engineers studied the bread-maker's practice for the specific purposes of isolating the baker's distinctive (yet tacit) way of stretching the dough in the process of kneading it (the intentionality limitation). Nonaka's notion of externalisation can be analogised as a water well. According to this analogy, tacit knowledge is the water at the bottom of a well. It does not arise (become explicit) of its own accord. Rather, converting the tacit into the explicit depends on an external mechanism, that is, the bucket and the rope (the *externality* limitation) and the deliberate will of a person to drop the bucket to the bottom of the well and to steadily draw it out (the *intentionality* limitation). These two limitations are intimately connected to the broader criticism levelled at Nonaka's SECI model, that is, that it is predicated upon a cognitivistic and rationalistic notion of knowledge (Souto 2013, 59), wherein knowledge is 'reified as a [pursuable and] transferable commodity' (Souto 2013, 60), which allows for 'its intentional and deliberate control' (Gherardi 2000, 213), as described above.

To overcome these two limitations, we must explore the prospect of re-imagining externalisation in the spirit of a practice-based epistemology (i.e., praxeologising Nonaka's externalisation), where *knowing* and *doing* are connected through practice, in which knowledge is treated as a living organism that is never complete, static, fixed, or finalised but is in fact dynamic, provisional, constructed, emergent, relational, processual, interactive, and continually reproduced in practice (Gherardi 2000, 2003, 356–57, 2006, 38–39; Gherardi and Nicolini 2003, 204–8; Corradi et al. 2010, 274–75; Souto 2013, 55, 62, 64 and 68; Cook and Wagenaar 2012, 5).

As explained in Chapter 1, this organic notion of knowing requires us to be attuned to the *unintended* and *internal* dimension and outcome of knowledge production, where knowledge cannot be pre-determined and controlled in the manner foreseen by rationalistic notions of knowledge (Gherardi 2003, 352). That in return means exploring the prospect of replacing the (i) externality and (ii) intentionality aspects of Nonaka's externalisation with (i) a practice-based *intrinsic* process(es), which accounts for (ii) *unintended* epistemic outcomes to ensue.

By doing so, we can conceptualise externalisation as a process that is consistent with a practice-based epistemology, which in return is far more suited to exploring the epistemic dimension of social movement practice. After all, if we are interested in the logic of practice, which is distinct from that of the practitioner, then the deliberate aim of the latter cannot necessarily speak for the outcomes to ensue from the former. Thus, the practitioner's 'deliberate intent' is far less useful to us in this respect than it is within a rationalistic framework of knowledge production. Moreover, the vast majority of movement practitioners do not adopt deliberate and calculating aims of knowledge conversion as described by Nonaka, which means that we must go beyond a form of externalisation that does.

Externalisation of Tacit Knowledge: Practice-based Epistemology

To achieve the above, I will replace the focus from the *outcome of externalisation* with the *input of (practice-based) internalisation*. That entails replacing the focus from the outcome of explicit knowledge and how it is extrapolated to the input of tacit knowledge and the corresponding force it creates on the production of explicit knowledge. As discussed earlier, if Nonaka's model is analogous to the drawing of water from a water well, where the onus is on an external mechanism and the deliberate will of an individual to draw water, my reconceptualisation is akin to a water spring whereby water breaks the ground level (e.g., the level of reflexivity) owing to its own internally built-up pressure (e.g., the force of internalisation organically leading to a form of externalisation). Reconceptualising externalisation in this fashion overcomes the twin limitations of Nonaka's model and its cognitivistic and rationalistic premise.

As explained in Chapter 1 on the basis of habitus and social learning, practice precipitates pre-reflexive internalisation through the act of doing. In other words, the force of internalisation ensues as a result of participation in practice. But how does a focus on practice-based internalisation help us conceptualise an organic form of externalisation? What links the force of internalisation with the outcome of externalisation? It is at this juncture that I propose using two concepts from social psychology: cognitive compromise and cognitive dissonance. We can use these concepts to help explain how a practice-based pre-reflexive internalisation can produce tacit knowledge, which in turn can sustain, produce, or change explicit knowledge, that is, result in externalisation. In this reconceptualised notion of knowledge conversion, externalisation ensues as the unintended organic outcome of a practice-based intrinsic process of internalisation (which is then re-internalised through recursive practice). Here, the outcome naturally ensues (as in the case of the water spring) as opposed to being deliberately pursued (as in the case of the water well).

Cognitive Compromise
Social phenomena such as social conformity (Asch 1951), group norm (Lewin 1947), groupthink (Janis 1982), religious syncretism (Droogers 1989), hybridisation, and cross-cultural fertilisation all point to the relativising effect of social interaction, which Peter Berger and Anton Zijderveld describe as 'cognitive compromise' (2010, 10–11). What's more, a number of studies have applied some of the aforementioned theoretical perspectives to Hizmet's practice, which I will explore more closely in Chapters 3 and 4 (Hällzon 2008; H. Yavuz 2003a; Grinell 2015; Conway 2014; H. Yavuz 2013; Pandya 2009). According to this view, 'in the absence of some type of cognitive defense, the relativising effect of conversation with "those others" will inevitably set in. What must happen then is a process of cognitive bargaining, leading to some type of cognitive compromise' (Berger and Zijderveld 2010, 33). This suggests that the more sustained the social interaction and the less cognitive the defence, the more substantial the cognitive influence.

The premise of this argument is rooted in the classical psychological 'line experiments' conducted by social psychologist Solomon Asch in the early 1950s. Through these experiments, Asch aimed to explore the effects of group pressure upon the modifications of judgements or social conformity. In doing so, he demonstrated the substantial influence to conform with the majority even where that majority was glaringly wrong (1951, 1955). Subsequent research confirmed and complexified the notion of social conformity. For example, Herbert C. Kelman's research focused 'on the depth and durability of change produced by social influence' (2005, 3). Kelman's work suggests that under certain circumstances, social interaction can produce a form of social influence that changes not just the public (say, explicit) but also the private (say, tacit) beliefs and opinions of those who partake in it. A change in private belief is likely to exemplify itself in a change of public belief or to reinforce a publicly stated position that was not in fact genuinely held. This would suggest that social interaction can precipitate the change of a private belief, which in turn can bring about a change of public belief (Kelman 1958, 2005).

Omar Ashour's research on the deradicalisation of the armed Egyptian Islamic Group (IG) supports this view (2017). In the mid-1980s, IG was an armed organisation that had engaged in acts of terrorism. By the late 1990s and early 2000, this group had renounced violence (2017, 602). Based on one hundred interviews with members and former members of this group, Ashour concluded that four variables were responsible for this ideological (private/inner) and behavioural (public/outer) change: state repression, selective inducements by the state, social interaction with the 'other,' and leadership (2017, 603). One form of social interaction with the other occurred in the 1990s when the Islamist leaders of this group were housed in the same cells as secular liberals and human rights activists in Egypt's political prisons. This led to in depth discussions about Islamism, democracy, and human rights (2017, 618–19). While IG leaders have not admitted to being influenced by these interactions, they have expressed 'their gratitude for those secular intellectuals,' which they would have targeted under their previous ideology (2017, 619). Moreover, new IG literature also reflects those 'mixed cell' debates, which includes a defense of post-modernist ideas, such as 'upholding ideological and theological uncertainty,' 'cultural and historical dynamism,' 'cultural dialogue,' and the 'necessity of renewing religious rhetoric' (2017, 619). If the cessation of violent acts demonstrated behavioural (outer/public) change, the production of literature and public statements to legitimise this transformation demonstrated ideological (inner/private) change. This demonstrates that among other dynamics, social interaction can precipitate change, even among members of an armed terrorist organisation.

Collectively, these studies suggest that practices that precipitate social interaction can bring about change at both the inner and outer, private and public, ideological and behavioural, and tacit and explicit levels and that one influences the other. Therefore, social movement practice, which produces social interaction with the other, is likely to precipitate the relativisation and moderation of the private and public views, beliefs, and positions of its participants in the manner described above. This helps us to overcome the *externality* and *intentionality* limitations in Nonaka's notion of externalisation as we discussed earlier. Internalisation is not an external but an intrinsic process that flows from social interaction; where practice produces social interaction, social interaction is likely to precipitate the internalisation of the other's views, beliefs, and dispositions in the manner just described. What's more, as I have already noted, internalisation does not depend on intent or deliberate will; it can ensue regardless of either at both the private and public level of belief. Thus, according to this view, as a form of practice, social interaction can, of its own, explain the changing within a tacitly held private view or belief (i.e., tacit-to-tacit change) as well as account for the changing of a privately held tacit to a publicly stated explicit view or belief (i.e., tacit-to-explicit change) without the need for an external hand or deliberate will to do so.

Cognitive Dissonance

The concept of cognitive dissonance was put forward by Leon Festinger in 1957. Its basic proposition is that 'the individual strives toward consistency within himself' and that the 'existence of dissonance, being psychologically uncomfortable, will motivate the person to try to reduce the dissonance and achieve consonance' (Festinger 1957, 1, 3). Dissonance is said to occur where 'the obverse of one element would follow from the other' (Festinger 1957, 13) or, to put it more simply, when one view is 'inconsistent' with another (Cooper 2007, 2–3). The resultant 'psychological discomfort' (Festinger 1957, 2) becomes a 'motivating factor' that 'leads to activity orientated toward dissonance reduction just as hunger leads to activity oriented toward hunger reduction' (Festinger 1957, 9–10). The reduction of dissonance is not merely a preference but a drive and a need, '[p]eople do not just prefer eating over starving; we are driven to eat' (Cooper 2007, 3). Where dissonance exists between two elements, 'this dissonance can be eliminated by changing one of those elements' (Festinger 1957, 18). The more important these conflictual elements are to the person, the greater the dissonance, which in turn amplifies the 'strength of the pressures to reduce the dissonance' (Festinger 1957, 16).

Although this theory has been complexified and critiqued over the decades, its basic proposition has been confirmed by subsequent and more advanced research. 'We now know that dissonance is uncomfortable.... We also know that dissonance is arousing. We know it because we can measure it physiologically... the evidence is compelling that Festinger was correct in the motivational system he proposed' (Cooper 2007, 61). Thus, by many accounts, 'Festinger's theory of cognitive dissonance has been one of the most influential theories in social psychology' (Harmon-Jones and Mills 1999, 3).

To assess the relevance of this theory for the present purposes, we need to ask two questions. First, how can humans assimilate discordant views if they always strive for internal consistency (the second principle of cognitive dissonance), and what does this tell us about how dissonant knowledge is introduced through practice? Second, we began this discussion from a relatively safe premise: that practice produces tacit knowledge. Does this theory allow for (a practice-based) tacit knowledge to conflict with and thereby change explicit knowledge?

The first question raises a general objection to cognitive dissonance, which is also relevant for the present purposes. Festinger responds by suggesting that 'new information may become known to a person' without his or her control, where, for example, 'a person who is quite certain in his knowledge that automatic transmissions on automobiles are inefficient may accidentally come across an article praising automatic transmissions' (1957, 4–5). Festinger's example is based on a 'mentalistic,' if accidental, form of knowledge processing. The case for assimilating (what turns out to be 'dissonant') knowledge through practice is far more plausible. After all, the byproduct of practice is to pre-reflexively internalise a set of underlying values, norms, assumptions, dispositions, and skills (or 'cognitions' as Festinger refers to it). Thus, a person might engage in a form of practice without necessarily appreciating the knowledge-based implications of doing so. Furthermore, different forms of practice can introduce new ways of changing pre-existing views and beliefs, such as practice-based social interaction moderating a pre-existing belief or view through cognitive compromise. A moderated belief or view might come into conflict with other 'unmoderated' pre-existing forms of knowledge. Moreover, like practice, knowledge is organic; it can sprout, grow, connect, and evolve, as per vegetation (Gherardi 2006, 14). Thus, the practice-based knowledge in question may not have caused dissonance to begin with but may have evolved in a way to challenge the status quo later on. In short, Festinger's theory allows for a practice-based form of (dissonant) knowledge production.

As for the second question; by treating any '*piece* of knowledge' as 'cognition,' Festinger equalises different forms of knowledge as one (my emphasis) (Cooper 2007, 6). These forms of knowledge include cognitions that are more readily associated with explicit knowledge (e.g., data and opinion) as well as cognitions that we are unaware of (Cooper 2007, 6) and that are often understood as tacit knowledge (e.g., culture, behaviour, attitude, and values) (Cooper 2007, 9–10, 14, 19). Additionally, one of Festinger's most oft-repeated examples is the dissonance between the 'knowledge' that smoking is harmful (data-based cognition) versus the continued act of smoking (action-based cognition) (1957, 5–6). These two cognitions are asymmetrical; '[a]n action is different from an attitude which, in turn, is different from an observation of reality. However, each of these has a psychological representation' (Cooper 2007, 6), which allows them to conflict.

Thus, Festinger does not require symmetrical opposition (e.g., tacit versus tacit) for dissonance to occur; asymmetrical cognitions (e.g., tacit versus explicit) can also produce cognitive dissonance. The only caveat is relevance; irrelevant cognitions cannot conflict within or across different forms of knowledge (Festinger 1957, 11–12). Therefore, Festinger's theory suggests that dissonance will occur between conflictual (and thereby relevant) forms of tacit and explicit knowledge. That in return suggests that a practice-based tacit knowledge can cause the revision of a pre-existing form of explicit knowledge.

Bringing It Together

Having discussed both cognitive compromise and cognitive dissonance, we can now ask how these two theories help us to explain the processes of internalisation and externalisation in the context of practice-based knowledge production? The following example will help answer that question.

Let us envisage a pious traditionalist Muslim encountering the following Qur'anic verse: 'O ye who believe! take not the Jews and the Christians for friends. They are friends one to another. And whoso among you takes them for friends is indeed one of them' (5:52). Let us assume that this Muslim adopts a traditionalist interpretation of this verse—that is, that Muslims are prohibited from befriending non-Muslims. In doing so, this religious interpretation becomes an explicit cognition. Let us now imagine a scenario where this person's day-to-day work brings him into sustained contact with his non-Muslim co-workers. In time, this person might find himself befriending his colleagues (or even becoming emotionally involved with one of them). Given his conscious opposition to such friendships, this outcome would have evolved at the pre-reflexive level of consciousness (cognitive compromise). As a traditionalist Muslim, this person would then be faced with one of two options according to Festinger's cognitive dissonance. He must either adopt a different

X	Intervening process				Y
Practice	Social interaction with non-Muslim work colleagues	This produces an evolving affinity towards non-Muslim coworkers at the pre-reflexive level of consciousness	Conflict occurs between explicit and tacit cognitions that non-Muslims can be befriended	Conflict produces discomfort, which produces urge for internal consistency	Reinterpretation of verse (explicit cognition) to allow for befriending of non-Muslim (colleagues)
	Internalisation		Externalisation		

Figure 2.2 An example—the intervening process for befriending non-Muslim co-workers

interpretation of the Qur'anic verse or cease his emotional affection for his non-Muslim co-worker(s).[13] Either way, a dissonance will have occurred between a text-based (explicit) cognition versus an experience-based (tacit) cognition. If he chooses the latter, then it can be said that a tacit cognition caused the revision of an explicit cognition through cognitive compromise and cognitive dissonance. Put differently, through his reinterpretation of this verse, this individual would have externalised a tacitly evolved cognition. Figure 2.2 illustrates the above intervening process, and Figure 2.3 lifts the level of abstraction of this theorised intervening process by reducing its case-specific identifiers.

According to Figure 2.3, practice precipitates social interaction, which in turn produces cognitive compromise. Here, social interaction-based cognitive compromise describes an internalisation process that is the relativisation effect that flows from internalising the views, beliefs, and dispositions of others. This relativisation/moderation occurs at the pre-reflexive (tacit) level of consciousness. However, the moderated tacit cognition (i.e., friendship towards others) now runs the risk of conflicting with other pre-existing forms of 'unmoderated' tacit and explicit cognitions. Where that happens, cognitive dissonance occurs, which produces psychological discomfort. That discomfort forces this moderated cognition to breach the level of reflexivity. Thus, the tacit cognition is no longer tacit but emergent. An explicit

---

[13] A third option is to become less religious, which would reduce the motivating force of the dissonance, which Festinger allows for in his exposition of cognitive dissonance. This would not remove the dissonance entirely, but it would ease the level of discomfort that it produces (Festinger 1957, 16).

X	Intervening process				Y
Practice	Social interaction	This produces cognitive compromise which moderates tacit cognition at pre-reflexive level of consciousness	Cognitive dissonance occurs between moderated tacit and unmoderated explicit forms of cognition	Dissonance produces discomfort which produces desire for consonance	Knowledge production (i.e., change) to achieve cognitive consonance
	Internalisation		Externalisation		

Figure 2.3 Lifting the level of abstraction of the intervening process of Figure 2.2

cognition is born when the person in question justifies the retention of his or her moderated view while 'dropping' the discordant other. A new form of explicit religious knowledge is born where the justification of this newly emergent moderated cognition relates to religious discourse. In this example, internalisation begins with social interaction, which produces cognitive compromise. Externalisation on the other hand begins with cognitive dissonance and ends with the effort to achieve cognitive consonance by justifying the revision of a pre-existing view in favour of the emergent one through re-interpretation of religious text.

This raises the following question. The above conceptualisation of cognitive compromise-based internalisation relies on social interaction; is that the only form of practice that produces this intervening process? Can we conceptualise other forms of practice as producing the same outcome? Any form of practice-based internalisation can trigger this outcome, cognitive compromise is merely one. The participation in any form of practice will precipitate the internalisation of the associated habitus, skills, knowledge, values, and dispositions through the recursive *act of doing*. For example, supporting the activities of an environmentalist group will precipitate the internalisation of its associated values and messages, even if this does not involve sustained social interaction with others. The key here is whether the internalised cognition (view, belief, disposition, skill, etc.) necessitates an externalisation through explicit justification. Cognitive dissonance describes *one* process whereby that occurs; there may be others. I have chosen these two concepts because they appear to be the most useful in making sense of Hizmet's practice and its epistemic effects.

This discussion raises another question; what happens where there is change but no conflict? In other words, could cognitive compromise produce an externalisation of a tacitly evolved cognition without cognitive dissonance? This is certainly possible, but the challenge for the researcher is identifying the epistemic effect of practice where the change is so subtle that it produces little to no contrast. Furthermore, as Nicolini, Gherardi, and Dvora Yanow explain, breakdowns and disturbances (e.g., conflicts) lead to reflexivity, which in turn produces reflexive (explicit) knowledge (Nicolini et al. 2003, 23). So far as cognitive dissonance is concerned, conflict is key for the relevant tacit cognition to (proverbially put) raise its head above the *reflexivity parapet*, but conflict is also key for the researcher exploring it because conflict produces contrast that allows it to be identified and 'reverse engineered'. Thus, I am exploring knowledge production in the context of conflict/contrast-producing change.

Therefore, through the use of cognitive compromise and cognitive dissonance, we can replace the focus from the *outcome of externalisation* to the *input of practice-based internalisation*. In doing so, we can reconceptualise Nonaka's mechanical externalisation, which relies on external and deliberate interventions, with one that is organic, relying on, and thereby accounting for, the intrinsic dynamics and unintended outcomes of practice. This is far more suited for examining social movement practice. In this manner, we can reconceptualise externalisation as a process that explains that which naturally *ensues* as opposed to that which is deliberately *pursued*.

Before moving on, I should point out that the foregoing also allows us to re-imagine the symbiotic relationship between the experiential and formalised facets of religious knowledge, as discussed in Chapter 1, as the symbiotic relationship between tacit and explicit knowledge. This, however, raises the following question: a symbiotic relationship refers to a two-way interaction, whereas the tacit-to-explicit knowledge conversion (i.e., externalisation) appears to imply a one-way relationship; is this not a theoretical impediment to conceptualising the experiential and formalised facets of religious knowledge? No, it is not because what we have described as the reconceptualised notion of externalisation accounts for this two-way relationship. The confusion arises from the 'tacit-to-explicit' shorthand, which is somewhat misleading.

For example, I used cognitive dissonance to explain how a tacit cognition can displace (and/or change) an explicit cognition in the process of externalisation. On the face of it, this interaction appears to produce a one-way linear change. However, as explained above, when this occurs, the tacit cognition also changes as it becomes explicit itself. In so doing, the tacit cognition changes in nature and quite possibly in substance as well. After all, and as cognitive compromise would tell us, it is unlikely that two cognitions interact without co-shaping one another. Moreover, externalised explicit cognitions (i.e., explicit epistemic outcomes) face the prospect of being reinternalised (and thereby reshaping the tacit cognitions) on account of being 'attached' to a recursive practice. In other words, there is an ongoing feedback loop between that which is externalised (explicit knowledge) and that which is internalised (tacit knowledge) through practice. That means the interaction is not one-way linear but two-way circular, as also noted in Figure 5.1 in Chapter 5.

Contextualising the Conceptualised Intervening Process in Islam

Chapters 3 and 4 of this book will examine Hizmet's practice vis-à-vis knowledge production as it pertains to the Islamic discipline of *fiqh*. Thus, *fiqh* is the substantive epistemic context within which I will explore Hizmet's practice-based knowledge production. As a result, it is important to discuss and define the nature of knowledge within this discipline and how it is traditionally produced and endorsed. That will allow me to determine what we mean by knowledge (production) within the context of *fiqh* and the epistemic criteria that needs to be met in order for knowledge production to be recognised from within this discipline. Without this form of contextualisation, I might be able to comment on the production of knowledge in general but not on the production of Islamic knowledge in the form of *fiqh*, in particular. I will then explore the prospect of legitimising and/or theorising tacit-to-explicit knowledge conversion as discussed above within an Islamic framework, that is, from an *emic* perspective. This will help justify the *etic* perspective that I have adopted in this study. Thus, this section will be guided by two questions. First, what is the nature of *fiqh*, and what does it say about *how* knowledge is produced and legitimised? Second, what does Islamic epistemology and *fiqh* say about tacit/explicit forms of knowledge and tacit-to-explicit knowledge conversion?

The Epistemic Context: *Fiqh*

As noted in the Introduction, given Islam's emphasis on practice (on actualising faith through worship and 'correct action'), the primary science in Islam is not theology, as it is in Christianity, but *fiqh* (Esposito 1998, 68–69, 74–75). As a result, *fiqh* is the most developed, didactic, formal, and advanced Islamic discipline in the body of Islamic knowledge, which governs all aspects of a Muslims' life, including personal hygiene, sexual relations, family life, etiquette, personal and collective worship, social affairs, and matters pertaining to legal rules and the penal code (Schacht 1982, 1; Hallaq 2009, 28–30). Moreover, while Islam does not recognise any form of clergy, the *ulama* (i.e., Islamic scholars) and *fuqaha* (i.e., Islamic jurists) serve as the unofficial gatekeepers of Islamic knowledge (Gilsenan 1982, 30–31; Ramadan 2009, 3).

Fiqh is often translated as 'Islamic law,' which is a contested and misunderstood term. 'Islamic law' is often conflated with both the *Sharia* and *fiqh*. For the sake of clarity, 'God's law as an abstraction is called the *Sharī'ah* (literally, the way), while the concrete understanding and implementation of this Will is called the *fiqh* (literally, the understanding). The *Sharī'ah* is God's Will in an ideal and abstract fashion, but the *fiqh* is the product of the human attempt to understand God's Will' (Abou El Fadl 2001, 75–76). *Fiqh* was first produced in the circles of master jurists who fulfilled the role of a law professor according to Hallaq. As a result, 'legal authority, therefore, became epistemic (i.e., knowledge-based) rather than political, social or even religious. That epistemic authority is the defining feature of Islamic law' (Hallaq 2009, 35). Legal authority 'resided with the scholars, not with the political rulers or any other source' (Hallaq 2009, 35). Thus, *fiqh* is first and foremost human knowledge produced by and for humans.

The production of new knowledge within this Islamic discipline comprises a new interpretation of a particular issue in accordance with its established rules referred to as *usul al-fiqh* (the methodology by which *fiqh* is produced). In this manner, a new interpretation qualifies as a rule or dictum (*ahkam*). The four Sunni *madhhabs* (legal schools of law) are in broad agreement on the following four sources for producing new interpretations (Hallaq 1997, 1; Kamali 2008, 19): the Qur'an, Sunna, *ijma* (juristic consensus),[14] and *qiyas*

---

[14] Here, *ijma* (juristic consensus) refers to legal rulings that achieve the consensus of the jurists who represent the main body of Muslim believers.

(analogical reasoning)[15] (hereafter the primary sources). According to traditional *usul al-fiqh*, jurists must first consult the Qur'an and then the Sunna, which are represented in written texts (Fadl 2001, 38). If both are silent or ambiguous, then jurists are permitted to decide the issue at hand by *ijma* and/or *qiyas*. A new re/interpretation based on any one of these sources (the Qur'an, Sunna, *ijma*, or *qiyas*) is considered as equal to the other. Jurists can also use secondary methods to arrive at new interpretations. However, there is no consensus among the four Sunni *madhhabs* on these methods, which include *istihsan* (juristic preference), *istislah/maslahah* (public interest), *darura* (necessity), and *urf/adat* (custom) (Hallaq 1997, 1; Doi 1997, 81; Kamali 2008, 19; Hallaq 2009, 22–27; Baderin 2003, 37; Shabana 2010, 2).

With the exception of the Qur'an and Sunna, all of these primary and secondary sources are in fact methods. Thus, rules are derived *from* the Qur'an and Sunna but *through* these various methods (Hallaq 1997, 1, 22). As a result, all of these methods are in fact forms of *ijtihad*, that is, autonomous (legal) reasoning (Ramadan 2009, 22).[16] *Ijtihad* occurs where the Qur'an and/or Sunna do not dictate an explicit meaning 'or when the context imperatively needed to be taken into account in the implementation of texts' (Ramadan 2009, 22). In these instances, the jurist is required to exercise *ijtihad* to arrive at a practical meaning through use of one of the above methods. For example, jurists used *qiyas* to prohibit date-wine (which is not explicitly prohibited in the Qur'an) on the basis that it shared the same *ratio legis* (*illa*) as grape-wine (which is explicitly prohibited) by interpreting what that *ratio legis* was and by applying it to date-wine (Hallaq 2009, 23).

Since Islam pervades all aspects of a Muslim's life, Islamic law must, in one sense, be conceived as Muslim culture (Yilmaz 2005a, 192). Consequently, 'any new discourse is directly or indirectly a result of a new ijtihad, which does not have to be in the field of law only, as strictly defined and understood by legal modernity' (Yilmaz 2003, 217). Thus, *ijtihad* is not restricted to re/interpretations to *fiqh* either. Rather, it may be exercised by 'experts in other disciplines, provided that the person who attempts it acquires mastery of the relevant data, especially in the Qur'an and Sunnah, pertaining to his subject' (Kamali 2008, 165). After all, *ijtihad* and the broader renewal of Islam

---

[15] *Qiyas* refers to legal rulings that are achieved by analogising one situation, for which there is no clear ruling, with another, for which there is.

[16] See also the following definition: 'The Arabic word for *Ijtihad* literally means an effort or an exercise to arrive at one's own judgement. In its widest sense, it means the use of human reason in the elaboration and explanation of the Shari'ah Law' (Doi 1997, 78).

(*tajdid*) go hand in hand (Ramadan 2009, 22). *Tajdid* (literally, renewal) refers to the Prophetic prophecy which foretold that Islam would be renewed every century by a *mujaddid* (literally, the renewer), that is, the person who will undertake this task.[17] Therefore, *ijtihad* 'allows Islam to dynamically develop itself within practical life in accordance with changing conditions in different contexts' (Yilmaz 2005b, 34).

In theory, there are 'strict, and indeed legitimate, conditions for the practice of *ijtihad*' (Ramadan 2009, 23). However, before moving onto discussing them, it is important to point out the limitations of those conditions. Mohammad Hashim Kamali notes the private, civil, and unofficial nature of *ijtihad* and of the *mujtahid* (a person engaged in *ijtihad*) to underscore the point that there is no procedure to regulate the production of *ijtihad* and to identify who is or is not a *mujtahid* (2008, 163). This explains why the modern age has produced what Yilmaz refers to as 'micro-mujtahids', that is, non-expert 'young Muslims' who pick and mix from the major Sunni *madhhabs* while also deducing 'their own interpretations directly from the Quran and Sunna' (2005a, 198–99). In theory, while *mujtahids* should be qualified to a certain degree, 'the reality remained somewhat elusive and hardly any *mujtahid* volunteered openly to declare himself on attaining this rank' (Kamali 2008, 163). Moreover, Abou El Fadl reminds us of the Prophetic saying that claims that every *ijtihad* is worthwhile: 'If the *mujtahid* is correct in his or her *ijtihad* . . . , he or she receives two bounties, and if he or she is wrong, he or she receives one' (2001, 34). While this reinforces the notion of 'individual and egalitarian accessibility of the truth' (Abou El Fadl 2001, 34–5), it also makes it difficult to dismiss an *ijtihad* as outright wrong. Moreover, Abou El Fadl also points out that Muslim jurists 'regularly introduced innovations and changes in the law while claiming that they were, in fact, adhering to precedent or the true spirit of a precedent,' which in turn allowed the introduction of change without having to justify it (2001, 86). Although Abou El Fadl criticises some contemporary examples of *ijtihad* for being unsystematic or selective in substantiating a particular opinion, he does not deny that they are nonetheless *ijtihads* (2001, 350–51). Thus, '*ijtihad* could offer solutions to all sorts of problems except defining/identifying its own carrier and agent!' (Kamali 2008, 163).

---

[17] 'At the beginning of every century Allah will send to this Ummah [the Muslim community] someone who will renew its religion' (al-Sijistani 2008, 512, hadith no 4291).

Bearing those caveats in mind, it is nonetheless possible to elucidate some pertinent patterns in the production of an *ijtihad*. First, to remain within the established rules of the Sunni legal thought, an *ijtihad* must justify its position by the primary (e.g., Qur'an, Sunna, *ijma*, or *qiyas*) or secondary sources (e.g., *istihsan, istislah, darura, urf/adat*) of *fiqh*. After all, *ijtihad* is not unfettered reasoning with no point of reference (Hallaq 1997, 15). A *mujtahid* does not need to flout his opinions as *ijtihad*, but he should offer a justified opinion on the basis of one or more of the aforementioned sources. Second, a *mujtahid* must be an expert in a number of Islamic disciplines with a grasp of Arabic grammar, semantics, and morphology, as well as familiarity with the culture of the time (Hallaq 1997, 118; Kamali 2008, 163). Third, a *mujtahid* must be an observant, pious, trustworthy believer of the highest moral character (Doi 1997, 79). Thus, a *mujtahid* cannot simply be a scholar; he must also be a practitioner of the knowledge he possesses.

As for originality; while we might expect new phenomena to produce original *ijtihads*, it would be misplaced to seek substantive originality on longstanding issues. After all, the premodern and modern *fuqaha* have been prolific in producing all types of responses to real and hypothetical situations. Thus, even where there is consensus among the four Sunni *madhhabs*, there are always a range of minority and obscure views in the annals of Islamic tradition. As a result, very few *ijtihads* can lay claim to such substantive originality. Furthermore, unlike academia, the aim in religious knowledge production is not to be *original* but to be *authentic* to the will of God, which orientates towards *continuity* rather than *change*. Thus, a fixation on originality is misplaced in the context of *ijtihad* production. Moreover, my focus is on practice-based knowledge production, which is not limited by considerations of originality.

This discussion yields a number of important points for the present purposes. First, it suggests that when examining practice-based *knowledge* production within *fiqh*, I am in fact looking at practice-based *ijtihad* production. Second, it suggests that to recognise an epistemic outcome as a form of *ijtihad*, it should exhibit the following characteristics: (i) expressed in written or spoken word even if it is not flouted as an *ijtihad*, (ii) based on the primary and/or secondary sources of *fiqh*, (iii) articulated by an expert practitioner, and (iv) pertain to an issue that is open to interpretation (i.e., issues on which the Qur'an and Sunna are silent or ambiguous or that even where they are explicit, the change of context requires a change of interpretation). An interpretation that meets these conditions can be said to meet the established rules of *ijtihad* production of the inherited traditions of religious epistemology on *fiqh*. This provides us with the epistemic context for evaluating Hizmet's practice vis-à-vis knowledge production. While all of these considerations are subjective (after all, who has the authority to judge the merits and methodology of an *ijtihad* and the qualifications and piety of a *mujtahid*), the very basis of *ijtihad* is subjective as noted above.

This raises some questions in the context of the present case study. First, does Gülen claim to be engaged in *ijtihad*? Does his work amount to *ijtihad*, and has it been recognised as such? The answer to the first question is straightforward: Gülen does not claim to be engaged in *ijtihad* (in fact, he denies it; see Gülen 2012a; Weller 2008, 758), but we have already said that this is not a condition of *ijtihad*. As for the follow-up question; based on the above criteria, Gülen has made a number of statements that clearly qualify as *ijtihads*. I will not go into these statements here, as the focus of my study is not whether Gülen produces *ijtihad*, but whether practice (including those attributed to Gülen and the movement) produces it. Clearly, for Hizmet participants, Gülen qualifies as a *mujtahid*.[18] Moreover, numerous scholarly pieces describe Gülen's contributions either directly or indirectly as *ijtihads*.[19] While these appraisals are of course subjective, the entire premise of *ijtihad* production and its durability is subjective. The point in referencing these studies is to demonstrate that the claim that Gülen has articulated statements that amount to *ijtihads* is not controversial. If Gülen's statements amount to *ijtihads* (or any other form of knowledge production within *fiqh*), then we can treat these statements as the end-point of externalisation and reverse engineer the process(es) by which it was produced. In doing so, we can replace the focus from (knowledge-producing) *practitioners* to (knowledge-producing) *practices*.

Contextualising Knowledge Conversion within an Islamic Framework

This brings us to the following question: can we legitimise and/or theorise tacit-to-explicit knowledge conversion from within an Islamic framework?

---

[18] Acar discusses Gülen's *ijtihads* more closely while systematically explaining how Gülen qualifies as a *mujtahid*, according to Gazali's criteria in a book chapter published by Hizmet's own publishing house (2011, 65–84).

[19] For example, see Yilmaz 2003, 2005a, 2008, 2018; Yavuz and Esposito 2003a, xxxii; Bakar 2005; Beşer 2006; Ergene 2008; Albayrak 2011; H. Yavuz 2013, 47, 182.

That, in return, raises a more fundamental question: how does Islam address tacit/explicit knowledge? The epistemologies associated with practice and Islam both ascribe an important epistemic role to practice, which lends credence to the practice-based perspective of this book. Nonetheless, there are limitations to theorising about practice-based knowledge production from within an Islamic framework (i.e., an *emic* perspective), as we will see below.

For example, the Qur'an and classical Islamic literature equates knowledge (*'ilm*) with religious knowledge (Rosenthal 2007, 29, 31; Hallaq 1997, 15). According to this perspective, the purpose of knowledge is to find God, which cannot be achieved unless it is anchored by faith (*iman*) and guided by practice (*amal*) (Rosenthal 2007, 30). While the majority of Sunni *madhhabs* do not make religious practice a requirement of faith, all theological schools of thought agree on the intimate connection among faith, knowledge, and practice (Rosenthal 2007, 39). After all, '[t]he inseparable character of knowledge and action was at the center of all Muslim ethics, both religious and philosophical' (Rosenthal 2007, 67), which explains the condition of religious practice and piety for *mujtahids* and *ulama*, as discussed above.

The connection between practice and knowledge is further illustrated by the Sufi concepts of esoteric heart knowledge, that is, *marifa* (intuitive knowledge of God) and *yaqeen* (certainty), which are described as subjective, embodied, experiential, metaphysical, intuitive, immersive, and gnostic forms of mystical heart knowledge (Rosenthal 2007, 30, 99, 165; Gülen 2006b, 123, 146). This suggests that esoteric knowledge is primarily tacit in nature. According to longstanding Sufi teachings, esoteric knowledge is not *earned* (through practice or otherwise) but is *bestowed* (as a gift) by God (Rosenthal 2007, 170; Gülen 2006b, vii–viii, 124–25). It is here that we run into trouble. While practice is understood as a *precursor* to esoteric knowledge in Sufism, it cannot be conceptualised as a *condition* of this knowledge. This eschews the causal link between practice and knowledge. This raises an additional challenge; the recipient of this 'gift' is expected to *preserve*, not *develop*, it. The focus on practice in this context is to precipitate spirituality, which in turn helps preserve the 'purity' of the knowledge entrusted upon the recipient while allowing him or her to *seek* out more. Thus, while there are areas of overlap between the discussions on esoteric/exoteric knowledge in Sufi literature with that of tacit/explicit knowledge as discussed above,[20] there are also inherent limitations to theorising from this point of view.

As for *fiqh*, as discussed above, this discipline acknowledges *urf and adah* (literally, custom and convention) as a secondary method for producing *ijtihad* (Shabana 2010, 2). Juristically, *urf and adah* refers to good common practice, which is based on and evolves through unwritten (tacit) culture, societal disposition, and habit (Shabana 2010, 49–50). Similarly, tacit knowledge could also impress itself upon new *ijtihads* through other secondary methods such as *maslahah* (public interest) and *istihsan* (juristic preference). In such instances, it could be suggested that tacit knowledge has been externalised when recognised and endorsed in this manner (i.e., when an *ijtihad* is based on the changing customs of the time). However, these methods do not account for *how* tacit knowledge reaches a level of relevance or reflexivity to qualify as explicit knowledge (the process) but rather what happens when a jurist *decides* that it has (the outcome). Thus, this does not contribute to the theorisation of the *process*, so to speak.

Moreover, as discussed above, these secondary methods are contested and carry limited weight on their own. As a result, while we can certainly make the case for practice-based tacit knowledge from within an Islamic framework (i.e., an *emic* perspective), this is unlikely to allow for the theorisation of practice-based knowledge conversion (externalisation) as discussed above. Accordingly, we must adopt an *etic* perspective, that is, one from outside the Islamic epistemological framework, which is what this book has set out to do by drawing together a range of interdisciplinary theoretical perspectives. As shown in Chapter 1, numerous studies have discussed the production of Islamic knowledge from an *etic* perspective (Loeffler 1988; Bowen 1993; Lambek 1993; Jouili and Amir-moazami 2006; Bruinessen and Allievi 2011; Bruinessen 2011; Sunier 2015; Flaskerud 2018; Flaskerud and Leirvik 2018). Collectively, these studies posit that Islamic knowledge is not merely semiotic but also social, performative, embodied, and relational and that the everyday practice of Islam by non-specialist Muslims is capable of (re)producing Islamic knowledge. This lends credence to the *etic* approach of this book, which seeks to theorise the practice-based process of Islamic

---

[20] For example, Nonaka treats spiritual knowledge as tacit knowledge (Bratianu 2013, 216–17); Zigler comments on the tacit element of spiritual understanding, which he refers to as spiritual epistemology (2007); and Guemuesay notes that the nature of Sufi knowledge and its transference is in fact tacit on account of being experiential, relational, and social (2012, 1082).

knowledge production through the symbiotic relationship between tacit and explicit knowledge.

Conclusion

The methodological approach of this research will allow me to trace and analyse the causal relationship between Hizmet's practice and knowledge production. Given the elusive, latent, multidirectional, and complex nature of practice and practice-based outcomes, I have combined three methodological approaches to study the phenomena under consideration. I have shown how each is useful in its own right but also in its ability to work well with the other methodological approaches discussed herein. Moreover, I have also explained how these methodological approaches meet the methodological considerations set out in the introduction of this chapter.

In Chapter 1, I discussed how practice theory, practice-based epistemology, practical theology, and lived religion inform the theoretical paradigm of this study. Here, I have combined these practice-based approaches with organisational studies, social psychology, social movement theory, and Islamic epistemology to both conceptualise and contextualise the intervening process between practice and knowledge production. In doing so, I have operationalised these theoretical discussions into a methodological framework. This also ensures the ontological-methodological consistency of this research.

3
Apostasy in Islam
From 'Off with His Head' to Humanising the Apostate

In 1980, Gülen extemporaneously endorsed, justified, and normalised the premodern classical formulation of the Islamic doctrine on apostasy (the apostasy doctrine) during a 'question and answer' sermon at the Bornova central mosque in Izmir (Gülen 2006a). In 2014, Gülen provided religious justification for rejecting this doctrine outright (Gülen 2014). This chapter will ask how and why that outcome came about. By focusing on the processual nature of practice and the interplay within and between Hizmet's doings and (Gülen's) sayings (i.e., Hizmet's practices) over an expansive temporospatial axis, I will show that the change of position ('breakage') was produced naturally and gradually, without prior proclamation or intent, in and through Hizmet's practice. That change of position eventually required an explicitly stated 'theological fusion' which presented itself as an emergent reinterpretation (*ijtihad*). Thus, as explained in Chapter 2, this form of practice-based knowledge production precipitated through two basic movements: *internalisation*, which operates at the level of intuitive, implicit, and pre-reflexive tacit knowledge, and *externalisation*, which channels the tacit knowledge into universal, accessible, and formalised explicit knowledge. As discussed in the foregoing chapter, this form of practice-based internalisation/externalisation overcomes the twin limitations of Nonaka's 'knowledge conversion' model, that is, *intentionality* and *externality*.

I will begin this chapter by providing some background about the apostasy doctrine, including its epistemic origin, legal context, present-day significance, and implementation. This will help contextualise Hizmet's evolving position within the Islamic milieu. I will then examine Hizmet's practice vis-à-vis this doctrine by utilising the methodological framework set out in Chapter 2. My primary aim in doing so will be to elucidate how and why the observed epistemic outcome came about, which will be the focus of the intervening process (causal mechanism).

Apostasy Doctrine: Genesis, Context, and Present-day Application

As discussed in the Introduction and Chapter 2, *fiqh* (Islamic law) is an all-embracing body of duties that Muslims believe to be the commandment of God pertaining to every aspect of life (Schacht 1982, 1). There are three categories of penal law in Islam: *hudud* (crimes against God, whose punishment is fixed in the Qur'an and/or Sunna); *qisas* (crimes against an individual whose punishment is equal retaliation or monetary compensation) (An-Na'im 1996, 105); and *ta'zir* (crimes whose punishment is at the discretion of the ruler or judge) (Rudolph 2005, 7). Of these categories, the penalty for *hudud* offences is the strictest, with set punishments that are mandatory upon conviction (An-Na'im 1996, 107).

There are six *hudud* offences: *sariq* (theft), *haraba* (rebellion or highway robbery), *zina* (fornication or adultery), *qadhf* (unproven accusation of fornication), *sukr* (intoxication), and *riddah* (apostasy from Islam) (An-Na'im 1996, 108).[1] Of these offences, rebellion or highway robbery, adultery, and apostasy are capital crimes. While all of these capital offences are controversial, the apostasy doctrine is particularly challenging because it criminalises the fundamental basis upon which the modern human rights project was built, that is, an 'appreciation of the inherent dignity of each individual' (Klug 2000, 12), which in turn rests on the intrinsic value of human agency (i.e., the right to choose).[2] More specifically, to punish apostasy from Islam is a non-derogable duty upon the Muslim polity. When implemented, this amounts to an absolute derogation of an absolutely non-derogable right of the *forum internum* (the right to hold and change religious belief) of article 18 of both the Universal Declaration of Human Rights 1948 and the subsequent International Covenant on Civil and Political Rights 1966 (M. Evans 1997, 295; Ghanea-Hercock et al. 2007, 46).

The legal grounds for criminalising apostasy in Islam, which can be committed in word or act,[3] is the *ijma* (juristic consensus) of the *madhhab* (school of law) founding premodern jurists, who in turn based their *ijma*, ostensibly, on a small number of *hadiths* (i.e., sayings attributed to the Prophet

---

[1] There is some debate among the jurists as to whether apostasy is a *hudud* or *tazir* offence (Saeed and Saeed 2004, 56).

[2] The Universal Declaration of Human Rights includes six references to the 'inherent dignity' of humans (1948).

[3] For a discussion of what amounts to apostasy in word and deed, see Friedman 2003, 121; Saeed and Saeed 2004, 44–48.

Muhammad), such as '[w]hoever changes his religion, kill him' (Saeed and Saeed 2004, 51). It is important to point out that the Qur'an does not stipulate any temporal punishment for apostasy. To the contrary, the Qur'an includes verses such as '[t]here is no compulsion in religion: true guidance has become distinct from error' (2: 256) and '[n]ow the truth has come from your Lord: let those who wish to believe in it do so, and let those who wish to reject it do so' (18: 29). As will be discussed further below, the words attributed to the Prophet, on the other hand, are contested on the grounds that there are other versions of the same *hadith*, which support a different interpretation of what the Prophet was actually counselling than the one provided (Kurucan 2007, 145–46). Nonetheless, this is the basis upon which the premodern juristic consensus was achieved.

This consensus was reached when the newly founded Muslim religion and polity was under constant threat, from both within and without. Accordingly, the early jurists divided the world into the mutually exclusive binary of *dar al harb* ('abode of war') and *dar al Islam* ('abode of Islam')—terms they introduced to Islam, which is illustrative of the prevailing concerns during this formative period (Afsaruddin 2007, 118–19; Kuru 2019, 27). In this war-based bordering context, a deserter of one group often became a combatant for the other. Thus, '[t]he traditional position is that an apostate is automatically considered to be a dangerous enemy of the Islamic state' (Peters and De Vries 1976, 17). Consequently, renouncing Islam was equated with high treason. This historic milieu suggests that the early jurists were motivated by what Ramadan refers to as a 'protectionist mindset' (Ramadan 2009, 41–43, 85–86), rather than merely being concerned with renunciation of faith per se (Saeed and Saeed 2004, 86).[4]

What the premodern jurists do not agree upon is whether the apostate's opportunity to repent is mandatory or recommended and whether the capital offence also applies to female apostates. Gülen and an overwhelming majority of Turkish Muslims follow the Hanafi *madhhab*. On the question of punishing male apostates, 'the Hanafis are near the farther end of the severity scale' (Friedman 2003, 158). For example, according to the Hanafi *madhhab*, the opportunity to repent is not mandatory but only recommended. As for female apostates, the founding jurist of the Hanafi *madhhab*, Abu Hanifa, takes a different view. He says that female apostates should not be killed because they cannot take arms against Muslims once they apostatise,

---

[4] For an elaboration of this point, see Friedman 2003, 121–27.

which underscores the political motivation of this doctrine as noted above (Kurucan 2006a, 126). While the early jurists shared this motivation, most of them argued that there should be no 'penal discrimination' between male and female apostates and that they should both be put to death (Friedman 2003, 158).

Contemporary scholars have adopted two broad approaches to the apostasy doctrine. The first approach is to endorse the premodern position by defending the doctrine either outright (Peters and De Vries 1976, 16) or subject to certain limitations (Saeed and Saeed 2004, 90). The second approach, on the other hand, calls for a reinterpretation (*ijtihad*) of the doctrine on the grounds that Islam extols human agency and dignity, that the Qur'an recognises the diversity of religion and faith, and that it explicitly prohibits forced conversion (Saeed and Saeed 2004, 69–87). The conciliatorists discussed in Chapter 1 fall into the 'far end' of the second approach. According to Sachedina, 'the majority of the jurists in the Muslim world continue to affirm the traditional rulings in this matter and, at least theoretically, maintain the validity of the classical formulations regarding apostasy' (2009, 188).[5] Thus, those who support the reinterpretation of this doctrine are 'white crows amongst the "ulama"' (Peters and De Vries 1976, 22).

Apostasy is criminalised explicitly in eight countries and implicitly in thirteen worldwide, all of which are Muslim majority states.[6] Apostasy is also being punished under blasphemy laws—that is, the alleged act of insulting a religion (Global Legal Research Centre 2014, 1). According to the U.S. Commission on International Religious Freedom, thirty-two of the seventy-one countries that outlaw blasphemy are Muslim majority states (2018, 1). While the enforcement of the death penalty varies, twenty-five men were charged with apostasy in Sudan in 2015 (Salih 2015) and 1,500 Pakistanis have been charged with blasphemy by Pakistani authorities since 1986, of which seventy have been killed by mob attacks (Kermani 2018). Furthermore, according to a 2013 Pew Survey, 75 percent of those surveyed across the Middle East and North Africa, sub-Saharan Africa, South Asia, and Southeast Asia supported making Islamic law the law of the land (2003, 16). Among those who supported the making of Islamic law the law of the land, support for the implementation of the death penalty for apostasy was

---

[5] See also, Peters and De Vries 1976, 16, 25; Saeed and Saeed 2004, 88.

[6] I arrived at this figure by triangulating the findings of two reports: *Laws Criminalizing Apostasy in Selected Jurisdictions 2014* (Global Legal Research Centre, 1–2) and *The Freedom of Thought Report 2017* (International Humanist and Ethical Union, 18).

76 percent in South Asia, 56 percent in the Middle East and North Africa, and 27 percent in Southeast Asia (2003, 23).

In addition to state law, ex-Muslims also face the risk of mob attack, social stigma, and ostracisation from family and the wider community (Anthony 2015). The first major sociological study of its kind on apostasy from Islam examines the social and familial pressures experienced by young ex-Muslims in Britain and Canada, which demonstrates the deep-rooted significance of this particular doctrine for Muslim communities, including the Muslim diaspora in the West (Cottee 2015).

Thus, the Islamic doctrine on apostasy is strict and robust inasmuch as it is classified as a *hudud* offence by the *ijma* of the premodern classical jurists. Furthermore, '[f]or many Muslims a close relationship exists between colonialism, Christian missionary activities among Muslims, conversion and apostasy' (Saeed and Saeed 2004, 116). Therefore, colonialism, as a form of reality, memory, and historical narrative provided, and continues to provide, the apostasy doctrine with a newfound relevance in the modern age. Moreover, this doctrine serves another function; it allows the religious and political establishment to perpetuate their authority by threatening to excommunicate political critics and opponents as apostates (Saeed and Saeed 2004, 102–7). Consequently, the doctrine has religious, historic, social, and political roots and utility, which suggests that its revision is a significant undertaking, especially for those attempting to work from within an Islamic framework while doing so.

Overview: Timeline and Intervening Process

As discussed in Chapter 1, practice can be conceptualised as a set of doings and sayings (i.e., a bodily action that says something) (Schatzki 2001b, 56–58). According to this conceptualisation, Hizmet's practices comprise Hizmet's doings and sayings that relate to the issues under consideration. At times, I use the terms 'doings' and 'practices' interchangeably but always in accordance with the definitional discussion of practice presented in Chapter 1. As for Hizmet's sayings; while they include that which is said during the performance of the practice in question (e.g., running a dialogue event), by definition those sayings must also include those sayings that were/are said as part of the performance of a broader/priori practice (e.g., preaching, sermonising, leading) that helped to give birth to and to sustain the practice in question as well. My reference to Hizmet's sayings relates primarily to the latter. Hizmet's sayings that are uttered in the practice of communicating to, and/or on behalf of, Hizmet is often but not exclusively performed by Gülen through his spoken (sermons, speeches, interviews, etc.) and written (articles, books, etc.) words. While these sayings are an integral part of Hizmet's doings, Hizmet's doings also shape, influence, and guide Hizmet's sayings.

Figure 3.1 provides a chronological timeline of the interplay between Hizmet's doings and Gülen's sayings over an extended period of time and terrain. A chronological view of Hizmet's practices allows me to 'mov[e] between practices' (Nicolini 2013, 229) by 'following them in space and time' (Nicolini 2013, 231). My aim here is to explore *what* happened, that is, the connections between practices and practices and their effects, the trajectory and (the emerging) points of change, and the points of fusion. That, in return, has helped me to determine the points of interest for further exploration. According to this appraisal, Hizmet's practices associated with *hicret* (pronounced *hij'ret*, literally, 'migration,' relocating from one place to another for the sake of God), education, and dialogue were particularly important in producing the observed epistemic outcome.

A closer examination of these three practices (*hicret*, education, and dialogue), situated within the wider context in which they occurred, helped me to map out the intervening process, which focuses on the causal relationship by asking how and why the said practices produced the observed epistemic outcomes under consideration. This is shown in Figure 3.2, where the aforementioned three practices, represented as empirical entities or links within the intervening process, are supported by two theoretical explanations: cognitive compromise and cognitive dissonance. The empirical entities and theoretical explanations are subdivided into two basic movements: internationalisation and externalisation. My aim here is to provide a 'minimally sufficient explanation of an outcome' (Beach and Pedersen 2019, 282), by showing how the empirical and theoretical entities of the intervening process support one another to account for the observed epistemic outcome. The straight arrow indicates how one entity leads to another. The reverse arrow suggests that there is a 'feedback loop' between the two entities, as shown in the intervening process, where (in the present case) Hizmet's dialogue reinforces Hizmet's *hicret* and education and vice versa (Beach and Pedersen 2019, 77).

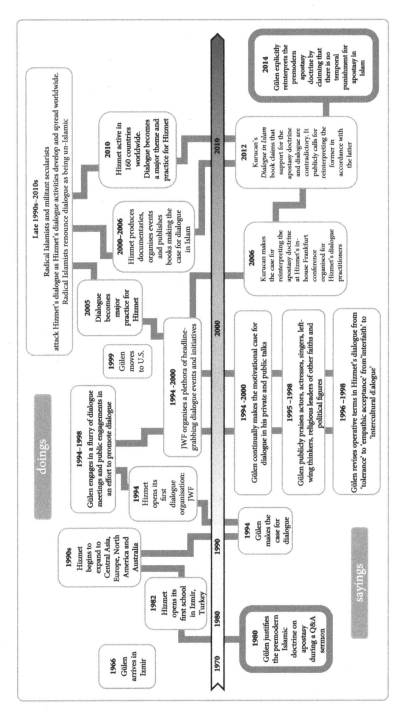

Figure 3.1 The timeline of the interplay between doings and sayings on the apostasy doctrine

X	*Hicret* and education	Dialogue	Dissonance	Consonance	Y
Practice	Hizmet's *hicret* and education practices precipitate social interaction, which humanises the other through cognitive compromise	Hizmet's dialogue reinforces this social interaction. It also causes Hizmet to internalise a dialogic habitus. Both have a humanising effect	Attack on, and Hizmet's defence of, dialogue complexifies the issue, which catalyses the awareness of the dissonance between Hizmet's dialogue practice and the apostasy doctrine	Hizmet reinterprets the apostasy doctrine in accordance with the humanising effect of its preceding practices	Knowledge production
	Internalisation		Externalisation		

Figure 3.2 The intervening process on the apostasy doctrine

I have structured this chapter according to Figure 3.2 with the appropriate socio-historic context to help situate and examine the aforementioned entities in the intervening process. I will pay particular attention to Hizmet's practices, while connecting these practices, where appropriate, with the theoretical discussions from the preceding two chapters. Before examining how and why Gülen's views changed, and the epistemic implications of doing so, we must first establish what they were, which is what I will turn to next.

Point of Departure: Gülen on Apostasy I

The first historic account of Gülen addressing the apostasy doctrine occurred during a 'question and answer' (Q&A) sermon at the Bornova central mosque (Bornova Merkez Camii) in Izmir, Turkey, in 1980. Between the late 1960s and early 1990s, Gülen delivered hundreds of sermons to tens of thousands of worshippers across and beyond Turkeys. These sermons were emotionally charged and yet thematically planned and delivered over several consecutive weeks and months (Pahl 2019, 141; Özyürek 1997). It is during this period that Gülen began delivering Q&A sermons. The format of these sermons was straightforward. Congregants would write down their questions on small pieces of paper, which would be passed to the pulpit. Gülen would read the questions out loud and then proceed to answer them. Thus, Gülen's answers were spontaneous, which is regarded as being more reflective of the speaker's mind than those questions that are pre-planned (Bennett and Checkel 2015, 33, 182–83). Gülen answered a total of 131 questions during the course of these Q&A sermons from 1976 to 1980 (Mercan 2008, 68–69). A selection of these questions and answers was published as a four-volume book in Turkish (Şahin 1985),[7] which has since been translated into several languages, including English (1993).

It is in this context that Gülen read the following question from the pulpit: 'The Qur'an says: There is no compulsion in religion (2:256); what does this mean?' (Gülen 2001). Gülen began his response by stating that '[c]ompulsion is contrary to the meaning and purpose of religion. . . . Intention and volition are necessary bases of all actions . . . , attitudes, and thoughts for which the individual is religiously accountable. Without that basis, accountability has no meaning' (Gülen 2001), and Gülen continued to stress the importance of freedom from compulsion for most of his talk. In the final few minutes (i.e., the last three paragraphs of his transcribed talk), he discussed the apostasy doctrine:[8]

> For example, a person who leaves Islam becomes an apostate. If that person does not repent within the time frame given to them then they are killed. *This is the punishment for breaching a contract. And it is all about protecting a system.* The state functions on the basis of a set system. *It is not possible to run such a system on the basis of the changing whims and desires of all people.* Therefore, to protect all the rights of Muslims, Islam does not allow the right of life for apostates.
>
> Those who enter Islam are required to do and not do certain things. *This has nothing to do with coercion.* For example, an adult who laughs while performing his prescribed prayer is met with the punishment of the

---

[7] Gülen's first books were published under his pen-name, M. Abdulfettah Şahin. Gülen's official website includes these questions and answers in various languages.

[8] There are three sources for this response. First, there is a partial video, which appears to be a recording of Gülen's 1980 response. This video, which has been uploaded to YouTube, ends before showing Gülen's comments on the apostasy doctrine (Gülen 2007). Second, there is an edited Turkish transcript of Gülen's response, which was published as a book chapter in a book by Gülen (2006a). Finally, there is an English translation of this Turkish transcript, which Gülen also published in book form. The English translation, however, is not in keeping with the Turkish transcript. This problem is most obvious in that part of the text that deals with the apostasy doctrine. Here, the English translation provides us with a 'sanitised' and 'moderated' response, and the tense has been changed from present continuous to past tense, giving the impression that Gülen was speaking about how the doctrine was originally construed, as opposed to how it ought to have been construed at the time of his response (Gülen 2001). Thus, I have relied on Gülen's (edited/published) Turkish transcript (2006a) in the absence of the actual recording (or the unedited transcript) of his original response. For the sake of accuracy, I have translated this Turkish response (2006a) into English myself.

annulment of both his prayer and his ablution, which requires him to repeat both.... Similarly, while Islam does not force anyone to enter its fold, it does not leave those who enter it freely to do as they please thereafter. *It is normal for Islam to have its own set of rules that oblige and forbid certain actions and for it to ask that Muslims follow these.* In this vein, it will require Muslims to pray, fast, give alms and undertake pilgrimage and will forbid alcohol, gambling, adultery and theft. It will prescribe penalties for those who contravene that which it has forbidden and *this has nothing to do with religious compulsion.*

In fact, when we take a moment to consider these, we will realize that such rules deter people from harmful acts, which is for their benefit. Such penalties protect people and society in this world and the afterlife. *In this sense, there is compulsion in religion and this is tantamount to forcing people into heaven* (my translation, my emphasis) (Gülen 2006a).[9]

Thus, with the above response, Gülen clearly endorses, justifies, and normalises the apostasy doctrine. In doing so, he belittles the converting out of (but presumably not the converting to) Islam as the 'changing whims and desires' of people. Furthermore, he adds that 'forcing people into heaven' was justifiable, given the outcome (i.e., heaven), while also claiming that the criminalisation of apostasy as a capital offence 'has nothing to do with coercion.' This allows Gülen to simultaneously uphold freedom of thought and defend the apostasy doctrine in the same breadth.

---

[9] With the exception of his 2014 interview, Gülen has commented on this issue from time to time in an ad hoc passing manner, while often discussing another issue. Most of these comments (a sentence or paragraph), originally stated during a sermon or talk, have found their way into books published in Gülen's name (the one exception being Gülen's interview with the Netherlands-based TV station, NMO, in 1995). Thankfully, Kurucan has collated these additional snippets and excerpts into one place (2021, 183–89). In essence, in all of these comments, Gülen is reinforcing his 1980 response. For example, in one comment, he simply says, 'an apostate has no right of inheritance just as s/he has no right of life' (my translation) (1996, 172). In another, an interview with a Netherlands-based TV station (NMO), Gülen begins by appearing to give a more nuanced response as he distinguishes between those who wage war on Muslims upon apostatising and those who merely renounce their Islamic faith. However, he soon conflates both categories into one as he treats apostates as a degenerative virus, whom he says Islam likens to a 'poisonous snake.' In so doing, he normalises the imprisonment of apostates, while treating the question of apostasy as a political issue, as he did in his 1980 response. That, in return, means that he fails to renounce (to the contrary, he defends) temporal punishment for the act of apostasy (Gülen 1995d). Furthermore, unlike his 1995 NMO interview, Gülen's 1980 response is published in (Turkish) book form and was reprinted several times from the 1990s to 2010s without revision. Thus, it is fair to take Gülen's 1980 response as representative of his position on this issue in the 1980s and 1990s as this chapter has done. Kurucan arrives at the same conclusion (2021, 184, 187–89).

APOSTASY IN ISLAM   109

That said, to appreciate Gülen's response, we need to situate it within the temporospatial context of Hizmet's socio-historic development, which can be subdivided into the following periods: religious community building (1966–1982), education and media (1982–2000), interfaith and intercultural dialogue (1994–2010), transnationalisation (1990s–2010), politicisation in Turkey (2006–2016), and criminalisation and persecution (2013–ongoing).[10] These bracketed years do not tell us when one practice or development stopped and another began. After all, Hizmet's education, media, and dialogue practices continue to date, in tandem. Rather, these periods often pertain to major developmental shifts in relation to Hizmet—for example, the opening of schools in Turkey from the early 1980s onwards.

Gülen's response was clearly delivered during the formative period of Hizmet's evolution, which was marked by its focus on building a religious community through a series of practices that prioritised the raising of religious fervor, responsibility, literacy, and solidarity (H. Yavuz 2003b, 31; Sunier and Landman 2015, 84). To that end, Gülen's early practices centered around his sermons in mosques and talks in halls and coffee houses, the running of religious summer camps for students in Izmir, the founding of a religious monthly periodical (*Sizinti*, est. 1979), and the encouragement to found and run hundreds of student houses and dormitories across Turkey.[11]

Hizmet's religious practices during this period, at both the personal and social level, were deeply conservative, protectionist, formulaic, didactic, insular, and patriarchal, especially in comparison with its practices from subsequent periods of its socio-historic development. For example, and as discussed in the next chapter, it was common practice among Hizmet's female participants to wear the face veil (*niqab*) (Erken 1995, 70; Lötüs 1989) and to adhere to strict gender-based segregation in public during this period (Kömeçoğlu 2008, 71; Turam 2007, 62). Hizmet participants were discouraged from watching TV, which was strictly monitored in student houses. If they watched the news, they were encouraged to do so by placing a piece of cloth over the TV set to protect their gaze from watching a news presenter of the opposite sex. Hizmet shunned music, art, photography, drama, fiction (considering it a form of 'lie'), and the playing of pastime games, such as chess (Yakutcan and Ömür 1991). It was also obsessively sensitive about food

---

[10] Yavuz was the first to provide a sociohistorical categorisation of Hizmet's development (2003b, 30–43).

[11] Hizmet's first dormitory was founded in Izmir in 1968 (Pahl 2019, 150).

and beverage on account of its emphasis on avoiding even a miniscule consumption of impermissible ingredients, such as traces of alcohol rumored to be found in Coca-Cola (Turam 2007, 80). Thus, there is consistency between Hizmet's deeply conservative religious practices and Gülen's justification of the premodern apostasy doctrine. That said, let us now turn to how and why Hizmet's position changed so dramatically on this issue in the manner that it did.

Internalisation: *Hicret*, Education, and Dialogue

According to the intervening process, as shown in Figure 3.2, Hizmet's practices pertaining to *hicret*, education, and dialogue caused Hizmet to engage in sustained social interaction with the other (i.e., believers of other faiths, non-believers, and non-practising Muslims), which helped Hizmet participants to relativise and moderate their views about the other through the process described as cognitive compromise in Chapter 2. Given the Islamic reticence about the other, this form of relativisation and moderation helped Hizmet participants to humanise, and thereby, to de-securitise the other. That, in return, allowed Hizmet participants to appreciate the human dignity of the other, which was previously shrouded in a 'us versus them' dichotomous worldview. Before we begin to unpack these claims, we must first address the following question: how does the humanisation and de-securitisation of the general other relate to Hizmet's position on apostasy?

In response, I would point out that the general other (i.e., the non-(practising) Muslim other) is a broad 'church,' including, for example, Christians and Jews on the one hand and ex-Muslims on the other. Here, Hizmet's humanisation of the other occurred experientially and pre-reflexively, not analytically. Thus, a pre-reflexive humanisation and de-securitisation of the *general other* could not have occurred without having implications for the humanisation and de-securitisation of the *apostate other*. Furthermore, and as noted above and further discussed later in this chapter, a humanisation of the other allowed Hizmet participants to appreciate the human dignity and agency of the other. To appreciate the agency of others in general while supporting its continued criminalisation in the case of apostates in particular is inherently problematic. The dissonance between those two positions became increasingly apparent through Hizmet's dialogue-based practices, as well as the backlash these dialogue practices produced among Turkey's Islamists. Thus, Hizmet's practices (*hicret*, education, and dialogue) and their associated effects (relativisation, moderation, humanisation, and backlash) are linked to Hizmet's knowledge production on apostasy.

I will now place these practices within their socio-historical context to explain how and why they produced the types of effects that they did and how and why these effects are linked with the subsequent developments shown in Figure 3.2 to produce the type of knowledge production as discussed in this chapter.

Hicret and Education

If Hizmet's formative period (1966–1982) was based on religious community development, Hizmet's subsequent period was focused on diversification into education (1982–2000). From the late 1970s to early 1980s, Gülen began encouraging participants of the religious community that had formed around his ideas to open student houses (*isik evleri*), dorms, and eventually schools instead of mosques (Kuru 2003, 119). By 1982, Hizmet had founded its first school in Izmir, Yamanlar Koleji: a private, fee-paying, secondary school for boys that followed the national secular curriculum. Formally, these schools focused on providing excellent education (especially in the natural sciences) with a socially conservative ethos that had religious undertones at the informal level. Thus, these schools had no outward-looking Islamic feature whatsoever; Islam was not taught during school hours. However, the religious lifestyle, morality, and (at times) informal counsel of the pious *belletmens* (dorm masters employed by the school) did bleed through after school hours (Tittensor 2014, 109–25). The combination of excellent education in a 'safe' and socially conservative learning environment proved to be immensely popular in Turkey. Thus, Hizmet swiftly moved to open more schools (including primary schools), *dershanes* (tuition centers that prepared students for the all-important university entrance exam), and eventually universities, up and down the country.

By 1999, Hizmet had founded 150 schools and 150 *dershanes* across Turkey (Agai 2002, 27). From the mid-1990s onwards, Hizmet began expanding this educational model overseas by opening schools in the newly independent Central Asian Turkic republics (Balcı 2003). By 1997, Hizmet had founded between 250 and 300 schools abroad (Agai 2002, 27). This development was followed by the opening of schools in the Balkans, Europe, North America, Australia, Africa, the Indian Peninsula, and eventually the Muslim world, including the Middle East, following the national curriculum in each country. Hizmet founds fee-paying schools where the state in question does not subsidise the running costs of private schools (as in Turkey and the Central Asian states). Where it does, Hizmet opts for founding non-fee-paying private schools (as in charter schools in the United States and similarly styled schools in some European states). By 2016, Hizmet was running approximately 2,000 schools (as well as dialogue organisations, community centers, relief organisations, media outlets, business networks, and religious activities) in 160 countries worldwide.[12] What is unique about these schools is not so much what they are doing but the fact that they are being funded, founded, and run by an Islamic movement and its pious Muslim donors and teachers across the world, a point to which I will return in Chapter 4.

To found schools across and beyond Turkey, Gülen operationalised the Prophetic example of *hicret*, that is, the Prophet Muhammad's relocation from Makkah (his place of birth) to Medina (his place of relocation in order to continue his Prophetic mission). In the case of Hizmet, *hicret* translated into migration for the sake of serving as teachers and mentors in Hizmet schools overseas. Hizmet participants successfully negotiate this practice in all parts of the word, spanning across democratic to autocratic, liberal to conservative, religious to secular, and rich to poor countries worldwide (Ebaugh 2010, 44–45; Pandya 2009; G. Çelik, Leman, and Steenbrink 2015; Sykiainen et al. 2013).

Thus, Hizmet's *hicret* and educational practices of opening and running schools, brought Hizmet participants into sustained social, cultural, intellectual, and economic interaction with different people, communities, cultures, customs, local laws, and political structures, over an extended period of time and terrain, especially in the developed world where these schools were founded and sustained through support from the local (Turkish) community and cooperation with the local education authorities (Hällzon 2008, 303–4; Grinell 2015, 23; Conway 2014; H. Yavuz 2013, 20, 247). As Maria F. Curtis notes, '[w]hile Turkish women spend a great deal of time missing their homes' some say 'that when they go home, they become "bored," that their former lifestyles in Turkey no longer satisfy them. Their constant interaction

---

[12] There is no single database for Hizmet schools. Information has to be gathered piecemeal, anecdotally, or derived from proxy measures, such as the list of 934 schools taken over by the Turkish government on the pretext of being affiliated with Hizmet (*Resmi Gazete* 2016; Keles 2013, 205).

with Americans and discovering ways to interact with people from different backgrounds replaces the lifestyles they once had' (Curtis 2005). While this outcome ensued naturally, as a result of Hizmet's practice, it was also, at times, an explicitly sought-after goal of Hizmet's organisations abroad. For example, Hizmet's female participants ran an organisation called Golden Rose in Belgium that explicitly aimed to promote the social integration and socialisation of 'immigrant women' in Belgium (Kılıç 2012, 51–52).

The continuous mixing together complexified Hizmet's identity (Hällzon 2008, 309; Pandya 2009, 133, 143; Kılıç 2014). A number of researchers have referred to this process and its outcome as Hizmet's 'unique cosmopolitan sense of Islamic identity', 'travelling Islam,' (Curtis 2012, 129), or 'Gülen's stateless cosmopolitan Islam' (Yilmaz 2008).[13] This social interaction was reinforced and given new meaning and purpose with Hizmet's dialogue practices.

Dialogue

Gülen launched Hizmet's dialogue efforts in 1994 with the founding of its first dialogue organisation, the Journalists and Writers Foundation (the Foundation), of which Gülen is the honorary chairperson.[14] This development represented a type of 'coming out' for Gülen, who until then had not formally acknowledged his link to Hizmet, and vice versa. According to İştar B. Gözaydın, 'Gülen was the first spiritual leader in Turkey to express his views on the necessity of interfaith dialogues' (2009, 1223). Gülen's justification for dialogue during this period was based on human dignity (the quintessential quality of which is human agency), the idea that diversity of race and belief is God intended, the Qur'anic call for knowing one another, and the Sufistic notions of love, compassion, empathetic acceptance, and humility (Gülen 1993a, 2000a, 193–207, 2000b; Sleap and Sener 2013, 85–92). According to Gülen, dialogue should focus on that which unites rather than that which divides us, which instinctively nudges the dialogue away from an in-depth intellectual discussion on scripture, theology, and historic grievances towards the practice of social engagement that brings people

---

[13] There is literature on how this complexification has relativised Hizmet's position and practice on gender related issues, which I will discuss in Chapter 4.
[14] http://jwf.org/

together (H. Yavuz 2013, 183). Furthermore, Gülen did not grapple with the theological implications of promoting dialogue from an Islamic point of view vis-à-vis the scripturally rooted suspicion and derision of the other in Islam, nor was he clear about where he thought dialogue should lead (Sleap and Sener 2013, footnote 5, 85). Instead, he emphasised social engagement as both the means and the end, which will be picked up further below.

Between 1994 and 1998, Gülen personally led Hizmet's dialogue efforts in Turkey by meeting with Turkey's leading figures from the religious, political, media, economic, and arts world (Mercan 2008, 157). During this period, Gülen met with many religious leaders, within and outside of Turkey, including Pope John Paul II (1998), Greek Ecumenical Patriarch Bartholomeos (1996), Sepharadic Chief Rabbi of Israel Eliyahu Bakshi Doron (1999), as well as other religious community leaders in Turkey (Gülen 2006c, 140–46).

Gülen did not just meet these religious leaders but he promoted them by publicly bringing them together with Turkey's politicians and intelligentsia. Many of these individuals spoke at Hizmet's dialogue events and received positive coverage in Hizmet's print and broadcast media (Aksiyon 2001; İ. Yavuz 2009). By 1995, Gülen had met all of the political party leaders, including the then-prime minister, Tansu Çiller (Mercan 2008, 154). In the same period, Gülen had visited the headquarters of Turkey's leading national secularist newspapers, including *Hurriyet, Milliyet,* and *Cumhuriyet,* and had given a series of interviews to Turkey's broadsheets and TV stations. In 1995 alone, Gülen is recorded to have met ninety journalists and writers at his residence in Istanbul (Mercan 2017, 135). In addition, Gülen was particularly keen to meet people from the arts world, including actors, musicians, performers, painters, and comedians (Mercan 2008, 172, 174).

Through these meetings (and his public statements), Gülen displayed public affection for the likes of the left-wing politician, Bülent Ecevit (d. 2006); left-wing academic and writer, Toktamış Ateş (d. 2013); the Turkey-based spiritual leader of 300 million Orthodox Christians worldwide (CDE News 2020); Greek Ecumenical Patriarch Bartholomeos; Turkey's foremost ex-Muslim thinker and writer, Aziz Nesin (d. 1995); Turkey's foremost (cross-dressing) Turkish classical music singer, Zeki Müren (d. 1996); and prominent Turkish rock star, Cem Karaca (d. 2004) (Mercan 2008, 189; Pamir 2008; Gülen 2006c, 146).[15] Put differently, Gülen displayed public affection

---

[15] See also Mercan 2008, 172–74.

for personalities for whom Turkey's conservative religious circles were not known to harbor warm feelings. In that respect, Gülen can be described as a 'border-transgressor,' that is, someone who reaches beyond ideology- and identity-based borders (Grinell 2007, 205).

By meeting and promoting the non-Muslim other, Gülen helped to 'validate, accommodate, and humanize the "other" in order to open up religious space for interfaith activities' (Kayaoglu 2010, 166). To appreciate this outcome, we need to bear in mind that Turkish Islamic orthopraxy is predicated on the notion of deep suspicion and scorn of the non-Muslim other (disparagingly referred to as *gavur* in Turkish, i.e., infidel). Furthermore, since the founding of the Turkish republic, all minority issues in Turkey have been hyper-securitised and have been seen as an existential threat to the unitary nature of the Turkish secular state (Cagaptay 2006; Yilmaz 2013). Moreover, as an Islamic scholar and public figure, Gülen himself was considered a security threat by Turkey's secularist (military) establishment. Thus, Gülen's practice of legitimising and humanising minority religious leaders in Turkey was ground-breaking for the 1990s Turkish political landscape, which is evidenced by the political commentary and reaction it generated at the time.

For example, according to Niyazi Öktem, a scholar and commentator, '[u]ntil Gülen started meeting with those [ethnic and religious] representatives, it was unusual for a Muslim to engage in dialogue with a Christian or a Jew' (1998) (Gülen 2000a, 282).[16] Hadi Uluengin, a veteran columnist, characterised Gülen's meeting with Patriarch Bartholomeus as 'carrying historic significance' noting that it represented a 'first' since the founding of the modern Turkish Republic (1996) (Gülen 2000a, 262). Fehmi Koru, another veteran political commentator, described the same meeting as 'a first step toward the dispersal of centuries-old suspicions regarding the Patriarchate' and noted how the Turkish newspapers and TV stations had covered the 'meeting's symbolic value' for three days (1996) (Gülen 2000a, 264–65). With regard to Gülen's meeting with the Pope, Öktem claimed that it was 'one of the most important events of the twentieth century [and that] . . . it will have far-reaching consequences' (1998) (Gülen 2000a, 283). For Cengiz Çandar, the international relations commentator and columnist, Gülen's meeting with the Pope represented a 'security measure for Turkey's democratization' and indirectly contributed toward Turkey's stability (1998) (Gülen 2000a, 292).

---

[16] For the sake of accuracy, I will state the year the quote was made in brackets, immediately after the quote.

As for Hizmet's broader dialogue practices; these began under the auspices of the Journalists and Writers Foundation in Turkey. Between 1994 and 1999, the Foundation organised headline-grabbing, goodwill-promoting, large-scale dialogue events that platformed Turkey's cultural, ethnic, religious, and political diversity at award ceremonies, fast-breaking dinners, friendship dinners, and overseas trips. Since expunged, these events were extensively covered in Turkey's print and broadcast media at the time. They were significant because of the diversity of people they brought together, including those who considered themselves to be on the opposing end of the socio-politico-cultural divide, such as left/right, secular/religious, Sunni/Alawi, and Muslim/non-Muslim. Furthermore, these meetings were being facilitated by a Sunni Islamic group, whose theological genealogy was credited with perpetuating, not mediating, these bordering divides.

Fehmi Koru notes that the guests were surprised at each other's attendance at a Foundation event. He says, '[o]ne was surprised by the presence of Banu Alkan, the "local Aphrodite,". . . . Another mentioned Emel Sayın [a singer] . . . Perihan Savaş [an actress] also came. . . . For some, the most interesting guest was Phanariot Greek Patriarch Bartholomeos I. Others noticed members of the Jewish community . . . Üzeyir Garih, and Alber Bilen' (1996) (Gülen 2000a, 219–20). According to Ayşe Önal of the *Akşam* newspaper, 'it was clear that, in regard to those attending and the arrangements, this type of dinner had not been seen before in Turkey' (1995) (Gülen 2000a, 211). Mehmet Aydın, a prominent theology professor, on the other hand, opined on Hizmet's practice in relation to change in the context of Islamic orthopraxy, when he said, 'I come from a culture that debates the religious permissibility of watching movies yet here I am [at this Hizmet event] working together with my friend and actor [Bulut Aras]. If this is not change and development, I don't know what is' (my translation) (Mercan 2008, 178).

The Foundation's Abant Platform on the other hand functioned as a think tank organising an annual workshop that brought together Turkey's diverse intelligentsia to discuss Turkey's most divisive issues from 1998 onwards (Saritoprak 2005). The participants of these workshops were hosted at a remote resort in Abant (hence the name) where they were tasked with issuing a joint declaration on the issue at hand (e.g., Islam and secularism and Islam and democracy and human rights) following several days of intense discussion behind closed doors. Thus, according to Gözaydın, '[t]his platform is the first of its kind in Turkey, an environment where intellectuals could agree to disagree on sensitive issues such as laicism, secularism, peaceful co-existence, "faith and reason" relations, and the status of one of Turkey's minority religious groups, the Alevis' (2009, 1224). According to Nilüfer Göle, a sociologist and participant of these workshops, 'the Abant meetings have institutionalized our togetherness with one another which was denied and rejected through the post-modern 28 Feb 1997 coup' (Mercan 2008, 180).[17]

From 1998 onwards, Hizmet participants overseas began setting up their own dialogue organisations, such as the Washington, D.C.-based Rumi Forum in 1998,[18] the Rotterdam-based Islam and Dialogue Foundation in 1998,[19] and the London-based Dialogue Society in 1999.[20] It was relatively easy for the movement to set up these dialogue organisations and initiatives across the world where the movement was already well established. Thus, '[i]t is reasonable to suggest that in every country in which the movement is active today, there are some form of local, grass-roots, dialogue-focused activities taking place' (Tee 2016, 123). In fact, more than one can be found in every country. As Yavuz notes, '[i]t runs over 50 local interfaith dialogue groups in virtually every state in America' (H. Yavuz 2013, 193). Today, like education, dialogue has become a major practice for Hizmet.

Whatever the format (e.g., conference, roundtable, cooking class, book club, interfaith picnic, fast-breaking corporate/home dinner, overseas excursion etc.), Hizmet's dialogue events brought people together to 'cultivate interpersonal encounters at a local level' (Tee 2016, 130). As a form of practice, that involved meeting people to talk, listen, ask questions, respond, and partake in mundane activities such as travelling and eating together. This happens to be consistent with Gülen's conceptualisation of dialogue, as noted during one of his private talks on dialogue, where he says, '[w]hat is important in dialogue is for ordinary people ["halk"] to meet one another. Long-lasting and successful dialogue can only be achieved in this manner' (Gülen 2009a). As Frances Sleap and Omer Sener note, '[f]or Gülen, dialogue itself consists not of dialogue events but of the interactions that occur as a result of such occasions . . . moving beyond mere words . . . to undertakings that bring about real, substantial, meaningful encounters' (Sleap and Sener 2013, 85–86).

---

[17] For a comprehensive appraisal of the Foundation's Abant meetings, see Uğur 2013.
[18] http://rumiforum.org/
[19] This name has since been changed (Yukleyen 2009).
[20] http://www.dialoguesociety.org

Thus, Hizmet's dialogue precipitated social interaction with the other, which reinforced the social interaction to flow from Hizmet's practices associated with *hicret* and education. That in return triggered the outcomes associated with cognitive compromise as discussed at some length in Chapter 2, that is, a relativisation and moderation of one's views about the other, which I have described as the humanisation of the other.

According to Yavuz, this form of 'cross-fertilization of ideas' (2013, 189) and the humanisation of the other as a result of Hizmet's dialogue efforts was to be expected; after all, 'dialogue aims to transform the conflict and encourage participants to humanize the other. Ultimately, this, is the essence of establishing relationships: humanising the other' (2013, 179). The connection between dialogue and the humanisation of the other is made by numerous dialogue theorists, including Martin Buber and Daniel Yankelovich (Sleap and Sener 2013, 60, 179). Moreover, and as discussed in Chapter 1, Hizmet's participation in the (Bourdieun) 'field' of dialogue caused it to internalise a 'dialogue habitus,' which on the one hand pre-dates Hizmet's dialogue (as the dialogue field pre-dates Hizmet) and on the other hand, is a field and habitus, which Hizmet has helped to reproduce by contributing towards it through its teachings, practice, and presence (at the very least, by injecting thousands of young Muslims into dialogue 'fields' worldwide; Park 2007, 58). While it is challenging to determine the pre-reflexive parameters of a dialogic habitus, it is safe to assume that it includes a proclivity for connectivity, empathy, and mutual understanding, which when internalised would support the type of humanisation process described above.

Furthermore, Gülen appears to welcome this form of cross-cultural relativisation (i.e., cognitive compromise) when he says, '[y]es, this is a give and take. We will take those values from other people, groups, cultures and civilisations that we can benefit from. Similarly, we will share with others our values if we have any values worth sharing' (Gülen 2009b). More importantly, Gülen concedes the humanisation process of dialogue when he personally attests to how it influenced his interpretation of the Qur'an (epistemic outcome) in relation to the other. When asked during an interview for the *Atlantic* in 2013, '[s]ome statements concerning Jews or Israel in your early sermons [those delivered in the 1980s] have been perceived as anti-Semitic. How do you respond to this?' This was Gülen's response:

> The actions and attitudes of your interlocutors affect your views and expressions. During the interfaith dialogue process of the 1990s, I had a

chance to get to know practitioners of non-Muslim faiths better, and I felt a need to revise my expressions from earlier periods. I sincerely admit that I might have misunderstood some verses and prophetic sayings. I realized and then stated that the critiques and condemnations that are found in the Koran or prophetic tradition are not targeted against people who belong to a religious group, but at characteristics that can be found in any person. (Tarabay 2013, 6–7)

Gülen encouraged dialogue in 1994 with Christians and Jews while holding onto the traditional and disparaging interpretation of the relevant Qur'anic verses concerning them. According to his own account, he only began to question and then revise his original interpretation after he personally engaged in dialogue with Christians and Jews. Based on this account, it was not Gülen's discourse *on*, but his practice *of*, dialogue that caused him to revise his original interpretation. The order by which this change came about is important because it demonstrates the difference between (abstract) knowledge and knowing (in doing) and how the latter can change the former. It also demonstrates the role of practice and social interaction in the context of Islamic knowledge production. In this context, Hizmet's dialogue practice provided the alternative settings and experience that stimulated relativisation, moderation, and humanisation, which produced the type of epistemic outcome described above. Other examples that demonstrate the causal link between Hizmet's social interaction and the relativisation of its views (e.g., on gender-based segregation) will be discussed in the next chapter.

Two Challenges: Sequencing and Motive

The above notwithstanding, it is also important to point out that Hizmet's dialogue and humanisation process is not without its limits (H. Yavuz 2013, 194–96). For example, Gülen has always maintained a certain apathy for Turkey's Islamist Welfare (Refah) party and the Islamic Republic of Iran and Shia Islam (H. Yavuz 2013, 194). Moreover, Hizmet's efforts to promote interfaith dialogue did not (and are yet to) extend to intra-faith dialogue. These examples raise questions about the parameters of Gülen's dialogue, which in turn raise at least two challenges in the context of the foregoing discussion. First, if Gülen's teachings triggered Hizmet's dialogue practice, can we still claim that *practice* produced the observed epistemic outcome? After all, in this sequential narrative, Gülen's teachings precedes Hizmet's practice. Second, what if Gülen was disingenuous when he encouraged dialogue; would that not undermine the relativisation/humanisation process discussed above? I will now address these two challenges in turn.

The first challenge assumes that Gülen's teaching is somehow distinct from Hizmet's (collective) practice, but it is not. The act of guiding through sermons, talks, and writings is a form of practice in itself, which Gülen performed first as a state-license preacher and then as the spiritual leader of an Islamic movement, which played an integral role within Hizmet's collective practice. Thus, Gülen is not pontificating as an Islamic scholar in abstract; he is performing one form of practice (preaching) to encourage another (dialogue). Furthermore, as Gülen's response during the *Atlantic* interview demonstrates, calling for dialogue and partaking in dialogue are two different things. Gülen encouraged dialogue in 1994, but what caused him to revise his views about the Qur'anic verses vis-à-vis Christians and Jews (i.e., the epistemic outcome) was his sustained interaction with them in the context of a practice. This is why we should credit *practice* as opposed to the (practice of) *encouragement of practice* with the emergent reinterpretation on apostasy. As an extension of this point, while Gülen may have anticipated the relativisation/humanisation effect of dialogue, there is no reason to expect that he intended Hizmet's dialogue to produce the type of backlash that it did, which (as will be shown in the next section) was integral to the externalisation of the emergent reinterpretation on apostasy, nor was there reason to think that he expected that process to result in the emergent reinterpretation of the apostasy doctrine, as it did. Thus, the observed outcome ensued as a result of practice, not the teaching or intent of Gülen that preceded it.

As for the second challenge, this calls into question Gülen's motive for encouraging dialogue. Let us imagine that Gülen was disingenuous when calling for dialogue and that he had an ulterior motive, which was to appease Turkey's secularist establishment. Let's imagine that Hizmet's senior leadership shared this ulterior motive. The question is, would such an ulterior motive undermine the relativisation/humanisation process discussed above?

This challenge would be more plausible if Hizmet's dialogue was short lived and centered primarily around the activities of Gülen and his close group of companions, but it was not. Hizmet's dialogue-based activities have been ongoing since 1994 and are sustained through the effort of thousands of Hizmet participants in approximately 160 countries worldwide. The significance of Gülen's alleged motive in 1994 pales in comparison to the size, scale, duration, and participation of this practice. If anything, the temporospatial axis of this practice suggests that the original motive and intent have developed and matured, and have not remained static. This reinforces the view that practice-based knowledge production does not depend on (the supposed) intent of the practitioner and that it can ensue regardless of it (as in the case of apostasy) and despite it (as in the case of women's rights and freedoms, as will be discussed in the next chapter). Altogether, this undermines the attempt to attribute too much significance to Gülen's supposed motive at the time or thereafter.

In addition, there is some literature that conflates Hizmet's dialogue with public relations (Hendrick 2013, 208–17; Lacey 2014; Tee 2016, 130–33, 2018). The challenge associated with this literature is that it focuses on intended-external outcomes. My main focus on the other hand is on the unintended-internal outcomes of Hizmet's practice in relation to knowledge production, which causes me to look elsewhere. Furthermore, I have a methodological point of divergence with this literature as well. As discussed in Chapter 1, a practice-based approach eschews the conflation of practice and practitioner and the intent or logic attributed to one on account of the other. Moreover, an emphasis on what Gülen/Hizmet intended and the insistence on drawing a straight line between the practitioner's supposed intent and the practice's observed outcome causes us, at the very least, to overlook unintended (internal/external) outcomes.

For example, Hendrick argues that the intent behind Hizmet's dialogue is public relations on behalf of the movement and 'mere influence peddling' (2013, 208). Let us imagine for a moment that Hendrick's characterisation of Hizmet's intent is correct. That does not mean that the intended outcome ensued, nor does it preclude other (internal/external) outcomes from also ensuing. Aside from the challenge of determining the practitioner's intent, a narrow focus on intended-external outcomes misses the epistemological focus of this study. As Turam puts it, albeit in a different context, 'a closer look [at Hizmet] reveals that the sharp focus on the *deliberate* project-based aspects of [its] Islamic action obscures its *unintentional and unplanned consequences*' (my emphasis) (2007, 25). A practice-based epistemology attunes us to such unintended outcomes and allows us to account for them.

In conclusion, therefore, witnessing Gülen's practice of meeting and promoting the other and engaging in practices that precipitated social interaction with the other through *hicret*, education, and dialogue produced a legitimising, relativising, moderating, and humanising process, which (as noted above and is further unpacked below) helped to pre-reflexively de-securitise the other and the underlying logic of criminalising apostasy as a capital offence. I associate these processes and outcomes with *practice-based internalisation* because they ensued in practice at the pre-reflexive level of consciousness. That said, the other consequence of Hizmet's dialogue was that it produced conflict, which was crucial to the overall process, as discussed next.

Emerging Dissonance

While Hizmet's dialogue efforts were enthusiastically received by many, 'Gülen and his associates were strongly criticised by two groups: hardline secularists and some Islamists' (Gözaydın 2009, 1224). Although these groups were diametrically opposed to each other, they found common cause in attacking Hizmet's dialogue for conflicting but equally conspiratorial reasons. These attacks began in 1994, but they continued in one form or another until the Turkish government crackdown, which overtly began in 2014.

On the one hand, Islamists, including the Haydar Baş (*Yeni Mesaj*) movement, religious leader Ahmet Mahmut Ünlü (colloquially known as Cüppeli Ahmet), and columnists such as Ahmet Akgül and Mehmet Şevket Eygi, accused Gülen of being a secret cardinal, the awaited anti-Christ, an apostate, an agent of the West, and a 'Trojan horse' appointed to popularise a 'sanitised Islam' in the Muslim world through interfaith dialogue to undermine the Islamic resolve against Western cultural imperialism (Koç 2012, 37, 43–46).[21] On the other hand, 'hardline secularists,' including the Doğu Perinçek (*Aydınlık*) group and columnists such as Hikmet Çetinkaya and Ergün Poyraz, accused Gülen of being a secret Islamist wanting to Islamize the Turkish state and society by using dialogue as a ruse to hide his true intent and purposes (Koç 2012, 40–43).

---

[21] See also Yilmaz, who summarises some of the accusations made by Mehmet Şevket Eygi, the Haydar Baş group, and the *Yeni Hayat* journal (2000, 13).

Hizmet responded by retrospectively theologising the case for dialogue in Islam. Until then, Hizmet had made the 'motivational case' for dialogue with tentative references to Qur'anic verses and Prophetic practice. Now it was having to address specific accusations and theological objections on the basis of the Qur'an, *hadiths* (Prophetic sayings), and premodern scholarly interpretations that expressed hostility towards the 'disbelieving' others. While Hizmet had not yet been accused of reinterpreting the apostasy doctrine (as the emergent reinterpretation had yet to emerge), it was being accused of diluting the Muslim resolve against the non-Muslim other. To rebuke these accusations, Hizmet produced articles, books, and TV and radio programmes, and organised a plethora of seminars and conferences.[22]

Hizmet's most effective and popular epistemic response to these challenges came in the form of a short book by Ahmed Kurucan titled *Niçin Diyalog* (literally, 'Why Dialogue') (2006).[23] At the time of publication, Kurucan was a columnist with Hizmet's *Zaman* newspaper, a leading dialogue practitioner and a personal student to Gülen of many years,[24] with specialism in *fiqh*. The book, aimed at a general readership, was organised into questions and answers about dialogue on the basis of the Qur'an, Sunna, and historic archives, such as '[w]hat is the difference between *tebligh* [proselytism] and dialogue?,' '[a]re "*jihad*" and "dialogue" not contradictory concepts?, [h]ow should we understand verses which command war against unbelievers?, [d]id Muslims ever force others to convert to Islam in the past?' (my translation) (Kurucan 2006b, 5–7). In addressing these questions, Kurucan argued that a methodological and comprehensive interpretation of Islam's primary and secondary sources necessitated support for dialogue between people of faith or none; positive social engagement and relations; acceptance that diversity of faith is God-intended; and the idea that dialogue is neither appeasement nor a guise to convert (2006b, 5–7).

Outside of Turkey, Hizmet's dialogue gave occasion for Hizmet participants to be questioned about Islam by non-Muslims. Some of the

---

[22] See the Journalists and Writers Foundation catalogue for an extensive coverage of past events (Gazeteciler ve Yazarlar Vakfı 2014). For a list of books published by the Journalists and Writers Foundation dating back to 1999, see Nadir Kitap 2020. For the four-part TV documentary in Turkish titled 'Diyaloğun Meyvesi' (literally, 'Fruits of Dialogue') broadcast on Hizmet's TV networks in 2005, see YouTube 2013. This documentary features the positive impressions of Americans who had visited Turkey as a result of Hizmet's dialogue efforts.

[23] Hizmet promoted Kurucan's book as a rebuttal to these accusations by gifting the book to *Zaman* subscribers and promoting the book via its grass roots networks.

[24] For an overview of Gülen's postgraduate seminary where he teaches theology graduates, see Atay 2007 and Capan 2011.

most repeated questions put to Hizmet in this context pertained to Islam's position on apostasy and women. In fact, in a 2014 interview, which we will discuss further below, Gülen concedes that 'this [i.e., the apostasy doctrine] is probably the most repeated question I have faced by foreign journalists' (Gülen 2014).

Thus, Hizmet's dialogue precipitated friendly and unfriendly challenges from both within and without Turkey. While these objections occurred from outside the body of Hizmet, they were nonetheless a natural and organic reaction to Hizmet's dialogue practice. After all, innovative practices often produce positive and negative reactions, which often help to shape the practice going forward. This back and forth, primarily between Hizmet and its detractors, but also between Hizmet and its sympathetic audience outside of Turkey, helped complexify the issue of dialogue in Islam and Islam's attitude towards the other for Hizmet. This in return highlighted the dissonance between an Islamic interpretation, which necessitated dialogue with the other against another which criminalised apostasy as a capital offense. Proverbially put, complexifying dialogue in Islam caused the apostasy doctrine to raise its *head above the* (reflexivity) *parapet*.

This became particularly apparent during Kurucan's presentation at a two-day inhouse dialogue conference in 2006 at *Zaman's* European headquarters in Frankfurt. The event was organised by Hizmet's Germany-based dialogue organisation to help share best practice among Hizmet's dialogue practitioners worldwide. I was among the approximately one hundred and fifty dialogue practitioners in attendance, which featured presentations by a number of speakers. Kurucan spoke on the second day of the conference about his doctoral thesis (2002–2006) (2006a). He explained that Gülen had encouraged him to study for a doctorate on freedom of thought in Islam in 2002 without asking him to examine the issue of apostasy in Islam, far less to produce/or call for the production of an *ijtihad* on the matter. Furthermore, upon completion, Kurucan said that he presented his findings to Gülen and that Gülen encouraged him to speak at the forthcoming Frankfurt conference where he was due to present his insights and thoughts on dialogue.

Kurucan went on to explain that he did in fact examine the apostasy doctrine in his thesis and that he had come to the conclusion that this doctrine, which is an *ijtihad* itself, needed to be superseded with another *ijtihad* today (2006a, 123–39). His reasoning was straightforward: we cannot justify an interpretation of Islam that simultaneously upholds the necessity of dialogue with the other and the apostasy doctrine without contradicting ourselves.

This reasoning points to the role of cognitive dissonance as the motivating force in Kurucan's attempt to overcome the said contradiction (i.e., dissonance) through a superseding *ijtihad* on the apostasy doctrine.

Kurucan further explained that the present doctrine contradicted the letter and spirit of the Qur'an as well as the body of the Prophetic tradition. He questioned the historic basis of the three Prophetic sayings that were primarily used to justify this doctrine, showing that the chain of narration was either weak or that there were different versions of each saying which suggested a different meaning to the one being offered. He claimed that neither the Qur'an (2006a, 67) nor Sunna (2006a, 69) provided any temporal punishment for the mere renunciation of faith whatsoever. Kurucan argued that what was being punished in those instances was not the renunciation of faith but the alleged murdering of innocent people in the process of doing so (Kurucan and Erol 2012, 66–69).[25] As he went on to explain:

> [w]hen we consider early Islamic history we see that individuals and groups who left the fold of Islam were not only leaving their beliefs, but, almost always, were also joining groups that were actively waging war against the Muslims. As a result, the form of *irtidad* [apostasy] which was punished in the time of the Prophet (pbuh) was one that involved high treason, not the form of *irtidad* which was a mere renunciation of faith.... During the reign of Abu Bakr, communities abandoned Islam and rose against the central government; while renouncing their faith they were also engaging in political acts of rebellion against the state. Punishments inflicted on such people at that time, and in other eras when comparable political conditions prevailed, were effectively punishments for high treason, not for the renouncement of religious beliefs.... In addition, in books on jurisprudence we find that the matter of *irtidad* and associated punishments has been considered by scholars as a political issue and classed under international relations and the measures to be taken during times of war.... Since apostasy no longer implies high treason and political rebellion as it did when the traditional *ijtihad* was formulated, and since that *ijtihad* is at odds with clear teachings from the Qur'an and the Sunnah [which provide no

---

[25] A summary of Kurucan's Frankfurt presentation was incorporated into the English translation of Kurucan's book *Niçin Diyalog* (2006): *Dialogue in Islam: Qur'an, Sunnah, History* (2012). I am relying on the sub-section of this to relay the relevant segment of Kurucan's 2006 presentation.

temporal punishment for apostasy], it can be superseded by a new *ijtihad* today. (Kurucan and Erol 2012, 68–69)[26]

Kurucan's presentation created a palpable sense of excitement among the audience, which was reflected in the comments and response during the Q&A. Most of us appeared to appreciate the inherent dissonance that he was trying to overcome by calling for a new *ijtihad* on the apostasy doctrine. This effort was significant because, so far as anyone in the audience was concerned, this was the first time that the apostasy doctrine had been explicitly challenged from within Hizmet. Furthermore, while Kurucan appeared to be calling for an *ijtihad* to supersede the original one, we recognised that the very act of doing so was in fact an *ijtihad* in and of itself.

Alternative Explanation: Practice or Practitioner

Let us pause here to consider the following objection: how is Kurucan's presentation relevant to Hizmet's practice? After all, is this not one individual expressing a personal opinion on one particular topic? This objection is based on a flawed assumption. Ultimately, *someone* has to verbalise the emergent reinterpretation. That verbalisation does not negate the practice-based antecedent processes that produced it. Moreover, Kurucan framed the 'problem' and his solution on the basis of Hizmet's *dialogue practice* and the dissonance this produced when pitted against the apostasy doctrine and its underlying logic. After all, he was presenting his findings to Hizmet's *dialogue practitioners* at an inhouse *dialogue* conference. This point is further underscored by the fact that Kurucan's *Niçin Diyalog* (2006) was translated and published in English (with a co-author) in 2012 as *Dialogue in Islam: Qur'an, Sunnah, History*, where a question (and answer) on the apostasy doctrine was added. The said question is explicitly predicated on the aforementioned cognitive dissonance, as it asks: 'In Islamic law, apostasy from Islam (*irtidad*) is punishable by death. *How can this be reconciled with freedom of religion and the spirit of dialogue?*' (my emphasis) (Kurucan and Erol 2012, 66–69). Thus, it was Hizmet's *dialogue practice* that motivated Kurucan's recognition and resolution of the dissonance problem.

---

[26] See footnote 25.

Another related objection could be mounted in the following terms: Gülen encouraged Kurucan to complete a doctoral thesis on freedom of thought; this suggests that rather than being an organic outcome of practice, Kurucan's reinterpretation was in fact an outcome of human agency. This objection presents a number of problems, but I will only address three of them for now (I will raise further points below when responding to the alternative explanation for Gülen's revisionist comments in 2014). First, we do not know that Gülen wanted Kurucan to focus on the apostasy doctrine when encouraging him to research freedom of thought in Islam; even if he did, we do not know if Gülen's views on the issue had sufficiently changed by this point in time, that is, twelve years prior to his 2014 interview in which Gülen articulated a revised position on the matter. Second, and as already noted, I am not suggesting that agency plays no part in practice-based knowledge production, especially after the issue has risen to the level of reflexive consciousness. Neither am I claiming that Gülen played no role in the externalisation of this reinterpretation; he clearly did as we will see in the next section. Rather, relying on a practice-based epistemology, I am suggesting that practice is priori in the production of knowledge in this instance and that Gülen's position and discourse evolved accordingly. Third, without practice, we fail to account for how and why this epistemic outcome ensued as it did and how and why it was internalised by Hizmet as it appears to have been (as evidenced by the fact that the movement has increasingly expanded on this issue as shown further below).

Thus, there is a causal nexus between Hizmet's dialogue practice (the reaction this caused, Hizmet's efforts to retrospectively theologise the case for dialogue in Islam and the complexification of the issue as a result), the dissonance this produced between it and the apostasy doctrine, and the effort to achieve consonance by holding onto the former (i.e., dialogue and its associated implications) and, somewhat tentatively and privately, reinterpreting the latter (i.e., the apostasy doctrine). This was a muted (i.e., the conference was not open to the public, and no record of the event was kept) externalisation of the (emergent) reinterpretation.

Externalisation of Reinterpretation: Gülen on Apostasy II

By 2014, Gülen had been in self-imposed exile for approximately fifteen years. It had been almost two years since Recep Tayyip Erdoğan, Turkey's then Prime Minister, had declared war on the movement, promising to 'annihilate this virus' (Sabah 2014) and to 'split them [Hizmet] to their molecules' (Star 2014). By early 2014, Erdoğan had described Gülen as a 'terrorist leader,' 'false prophet,' 'fake saint,' 'bogus scholar,' 'conjurer,' 'spell binder,' and 'worse than Shia' (Woolf et al. 2015, para. 188). In the Islamic lexicon, these statements amount to *takfeer*, that is, the excommunication of Gülen and Hizmet as apostates and enemies of Islam.[27] While the Turkish government and pro-government media began accusing Hizmet of working with the West to topple the state from 2013 onwards, elements of the German media also began to target Hizmet during the same period on the grounds that it was a cult and that its participants were crypto Islamists who were attempting to infiltrate German society (Popp 2012; DW 2014).

It is in this broad context that in April 2014 Gülen gave an interview to Hizmet's Berlin-based Stiftung Dialog und Bildung organisation. This organisation describes itself as a 'foundation of people active in Hizmet' which 'provides answers to questions relating to Hizmet as a point of contact for . . . [among others] the media and politics.' (Stiftung Dialog und Bildung 2020). During this interview, which appears to have been conducted in writing,[28] Gülen was asked a number of questions, including his views on apostasy, equality, ethics in the production of scientific knowledge, and political Islam.

The second question of the interview was, '[w]hat are your views of freedom of religion or belief? What should happen when a person leaves Islam of their own will? Should they be killed?' Gülen began his answer by acknowledging the source of the question: his 1980 Bornova central mosque response, which he claimed to have been misunderstood and decontextualised. He stated that this was one of the most common questions put to him by foreign journalists. He claimed that in his 1980 response he explained that the capital punishment for apostasy was a political issue; that the pre-modern jurists equated apostasy with high treason and that it was *this* that they sought to criminalise when ruling on apostasy; and that he favored religious freedom then as he did now. He provided a number of reasons for arriving at this conclusion, which are strikingly similar to those reasons provided by Kurucan, as noted

---

[27] For a theological and historic perspective with an appraisal of modern-day *takfeer* practices, see Biesterfeldt, Günther, and Kadi 2016.

[28] This is not unusual for Gülen. Since relocating to the United States, he has restricted his media appearances and interviews. Until Turkey's failed coup of 15 July 2016, Gülen's interviews were conducted mainly in written form.

above (e.g., the war-ridden context at the time, the dichotomous worldview of the premodern jurists) (Gülen 2014). Gülen continued:

> From a religious belief perspective, individuals are free to believe or disbelieve in any religion they so wish according to the Qur'an and the teachings and practices of our Prophet. They are free to join any religion, and can leave whenever they want. . . . *On its own, without the commission of any accompanying criminal act, Islam does not prescribe temporal punishment for joining or leaving a religion.* . . . We must not forget this; freedom of religion or belief is a fundamental human right. Respecting these rights means fulfilling the responsibility that flows from that respect. To accept everyone as they are according to Islam requires ensuring that everyone can enjoy their rights and freedoms as equal citizens before the law (without infringing the rights and freedoms of others); to not impose a particular belief system or way of life upon others through political power; and to not diminish or discriminate people on the basis of their ethnicity, culture, religion or background. (my translation, my emphasis) (Gülen 2014)

Despite his protestations to the contrary,[29] Gülen clearly endorsed, justified, and normalised the apostasy doctrine in his original 1980 response, as discussed at the outset of this chapter. In his 2014 interview, that is, thirty-four years later, Gülen is clearly and categorically rejecting the apostasy doctrine on the grounds noted above. Thus, there is most certainly a fundamental change of 'opinion'. This raises the following question—how does this statement and change of 'opinion' amount to knowledge production?

In Chapter 2, I explained that knowledge production within the parameters of *fiqh* equates to *ijtihad* production, which must be (i) expressed in written or spoken word, (ii) based on the primary and/or secondary sources of *fiqh*, (iii) articulated by an expert practitioner, and (iv) pertain to an issue that is open to interpretation (i.e., issues on which the Qur'an and Sunna are silent or, even where they are explicit, the change of context requires a change of

---

[29] In his 2014 response, Gülen appears to suggest that he was always opposed to the capital punishment of the apostasy doctrine by quoting an interview he gave in 1996 (he says 1997, but the first print of this interview is dated 1996), where he says, '[w]ithin a democratic framework, whosoever wants can become a Muslim, remain a Samanist; whosoever wants can choose your way, whosoever wants can choose the way of another' (Can 1996, 70). Gülen's 1996 response is carefully crafted; it refers to the right to adopt Islam or another religion, but the 'right to adopt' a religion is not the same as the 'right to change' a religion once it has been adopted, which is the issue at stake in so far as the apostasy doctrine is concerned.

interpretation) in order for the new *ijtihad* to conform with the inherited traditions of *fiqh* and its associated epistemology (*usul al-fiqh*). I also explained that an *ijtihad* does not need to be labelled as an *ijtihad*; nor does it need to be original, to qualify as one.

How does Gülen's 2014 response fare in relation to the above conditions? First, Gülen's statement, which contradicts the apostasy doctrine, is stated in written word. Second, Gülen justifies his position by reference to the Qur'an and Sunna. He quotes two Qur'anic verses (18:29 and 2:256), and he refers to the general and specific Prophetic tradition (Sunna) of not forcing others to believe during his mission. He explains the logic and reasoning of the premodern jurists and explains how the operative context that influenced their reasoning does not apply today. He references the general spirit and teachings of Islam and how punishing the renunciation of faith contradicts it. Third, according to numerous outsider appraisals, Gülen is an Islamic scholar and practitioner as discussed in the Introduction and Chapter 2. Fourth and finally, the apostasy doctrine is open to interpretation because it is itself an *ijtihad*; the Qur'an is silent on the issue; the Sunna is, at most, conflicted; and finally, the premodern context is of course changed. Thus, this would suggest that Gülen's 2014 response on this issue does qualify as an *ijtihad*.

Challenge and Alternative Explanation: Causality and Appeasement

Once again, this brings us to the question of causality—how is the *ijtihad* related to and an outcome of Hizmet's practice? We can further complexify this issue by challenging it with an alternative explanation that explains the causality not by reference to Hizmet's practice but by Gülen's supposed motivation to appease the German press. After all, Gülen gave this interview to a Germany-based Hizmet organisation when Hizmet was being targeted by the German tabloids for being crypto Islamists. Does this supposed motivation not undermine the case for practice-based knowledge production?

I have already dealt with the role of human agency vis-à-vis practice-based knowledge production above (see the section titled Alternative Explanation: Practice or Practitioner). Rather than repeat those points here, I will note some additional considerations that apply in this instance. For example, Hizmet's expansive, inclusive, and dialogic practices (through primarily dialogue, *hicret,* and education) precipitated sustained social interaction with the other, which helped to relativise, moderate, legitimise, and humanise the other. That, on its own, necessitated Gülen's 2014 revision.

Furthermore, as shown earlier, there was a fundamental dissonance between Hizmet's explicit support for dialogue and its implicit support for the apostasy doctrine. One way or another, that needed to be overcome. By making dialogue a central plank of its praxis and by increasing its dialogue efforts year on year, Hizmet had already made an inadvertent choice between the values and teachings associated with dialogue and the premodern apostasy doctrine. What remained was recognising the theological implications of doing so, which is what Gülen's 2014 interview does. In addition, Gülen's said comments mirror Kurucan's arguments, aired in 2006 and published in 2012, which framed the case for reinterpreting the apostasy doctrine on the basis of the contradiction it presented with Hizmet's dialogue practice (Kurucan and Erol 2012, 66–69). This, in turn, further reinforces the case for connecting Gülen's 2014 comments with Hizmet's dialogue practice.

Moreover, the fact that Gülen has not offered a reinterpretation of equally challenging issues, such as the prohibition of homosexuality and the punishment for other *hudud* offences, including death by stoning for adultery, the amputation of limbs for theft, and the lashing for fornication—matters on which Hizmet is *not* engaged in correspondingly dissonant practices—supports the centrality of practice in the process discussed herein.

As for the alternative explanation; the negative German media coverage may have contributed to 'the when' and to 'the whom' Gülen's statement was made, but it was not the basis upon which his substantive views were formulated. After all, Gülen and Hizmet were defending their position and practice on dialogue against radical Islamists and militant secularists from 1994 to the 2010s, when Hizmet was not being attacked by the Western media. In other words, Gülen and Hizmet have been consistent in their defence of dialogue and its eventual epistemic implications (i.e., in this case, the reinterpretation of the apostasy doctrine), regardless of the reaction it evoked. The alternative explanation could be revised to ask if Gülen's reinterpretation was not an attempt to redress a 'problematic' statement that he had made in the past (i.e., his 1980 response on apostasy). That, however, would not explain Gülen's failure to 'redress' similarly problematic statements, such as his disparaging remarks about homosexuality.[30] As a result, this alternative

---

[30] In one excerpt, he equalises homosexuality with incest and characterises it as 'moral confusion and viciousness' (Gülen 2005, 210, originally published in 1991).

explanation does not provide us with a better explanation for the observed epistemic outcome under consideration, nor does it undermine this chapter's preferred explanation either.

Thus, given the foregoing, Gülen's 2014 revisionist comments (which I have already described as an *ijtihad*) and Kurucan's earlier spoken and written word, externalised (affirmed) Hizmet's emerging reinterpretation on the apostasy doctrine as indeed emerged. In doing so, they formalised the pre-propositional tacit cognition to flow from Hizmet's practice-based internalisation (e.g., relativisation, moderation, humanisation, assimilation of a dialogic habitus) into explicit knowledge.

Conclusion

As explained in Chapter 2, case-centric process tracing stops when we have crafted a 'minimally sufficient explanation of an outcome' (Beach and Pedersen 2019, 282), which is achieved when we arrive at the conclusion that 'all the relevant facets of the outcome have adequately been accounted for and whether the evidence is best explained by the developed explanation rather than plausible alternatives' (Beach and Pedersen 2019, 286). I have aimed to satisfy that criteria by unpacking the intervening process that explains how and why the observed epistemic outcome ensued in the manner that it did.

This has shown that the intervening process includes two fundamental movements: internalisation and externalisation. *Internalisation* occurred primarily by two means. First, Hizmet's practices associated with *hicret*, education, and dialogue precipitated cognitive compromise, which in turn caused Hizmet participants to relativise and moderate their views and attitudes towards the other. Second, by participating in the dialogue 'field,' Hizmet participants internalised a dialogic habitus. Together, these processes caused Hizmet participants to humanise the other at the pre-reflexive level of consciousness. *Externalisation* occurred as and when Hizmet began to appreciate the cognitive dissonance between its dialogue practices and Islam's premodern apostasy doctrine and its efforts to achieve cognitive consonance by reinterpreting the apostasy doctrine in accordance with the humanisation effect of what was described as its *internalisation* process.

Thus, this practice-based cumulative process of knowledge production occurs through an interactive loop connecting societal disposition (internalisation) with scriptural justification (externalisation). The emergent reinterpretation ensues naturally, gradually, and securely, without prior proclamation or express intent, in and through Hizmet's collective practice, passing through the level of intuitive, implicit, and pre-reflexive tacit knowledge before being externalised into universal, accessible, and formalised explicit knowledge, which feeds back into the interactive loop. This way, consensus on the emergent position is achieved in the process of developing and delivering it, where knowledge *arises* from the (doing) body to the (reflexive) mind and not vice versa. As a result, this form of practice-based knowledge production eschews the duality problem as identified in the rapprochement literature on Islam and human rights in Chapter 1, by combining both facets of religious knowledge (formalised/experiential, explicit/tacit, official/lived) as elements that are present in the performance of practice, without denying one or the other or the symbiotic interaction between the two. Thus, practice-based knowledge production succeeds (to explain) where an exclusive focus on scriptural exposition or societal disposition was shown to have failed.

Furthermore, I have shown that the processes associated with these two movements (internalisation and externalisation) were not dependent on Gülen's or Hizmet's intent. Neither did the externalisation occur as a result of some external hand that aimed to deliberately convert Hizmet's tacit knowledge into explicit knowledge. Instead, the pressure of (practice-based) internalisation precipitated externalisation. Thus, this overcomes the twin limitation of Nonaka's model of knowledge conversion as explained in Chapter 2, that is *intentionality* (the deliberate intent to produce tacit-to-explicit knowledge conversion) and *externality* (the use of a process or tool that is external and artificial to the practice under examination to produce tacit-to-explicit knowledge conversion). This in return ensures that what we have examined here is in keeping with what was conceptualised as a form of knowledge conversion that is better suited for the unintended and organic epistemic outcomes to ensue from social movement practice.

That said, there are certain limitations that are associated with this example (i.e., the apostasy doctrine). First, this is one example, and we need to examine practice-based knowledge production in relation to other thorny issues as well. Second, there is the issue of vested interests. Hizmet is a theologically traditional (sociologically modern) movement. As such, it is concerned with (and has an interest in) operating within the inherited tradition of religious epistemology. Therefore, it is possible to argue that it produced its emergent reinterpretation despite this interest. However, whatever interest Hizmet had in the apostasy doctrine, it was theoretical, not practical. In other words, Hizmet did not partake in either the criminalisation or punishment of apostates; neither did it have anything to gain from its perpetuation. Consequently, when Hizmet's dialogue practice was pitted against the apostasy doctrine, the 'competition' was between a practice in which Hizmet was practically invested in against an Islamic doctrine in which it was not. This does not diminish the significance of this particular reinterpretation; after all, it goes against the consensus of the *madhhab*-founding jurists. Nonetheless, it would be helpful to examine Hizmet's practice in the context of an Islamic doctrine in which Hizmet was practically invested in as well. The following chapter will do just that. It will not only trace Hizmet's practice in relation to a *number* of thorny issues but it will do so in relation to Hizmet's position on women's rights, an area in which Hizmet is practically invested in.

4
Women in Islam
From *Unseen Consumer* to *Active Producer*

In the 1970s and 1980s, Gülen's view of women and women's freedoms, rights, roles, and relations with men (hereafter, simply 'women's rights') was determined by the patriarchal formulations of Sunni Hanafi Islamic orthodoxy. According to this view, women are inferior to men in intellect and character, were created by God primarily as homemakers, and posed a risk to society if allowed to roam the streets unchecked. Thus, women should remain at home where possible and cover their bodies and faces in public when not. Furthermore, the public space should be segregated by sex, and girls should not attend school beyond the age of puberty (and thereby be forced to remove their headscarves). By 1997, however (i.e., until single sex schools were banned in Turkey), Hizmet was running forty-two schools and hundreds of *dershanes* (university preparatory centres) for girls in Turkey. By 2016, Hizmet's female participants were working as teachers, doctors, administrators, entrepreneurs, opera singers, TV personalities, journalists, engineers, and more while fulfilling a range of roles within Hizmet (Curtis 2015, 142). Furthermore, Gülen had called upon pious Muslim women to remove their headscarves to attend university in the face of the headscarf ban and claimed that women could lead men in any public role, including as head of state. Gülen justified his revised position (and Hizmet's revised practice) by recourse to Islam on account of the fact that the previous position/practice was also justified by recourse to Islam, as will be shown below. Thus, these 'organisational revisions' amount to emergent epistemic religious reinterpretations (*ijtihads*), as discussed in Chapter 2.

As per the previous chapter, this chapter will ask how and why that dramatic change of position and practice, and its underlying epistemic justification, came about. To do so, I will take practice as my basic unit of analysis as I examine the processual interplay within and between Hizmet's doings and sayings (i.e., practices) on women's rights over an expansive temporospatial axis (Schatzki 2001b, 56–58). As noted in Chapter 3, at times, I use 'doings' and 'practices' interchangeably but always in accordance with the definitional discussion of practice in Chapter 1. Moreover, I use 'Hizmet's sayings' and 'Gülen's sayings,' 'teachings,' 'views,' and 'statements' interchangeably as well owing to the fact that Gülen is often (albeit not exclusively) the one who verbalises Hizmet's sayings when performing the relevant practice that entails speaking to, and/or on behalf of, Hizmet.

Although this and the previous chapter pursue the same questions, the structure of these two chapters reflects the difference between how Hizmet's practices have interacted with the two topics being traced, that is, apostasy and women's rights, respectively. For example, in the case of apostasy, we were concerned with a single epistemic outcome, that is, the reinterpretation of the premodern Islamic doctrine on apostasy, whereas in the case of women's rights, there is no single issue of equal claim but several, which can vary from one polity to another. (I will discuss how I determined my issues of concern when introducing the broader topic of women in Islam below.) Furthermore, Hizmet's emergent reinterpretation on the apostasy doctrine evolved primarily through its interaction with Hizmet's dialogue practice. In other words, it was possible to trace one issue (apostasy) in the context of primarily one practice (dialogue). That is not the case with women's rights, where Hizmet's emergent reinterpretations have ensued through its interaction with a number of practices and practice bundles. In addition, these issues in relation to women's rights evolved interdependently in the context of Hizmet's practices. Therefore, it is very difficult to examine one issue without discussing the other. As a result, this chapter is forced to trace multiple (women's rights') issues in the context of numerous practices. Given the methodological framework of this study, that means producing multiple intervening processes, each with its own set of empirical entities and theoretical explanations to trace the issues under consideration. The upside of this, however, is a thicker, enriched, nuanced, and complexified appreciation of the relationship between practice and knowledge production, as will be shown below. This approach also guards against the risk of generalising what might otherwise be the anomalous outcomes and processes associated with a single issue.

Women in Islam: Background, Context, and Prevailing Approaches

The question of women in Islam (or the 'woman problem' as Fu'ad 'Abd al-Mun'im called it in 1976 (Mernissi 1991, 4)) is vast, complex, and deeply contested as it pertains to religious and political power, which 'are often intertwined' (Mernissi 1991, 10). It is a theologically rooted question that is ontological, legal, political, economic, social, cultural, anthropological, historical, and hermeneutical at the very least (Topal 2014, 1).

While the debate surrounding women's liberation in Muslim societies began to emerge at the end of the 19th century (Haddad 2011, 73–74), it took a new turn from around the 1960s onwards owing to a number of developments, including the social reforms of the newly independent Muslim majority states, such as universal education for boys and girls, the broader resurgence of political Islam across the Muslim world, the regression of women's rights where Islamists took control, and the emergence of feminist movements in Muslim majority societies (Doorn-Harder 2005, 3365). Thus, the liberation of women in the Muslim world became intimately connected to, and instrumentalised by, competing forces in the Muslim world in relation to these broader developments, including efforts to overcome colonial domination by the nationalists (Ahmed 1992, 129), modernise and secularise state and society by the reformists (Kandiyoti 1991a, 38–39), and mobilise grass roots political support by the Islamists (Salime 2011, 49).

The literature on this subject broadly organises the response from within the Muslim world according to three approaches or 'waves of reflection': secular feminism, Muslim feminism, and traditionalist reaction (Haddad 2011, 77; Doorn-Harder 2005, 3366–68; Hilsdon and Rozario 2006; Salime 2011, 37–41). Secular feminism 'refers to those whose activism is not directly based on the Islamic tradition but who struggle for women's rights within the framework of universal values and principles' (Doorn-Harder 2005, 3366). While diverse, the Western media often portray this group, according to Haddad, as 'self-flagellating, self-hating Muslims' such as 'Wafa Sultan; Tasleema Nasreen; Ayaan Hirsi Ali ... and Irshad Manji' whose work attacks 'Islam as a religion that subjugates and abuses women' (2011, 75).[1]

---

[1] See also Hilsdon and Rozario 2006, 332.

Muslim/Islamic feminism, on the other hand refers to those who advocate for change from within the Islamic tradition by arguing that '[w]e Muslim women can walk into the modern world with pride, knowing that the quest for dignity, democracy, and human rights . . . is a true part of the Muslim tradition' (Mernissi 1991, viii). Conciliatorists, as shown in Chapter 1 or Muslim feminists as mentioned above, argue for a rereading of Islam's primary sources by decoupling it from the patriarchal interpretations of premodern scholars to derive new interpretations suited to contemporary times and challenges (Hilsdon and Rozario 2006, 332-33; Ahmed 1992, 5). Leading figures within this approach include Fatima Mernissi (1991), Leyla Ahmed (1992), Asma Barlas (2002), Amina Wadud (1999), Nimat Hafiz Barazngi, Shirin Ebadi (2006), and Riffat Hassan (Doorn-Harder 2005, 3367; Haddad 2011, 76).

The traditionalist position, which includes the structures of religious authority such as the established *ulama*, *madrasah* and professional religious associations (Salime 2011, 14), the Islamists (Hilsdon and Rozario 2006, 332), and Islamist feminists (Doorn-Harder 2005, 3367), claim that the rights and roles of women should be determined by the classical formulations of (premodern) Islam, including the established *fiqh* (Islamic law) of the four main *madhhabs* (legal schools of law) (Haddad 2011, 74). Gülen's views on the subject in the 1970s and 1980s, as summarised above and unpacked further below, was determined by this framework.

The crux of the matter pertains to the difference between what is *written in* (i.e., God's *unknowable* intent) versus what is *read out* (i.e., humankind's *inescapable* interpretation) of scripture (Lambek 1993, 66). When the two are conflated, then human interpretation becomes immutable as the word and will of God. Thus, the question returns to the fundamental issue set out in Chapter 1, that is, balancing ontological absolutism against epistemological uncertainty or, to put it another way, recognising what is immutable and what is open to change in religion (Hilsdon and Rozario 2006, 333; Doorn-Harder 2005, 3370).

In practical terms, the issues raised in relation to women in Islam change from one region to another (Kandiyoti 1991b, 1). At the broadest level, the issues can be summarised as relating to inequality, discrimination, violence, sexual harassment, abuse, female genital mutilation, and honour killings, which manifest in both the private (e.g., marriage, polygamy, divorce, family life, child custody, inheritance) and public (e.g., education, employment, penal law, political representation) domain

(Bielefeldt 2000, 103; Doorn-Harder 2005, 3365; Hilsdon and Rozario 2006, 332; Haddad 2011, 77; Mayer 2018, 85–86). According to Césari et al., almost all human rights issues for European Muslims relate to women, including forced marriage, divorce, equality of women in marriage, and the custody of children (2004, 3). All of these issues are rooted in premodern interpretations of the Qur'an and/or Sunna. Thus, they need to be addressed by those attempting to reinterpret religious doctrine from within an Islamic framework.

This brings us to the question of which issues to trace in relation to Hizmet and women. That question is not the same as asking what are the central issues for women in Hizmet today. After all, my research is a historical study of Hizmet's evolving practices from 1966 to date and their epistemic outcomes along the way. Furthermore, practice-based knowledge production requires time and terrain to ensue, which counsels against a narrow focus on recent issues. Moreover, the central issues pertaining to Hizmet and women in Islam (or the central issues of women in Hizmet and Hizmet on women) are not necessarily detached from the broader issues faced by pious Muslim women in Turkey either.

Thus, based on that perspective, I have determined my issues of concern for this chapter by triangulating three sources. The first are the broader issues faced by Turkey's pious Muslim women and their implication for their religious belief, understanding, and manifestation, from the 1970s onwards (Kandiyoti 1991a; Kadıoğlu 1994; Göle 1996; Gül and Gül 2000; White 2002; Aksoy 2005; Ozcetin 2009; Arat 2010; Kaya 2011; Arik 2012; O'Neil and Toktas 2014; Okuyan and Curtin 2018). This in turn is connected with the clash of at least two forces: the modernisation/secularisation project of the Kemalist elite of modern Turkey from 1923 onwards (Kandiyoti 1991a, 38–39), wherein 'Muslim women were burdened with being the litmus test for the modernity of a whole nation' (Topal 2014, 2), on the one hand, and the resurgence of religion within the public and political domain of Turkey from the 1970s and 1980s onwards, on the other (Hiro 1986). This clash, which had far-reaching consequences, was most obviously symbolised by the wearing of the Islamic headscarf (*türban*) in public (Göle 1996; Elver 2012, 19). I will draw on this background as necessary in the body of my analysis.

The second source is Hizmet's response to these broader issues and to those issues pertaining to women in Hizmet. I have elucidated these issues from the repeated questions put to Gülen in media interviews as well as Hizmet's changing position and practice on women in Hizmet.

The third is a survey of the most commonly discussed issues in the scholarly literature on Hizmet, Gülen, and women, including those claiming that Gülen is a champion of the patriarchy.[2]

According to this survey, the most significant issues for women in Hizmet and Hizmet on women since the 1970s are (i) the right to education for girls (both as individuals but also as a form of practice for Hizmet), (ii) the wearing of the headscarf in the context of formal education and the headscarf ban, (iii) gender-based segregation in the context of piety in the public space, and (iv) the role of Hizmet's female participants within and beyond Hizmet.

The common thread in all of these issues is their relation to how women interact with and through Hizmet as a patriarchal space. In that sense, these issues relate primarily to the freedom of women, while some aspects of it relate more narrowly to women's rights and equality (e.g., the right to education for girls). Furthermore, all of these issues are relevant to the question of knowledge production on Islam and human rights since they relate to the ontological nature of women; the relationship between men and women; human dignity, equality, and non-discrimination; the nature, role, and rights of women; the right to education and work; and the flexibility of religious knowledge production on intransigent issues relating to women. For the sake of expediency, this chapter will characterise the aforementioned four contentious issues simply as 'women's rights,' while noting that they are, in fact, more expansive than that.

Overview: Direct and Cumulative Outcomes

The importance of contextualising Gülen's sayings against Hizmet's doings in a manner that is sensitive to the processual nature of practice is demonstrated by the literature on Gülen and women's rights that fails to do so. This literature can be broadly categorised into two groups. The first and more populous group of the literature claims that Gülen is progressive or a champion of women's rights (Najjaj 2009; Erken 1995; Özdalga 2003; Curtis 2005, 2012, 2015; Andrea 2006; Stephenson 2007; Rausch 2008, 2009, 2015; Gurbuz-Kucuksari 2008; Hällzon 2008; S. Yavuz 2008; Pandya 2009; Hassencahl 2009; Kılıç 2012). The second group, however, argues that Gülen is in fact a champion of patriarchy (Fougner 2017; Çobanoğlu 2012). The methodological

---

[2] I will cite the references for the second and third source when unpacking them below.

problem with both groups of literature is that they overemphasise Gülen's teachings from one period over another.

Gülen was far more conservative and traditionalist at the beginning of his mission, and some of that traditionalist and essentialising mindset persists; in this regard, the second group of literature is correct. But Gülen has increasingly become more progressive on women's rights, and so, in that sense, the first group of literature is correct. The first group of literature relies primarily on Gülen's more contemporary statements and interviews (1995–2010), at the exclusion of his earlier sermons (1970s and 1980s), while the second group does the reverse. Furthermore, the second group of literature does not pay close attention to Hizmet's practice. As a result, this group of literature places far too much emphasis on Gülen's earlier views and their assumed impact on Hizmet today. Furthermore, neither of the two groups of literature pays close attention to the processual and evolving nature of Hizmet's position and practice on women and women's rights. Consequently, they both overlook the *trajectory* of change, which undermines the diametrically opposed conclusions they respectively reach.

To avoid this pitfall, I will apply the theoretical-methodological framework set out in Chapters 1 and 2, which includes tracing the interplay within and between Hizmet's doings and Gülen's sayings (i.e., Hizmet's practices) over an extended period of time and terrain. Figure 4.1 provides a chronological view of that interplay by looking at *what* happened. This figure begins to map the connections within and between the key sayings and doings on the four issues under consideration.

Furthermore, I have traced the causal relationships among Hizmet's doings, Gülen's sayings, and the observed epistemic outcomes under consideration through the elaboration of an intervening process (i.e., causal mechanism) for each issue. This has shown that Hizmet's practices associated with education (one version or another) is the most common, significant, empirical entity for all of the issues discussed. Moreover, while cognitive compromise featured as a theoretical explanation in two of the issues discussed (role of women and gender-based segregation), cognitive dissonance, on the other hand, featured in all of them.

In addition, by tracing multiple issues in the context of numerous practices, I was able to complexify the nature of practice-based knowledge production to the point of distilling its direct and cumulative forms. In the case of the former, I found that a specific Hizmet doing influenced a correspondingly specific Gülen saying in a relatively prompt and linear manner.

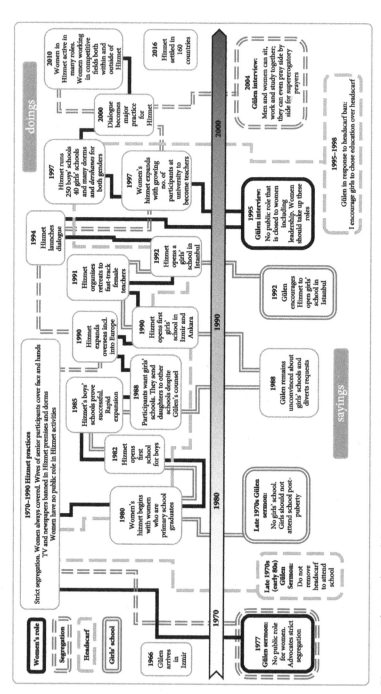

Figure 4.1 The timeline of the interplay between doings and sayings on women's right

In the case of the latter, multiple doings and sayings collided to co-shape and co-influence one another and the epistemic outcome under consideration in a far more cumulative, unassuming, incremental, and long *dureé* fashion. In both instances, practice produced unintended internal outcomes, which is the focus of my inquiry (Suh 2012, 2.4).

Again, in both instances, Gülen justified Hizmet's evolving practice by reference to Islamic knowledge. In so doing, he did two things. First, he affirmed the emerging revision as indeed emerged; in other words, he externalised Hizmet's tacitly evolving position and practice into explicit knowledge (Choo 2006, 8). Second, he 'converted' the affirmation of what was an organisational revision (of position and practice) into a religious one, that is an *ijtihad* (religious reinterpretation), as discussed in Chapter 2. To understand how and why that came about, we must first establish a point of departure for Gülen's sayings and Hizmet's doings, which is what I will turn to next.

Point of Departure: Gülen on Women

Four points of historical background are relevant to any reading of Gülen's position on women. First is Gülen's theological heritage, which is thoroughly patriarchal, being rooted in the Sunni Hanafi-Maturidi tradition of Islamic orthodoxy (Uğur 2004; Leaman 2007; Bruckmayr 2008, 175–76; Acar 2011, 71; Çobanoğlu 2012, 79). Second, Gülen's emphasis on *taqwa* (Islamic piety) and *tasawwuf* (Islamic mysticism), which connect spiritual purity with a firm control over carnal desires and an abstinence from not just what is sinful (*haram*) but what is religiously doubtful, especially on matters pertaining to interaction with the opposite sex (Gülen 1995b, 2006b, 47; H. C. Kim 2008, 124, 153–54; Saritoprak 2003, 161; Tittensor 2015, 170). Third is the significance of Said Nursi's (d. 1960) personal example, which informs Gülen's notion of *adanmışlık*, that is, devotion to cause, where Islamic activism is prioritised above all forms of personal ambitions, including familial (Gülen 2002; Ergene 2008, 19, 160; Saritoprak 2011; Bruckmayr 2008, 167–69; Barton 2004, 24, 2005).

These three points (with the fourth point to follow later in this chapter) help explain Gülen's personal sensitivity on the topic of women, with implications for his views on women's rights, roles, equality, and the interaction between the sexes in Hizmet and in broader society (Pahl 2019, 132). Many examples from his life help illustrate this sensitivity, not least of which is the fact that

Gülen, like Nursi, remains a celibate by choice. Celibacy is highly unusual for an Islamic scholar (which Gülen is) or even for a self-denying Sufi master (which Gülen is not) since many Islamic teachings encourage marriage and disparage celibacy (K. Ali 2006, 6). Nonetheless, Gülen justifies his celibacy, while discouraging others from emulating him (Jon Pahl, 2019, 168), on the grounds that he has dedicated his entire life to the service of God (Kurtz 2005, 375; Pahl 2019, 133). In the *Nurcu* circles (i.e., among those who self-identify as followers of Said Nursi's teachings), this level of dedication is sometimes referred to as *kendini vakfetmek*, that is, 'to dedicate your life for the cause' (Bulut 2020).

Another telling example of Gülen's sensitivity on the topic of women took place in the 1960s when he was appointed as an imam to Turkey's Üç Şerefeli mosque in Edirne. Gülen insisted on sleeping on the (deep and wide) window sill of the ancient mosque for two years as opposed to renting a nearby apartment or room so that he could avoid the unwanted gaze of women as he travelled to and from the mosque (Gülen 1995b).[3] This level of scrupulous behaviour only makes sense within the context of *taqwa*, *tasawwuf*, *adanmışlık*, and *kendini vakfetme* as discussed above, and is likely to explain the basis for his views, which he expressed for the first time during a comprehensive ten-week sermon series he gave in 1977, titled 'Women and Family in Islam' (*Islam'da Kadın ve Aile*).[4]

This brings me to my fourth point. Gülen delivered his sermon series on women in 1977 during the formative period of Hizmet's socio-historic development. As discussed in Chapter 3, Gülen's emphasis during this period was on raising religious sensibility and solidarity through religious practices that were deeply conservative, protectionist, formulaic, didactic, insular, and patriarchal. Thus, the timing of this sermon series is likely to have reinforced the substance of Gülen's views and the preceding three contextual dynamics that helped to produce them in the first place.

Let us turn now to the substance of Gülen's views on women during this period. For this discussion, I will rely primarily on the aforementioned 1977 sermon series for the reasons I just explained. I will supplement that discussion with other pieces and responses Gülen provided during the

---

[3] See also Jon Pahl, 2019, 132.
[4] This sermon series is also referred to by another name: 'Women in the Qur'an' (*Kur'an'da Kadın*) (Gülen 1999). Another early piece includes a 1977 sermon series titled 'The Upbringing of Children' (*Çocuk Terbiyesi*) (Gülen 1999), which was later transcribed into book form (Gülen 2011b). In addition, Gülen returns to this topic in an ad hoc manner in some of his talks and writings.

same period. But despite its obvious significance and my best efforts, I was unable to locate this sermon series, be it in audio, video, or written form. While it was circulated among the faithful on audio tapes at the time, apparently this particular sermon series was never digitised or at least shared in digital form by Hizmet's media outlets such as Kaynak, Nil, or Gülen's website, which includes other sermons from the same period (e.g., Gülen's 1977 'The Upbringing of Children' series; Gülen 1999). Given its content and in the absence of any explanation to the contrary, it appears that Hizmet's media outlets censored this particular sermon series because it was no longer in keeping with Hizmet's practices and Gülen's subsequent sayings. Nonetheless, I have located a doctoral thesis by Sevim Erken (Erken 1995) in Turkish, which provides extensive quotes from this sermon series on which, in return, I will gratefully rely.[5]

An examination of Gülen's teachings on these four contested issues from this period (1970s) marks our point of departure for our historical analysis in this chapter. According to Gülen's teachings from this period, women were created to be mothers for their children, wives for their husbands, and inhabitants of their homes, where they were meant to spend most, if not all, of their time. Gülen believed that it was his responsibility to remind women of 'the most distinguished role bestowed upon her by God, [which would] prevent [women] from wasting time seeking out alternative past-times' at a time when the modern world was trying to 'give women new roles and positions' (Erken 1995, 65). According to Gülen, 'the salvation of society depends on segregating man and woman with a curtain. To involve women in public life, to let women *loose* onto the street is tantamount to seducing man and goes against Islamic law and the nature of women' (my emphasis) (Erken 1995, 66). Thus, a woman should not only cover her head and body but also her face, upon which her beauty is concentrated: '[y]ou will cover your hair. With that covering you will cover up to your eyebrows and even cover one eye' (Erken 1995, 70). For Gülen, gender-based segregation and veiling was a form of 'damage control'. A former Hizmet participant, (allegedly) turned state informant Latif Erdoğan, says that in the formative years, 'Gülen described the face veil in his private and public talks as a *fard*', that is, as a religious obligation, when in fact it is not (Erdoğan 2015). In one of his public talks originating from the 1970s, an extract of which has since

---

[5] I personally translated the quotes attributed to Gülen in Erken's (Turkish) study which I have used in this book.

been uploaded to YouTube, Gülen says that girls should not remove their headscarves or compromise on it in any way whatsoever, even if that means expulsion from school (Gülen 2013b, secs. 00:00–02:00).[6]

During his 1977 sermon series, Gülen claimed that women were inferior to men in intellect and character. After all, 'Einstein, Descartes or Hegel did not come from among women but men. Such people can only come from among men. There are no leading women in the field of philosophy, literature, or military affairs' (Erken 1995, 66–67). Thus, he maintained, women had little to contribute to society, which justified them remaining at home. According to Gülen, the children of working women are raised by caregivers, which will lead to a 'generation of children who lack respect and deference' (Erken 1995, 67). These two propositions—that women are ontologically unfit to contribute to society and that caregivers are unfit to raise 'respectful' children—coupled with the requirement that women remain at home and cover up in public to minimise their corruption of society—appears to explain why Gülen was opposed to girls being formally educated beyond the age of puberty and foresaw a rather limited role for women during the formative period of Hizmet. As for the inferiority of character, Gülen gave the following explanation in the late 1970s[7]: '[w]omen are at your disposal. They will do the things you want; they will continue your lineage. You, on the other hand, will guide them like a spiritual teacher.... They have some weaknesses and flaws. You must support them against these and show them the right way,' including by 'light physical chastisement . . . as a last resort,' where she 'cannot be disciplined and whose character cannot be put right any other way' (my translation) (Gülen 2011a, 130–31).[8]

Therefore, given the foregoing, it is not surprising that Hizmet's early practices were in line with these teachings. For example, from the 1970s to the early 1990s, all Hizmet space was strictly segregated (Kömeçoğlu

---

[6] Also, see Lötüs 1989, a book published by one of Gülen's personal students on women's attire in Islam, which supports Gülen's early views on this subject, as discussed here.

[7] Although published in book form in 2011 as *Asrın Getirdiği Tereddütler*, this statement is likely to have originated from a response Gülen gave in the late 1970s during a 'question and answer' sermon series at Bornova (Izmir) mosque, where, among other things, he was asked about issues concerning women in Islam. These questions on women in Islam date back to 1977–1979. This particular excerpt is likely to have originated from his response to one of the questions from this period (Gülen 2020).

[8] I will not trace Gülen's evolving position on intimate partner violence in this chapter. As per the other issues that are traced, Gülen has revised his position on this particular issue as well. Gülen's 2008 comments on this issue suggests that he considers intimate partner violence to be grounds for divorce for women in Islam. In the same comments, Gülen also calls upon women to learn martial arts to protect themselves against abusive husbands (Kurucan 2008).

2008, 71; Turam 2007, 62). Boys and girls attended separate schools (until single-sex schools were banned in Turkey in 1997) and dorms, and they lived in separate houses (Pahl 2019, 150–52, 156). Male teachers taught in boys' schools and female teachers taught in girls' schools. On the rare occasion when Hizmet's single-sex schools employed teachers from the opposite sex, they did so while providing these teachers with separate teachers' rooms and space to eat in the dining halls to minimise the mixing of genders, even among teachers, outside of the classroom (Özdalga 2003, 88). Hizmet participants applied the same rules at home when entertaining guests. The women of the household would remain out of sight as they served tea and dinner from behind closed doors (Turam 2007, 117–19). I know from personal experience that Hizmet's student houses were also strictly regulated during this period: television sets, newspapers, and magazines (including those published by Hizmet) were banned to avoid an inadvertent glance of the opposite sex.

While Hizmet's female participants did not wear the *burka* (or 'çarşaf' as it is known in Turkey), which is a full-body black gown, they did adhere to a strict dress code in public, which included wearing a full-length overcoat and the religiously sanctioned headscarf (Erken 1995, 70–71; Lötüs 1989). Many of Hizmet's female participants, especially those who were married to senior Hizmet participants (*ağabeys* or *abis,* literally 'elder brothers'), also wore the face veil, sunglasses, and gloves (Aydın 2016).[9] According to Erken, this practice was still prevalent in 1995, when she notes that '[t]oday, Fethullah Gülen's close relatives and Hizmet's female participants, especially those who are housewives, are very particular about wearing the face veil' (Erken 1995, 70; Lötüs 1989, 40). One Hizmet participant once told me that she only removed her face veil and gloves when she relocated to Thailand in 1994. During this formative period of Hizmet's development (1966–1982), Hizmet's female participants played no public role in Hizmet whatsoever (Aydın 2016), other than teaching other women about Islam in informal settings, as I will discuss further below.

---

[9] This citation refers to a critical Turkish newspaper article, which claims to be based on interviews with former participants and supporters, including Hüseyin Gülerce, Ahmet Keleş, and three unnamed women. The piece provides no right of response from the movement. Thus, I will use it sparingly to support noncontroversial claims.

Direct Outcomes: Education, the Role of Women, and the Headscarf

If Hizmet's formative period (1966–1982) was defined by its focus on building a religious community, what followed was a period focused on education (1982–1994). Hizmet founded its first school in 1982, and by the late 1990s, had established hundreds of schools and *dershanes* across Turkey (Agai 2002, 27). By 1997, Hizmet had founded between 250 and 300 schools abroad (Agai 2002, 27),[10] and by 2016, it had founded 15 universities, 934 schools (excluding *dershanes*), 109 student dorms, and 1,229 charities and associations in Turkey alone, of which a significant proportion were focused on education (Resmi Gazete 2016).[11] By the same year, 2016, Hizmet had founded and was running an equal number of schools and educational institutions outside of Turkey across 160 countries worldwide (House of Commons 2017, 89).

Hizmet's transition from close-knit religious community to nationwide education movement and the precipitating practice behind it (i.e., education) had significant implications for the changing nature of Hizmet and its attitude towards women. Hizmet harboured a number of external and deliberate aims via these schools. These included short-term aims, such as providing Turkey's pious Muslim families with alternative educational settings than the ones offered by the secular state, as discussed below; medium-term aims, such as achieving recognition and legitimisation by providing excellent education; and long-term idealistic aims, such as raising a new generation of pious Muslim youth ('Golden Generation') who would successfully navigate the challenges of living in the modern secularised world with their religious belief and morality intact (H. Yavuz 2013, 98). However, the practice of founding and running these schools also had unintended internal epistemic outcomes, some of which were direct, on account of ensuing from this practice in a prompt and linear manner. I came across this form of direct outcome when zooming in and out of Hizmet's practices on at least three occasions. These pertained to girls' education, women's role in Hizmet (as teachers), and

---

[10] See also Ebaugh 2010, 43.

[11] This publication in the *Resmi Gazete* (i.e., the Official Gazette of the Republic of Turkey) refers to the infamous Emergency Degree No. 667, which allowed the state to confiscate 934 privately owned schools on the pretext that they were affiliated with Hizmet. This decree also closed down thirty-five hospitals and polyclinics and nineteen trade unions on the same pretext. For an English translation of the decree, see Malaurie et al. 2016, 2–7.

the wearing of the headscarf in the face of Turkey's 1997 university headscarf ban.

Girls' Education and Discontent in Practice

As noted earlier, Gülen opposed the idea of girls attending school beyond the age of puberty. That meant discontinuing formal education beyond (the compulsory) primary school. His opposition lasted until 1990. In one sermon, Gülen sarcastically exclaimed that 'some say that girls should be educated so that they may raise children like Fatih Sultan Mehmet II [who conquered Istanbul]. What faculty did Fatih's mother graduate from'? (Erken 1995, 71).[12] Consequently, Gülen's two nieces, married to prominent movement participants, discontinued their formal education beyond primary school. However, despite Gülen's general opposition regarding the formal education of girls, Hizmet founded its first girls' school in 1990. Within a few years, Hizmet had opened ten additional girls' schools in Turkey and by 1997 was running approximately forty-two schools[13] and hundreds of *dershanes* for girls across the country (by 2015, Hizmet was running 430 *dershanes* for girls in Turkey).[14] By 2016, all of Hizmet's approximately 934 schools in Turkey were running as fully fledged coeducational schools. Gülen's objection evolved into outright support from 1992 onwards. The intervening process between these two positions is represented in Figure 4.2, which I will now unpack.

The key to understanding how and why Hizmet founded its first girls' school in 1990 (and how and why Gülen went from opposing girls' formal education to supporting it from 1992 onwards) takes us back to the founding of Hizmet's first boys' school. According to Gülen, Hizmet participants were reticent about founding secular schools in the early 1980s. He says that he

---

[12] See also Kılıç 2014.
[13] The forty-two girls' schools were founded by 1997, after which all single-sex schools were banned in Turkey, as discussed below. Thus, in time, all of Hizmet's approximately 934 schools in Turkey became fully fledged coeducational schools. The figures provided here are an estimate based on an analysis of the list of schools the Turkish government shut down in 2016, as shown in the annex to the Decree with Force of Law No. 667 (2016).
[14] Anecdotal evidence suggests that Hizmet was running approximately 1,200 *dershanes* across Turkey by 2015, of which one-third were for girls only. Information in the public domain (920 *dershanes* overall) comes close to this total estimate (Oda TV 2013). The Turkish government forced the closure of all *dershanes* in Turkey from September 2015 onwards in a bid to undermine Hizmet (Sözcü 2014).

X	Schools	Schools	Schools	Dissonance	Dissonance	Dissonance	Y
Practice	Gülen encourages the founding of boys' schools	Hizmet participants reluctantly agree	Boys' schools prove successful	Hizmet participants want to open girls' schools. Gülen opposes the idea	Hizmet participants send their daughters to school	Hizmet opens a girl's school. Schools are overwhelmed by demand	Gülen encourages the opening of girls' schools
	Internalisation process			Externalisation process			

Figure 4.2 The intervening process on girls' education

had to push, nudge, and prod the movement to found a private secular school in Turkey that would follow the national curriculum and be run in accordance with Turkey's strict secular laws. On one occasion, he says that he 'stood up, grabbed his wet coat that [he] had laid out to dry, and headed to the door to find new friends who would'. He says that it was only then that 'his friends' agreed and that Yamanlar College, an all-boys fee-paying boarding school, was founded in Izmir, Turkey, in 1982 (Gülen 1998).[15]

As noted earlier, within twenty years, Hizmet had found hundreds of boys' schools in Turkey and abroad. These schools became successful in a short period of time on account of the 'unusually high levels of commitment demonstrated by the teachers' and, in time, the school entrance test which selected students on aptitude (Tee 2016, 62). These schools were also sought after because they provided an alternative to the state-run mainstream secularist schools, which had a patchy record on educational attainment and were intolerant of religion, and the state-run (Imam Hatip) vocational religious schools that disadvantaged their students taking the national university entrance exam. Hizmet's schools, on the other hand, combined excellent education with a learning environment that was socially conservative with religious undertones (Tee 2016, 77). In this respect, these schools met an obvious demand.

The success of these schools had an unforeseen consequence. As Erken notes, '[t]he movement was unable to remain indifferent to the significant demand from girls and families with daughters, who were moved by the success of Hizmet's *dershanes* and schools aimed at boys in many parts of the

---

[15] This excerpt is based on my translation (1998) of Gülen's said talk from the late 1990s in Istanbul. The video recording of Gülen's original talk is no longer available because of the government crackdown. See footnote 1 in Chapter 2.

country' (1995, 68). Mustafa Başarı, a longstanding Hizmet participant, who led the effort to found Hizmet's girls' schools across Turkey, elaborates on this point. In his unpublished notes, he says,

> [T]hese schools came about because there was a demand for them by our people. Parents who had enrolled their sons to our schools began asking, 'what about our daughters?' This demand only increased as Hizmet opened more and more [boys'] schools and when these schools became successful. Many families who supported Hizmet wanted schools for their daughters. Some of the men I met wanted it simply to escape pressure at home. Others were genuinely concerned. One lawyer said, 'I have one daughter and her education was a big concern for me. *Hodjaefendi* [Gülen] was against girl's education so this was a big issue for me. I pray for you [Mustafa Başarı] day and night that these schools were founded'. (My translation, 2019)

In the absence of Hizmet's schools, socially conservative families from rural or middle/eastern Turkey were forced to send their daughters to schools and universities in far-flung metropolitan areas such as Istanbul, Izmir, and Ankara. According to Başarı, Gülen 'saw that families were sending their daughters to school anyway', despite his counsel to the contrary (my translation) (2019).

Başarı says that he asked Gülen if Hizmet should found a girls' school in 1988 and 1989. According to Başarı, Gülen diverted the question to the Akyazılı Foundation for Secondary and Higher Education board of trustees, which was responsible for Yamanlar Koleji (the all-boys school for 11- to 18-year-olds). Başarı says that whenever he raised the issue at the Akyazılı board meeting he was shut down by one or another member who regurgitated Gülen's 'did Fatih [Mehmed II]'s mother go to school' mantra. Failing to gain traction at these meetings, Başarı says he approached the board members individually, which included businessmen and donors. 'On a one-to-one basis they all agreed. I found out that some were even sending their daughters to school, in secret without telling the others, anyway. So, I was able to raise funds from them in that way. That's when we opened Malhatun in Izmir in 1990' (my translation, 2019). This was Hizmet's first girls' school, for 275 students.

Başarı explains that the first challenge they encountered was demand; there were too many families from within and without Hizmet who wanted to enrol their daughters in the school (2019). To meet this demand, the following year, Hizmet founded a girl's school in Turgutlu and Ankara (Safiye Sultan).

It is important to pause here to note that the movement's initial reticence about opening schools eventually evolved into ardent support for opening and running schools for both boys and then girls. This suggests that the movement internalised the inherent or, at the very least, the instrumental value of educating both boys and girls and that this internalisation was achieved in and through the performance of these educational practices and those associated with the opening and running of these schools. As noted earlier, the success of Hizmet's schools and *dershanes* for boys catalysed a corresponding demand for the same provisions for girls. This time it was Gülen who was reticent, and the movement participants who took action by enrolling their daughters in schools and universities in spite of Gülen's opposition; this was indeed a form of discontent in practice.

This development created dissonance between Gülen's teachings and practice (via his close family members): on the one hand, he opposed sending girls to school beyond the age of puberty, and on the other hand, Hizmet supporting families who nevertheless were doing so. The two propositions— Gülen's counsel against and Hizmet's support for the founding and running of girls' schools—were irreconcilable. This dissonance marked the point at which the process of externalisation on this particular issue began to emerge—that is, the conversion of that which was internalised (an appreciation of the inherent or, at the very least, the instrumental value of educating girls) into a form of explicit knowledge.

When Hizmet finally opened its first girls' school, its decision to do so was vindicated by the overwhelming demand for such schools and provisions for girls. This demand, coupled with Gülen's previous opposition, required an explicit revision. That revision initially came about through a telephone call Gülen made to Başarı in 1992, when '*Hodjaefendi* [Gülen] called me from the United States and asked that I help open a girls school in Istanbul, which we did the same year' (Başarı 2019). This school was named Çoskun Koleji and had capacity for 1,200 students. Since then, Gülen has justified the education of girls and women on the basis of Islam, to the extent that (as we will see below) he has called on women to remove their religiously sanctioned headscarves to attend university in the face of the 1997 headscarf ban in Turkey. In doing so, Gülen converted Hizmet's organisational revision (i.e., from opposing to supporting girls' education) into a religious reinterpretation (*ijtihad*). Thus, the unintended epistemic outcome of successfully running boys' schools and *dershanes* in Turkey was to precipitate Hizmet's emergent reinterpretation (*ijtihad*) on girls' education.

Women's Role in Hizmet

Previously, Hizmet's female participants were encouraged to prioritise their home and the raising of their children over participation in public life. From 1990 onwards, however, they were being encouraged to leave their homes, attain higher education qualifications, and join Hizmet's workforce to staff Hizmet's growing network of schools and *dershanes* for girls (Özdalga 2003, 97–99; Tee 2016, 53–55; Erken 1995, 69, 90; Kılıç 2014; Curtis 2015, 152) to the extent that they were being discouraged from taking maternity leave (Erken 1995, 69). Both positions were justified by recourse to Islam. The intervening process between these two positions is shown in Figure 4.3. According to Başarı, Hizmet began to frantically encourage its female participants to qualify as teachers after the founding of its first girls' school in 1990 (2019). To aid this process, Hizmet organised summer retreats to train prospective teachers for the following semester (Erken 1995, 68). Therefore, extending Hizmet's educational efforts and practices to girls produced a knock-on effect. Hizmet's schools and *dershanes* for girls required female teachers, mentors, and administrators (Kılıç 2014). That requirement, in return, meant that Hizmet had to revise its previous position and practice on the role and utility of women in Hizmet, and by extension, in society.

Thus, the practice-based process of encouraging and training Hizmet's female participants to qualify as teachers and to leave their homes to join Hizmet's workforce helped the movement to internalise the religious

X	Schools	Schools	Schools	Dissonance	Y
Practice	Hizmet begins opening schools and *dershanes* for girls	Hizmet's girls' schools require female teachers, administrators and mentors	Hizmet encourages its female participants to attend school and university and to join Hizmet's workforce	This contradicts Gülen's earlier teachings on the role of women in Hizmet and society	Gülen revises earlier teachings
	Internalisation			Externalisation	

Figure 4.3 The intervening process on women's role in Hizmet

legitimacy of doing so. By this point in time (i.e., the early 1990s), Gülen was no longer preaching that women should remain at home. Nonetheless, a latent dissonance lingered between Gülen's past statements and Hizmet's then-practice, which marks the beginning of the externalisation process on this topic. That dissonance was explicitly overcome when Gülen privately joined the call for women to qualify as teachers to join Hizmet's workforce in order to support Hizmet's schools, as evidenced by the movement's mobilisation to train female teachers beginning in the early 1990s.[16]

'To Wear or not to Wear': The Headscarf Ban

Turkey's history with the headscarf is a chequered one (Elver 2012, 15–40). Turkey's secular establishment has always considered the headscarf to be a symbol of political Islam and has long sought to ban it in one form or another. While the headscarf has never been banned in Turkey by law, it has been banned in practice and by departmental regulations. For example, a 1981 Ministry of Education directive states that all primary, secondary, and high school (*ilk*, *orta*, and *lise*) students, including private school students, must keep their heads 'uncovered' (*baş açık*) in school at all times.[17]

It is in this context that Gülen, during a 'question and answer' sermon from the 1980s, was asked the following question: 'should my sister remove her headscarf to attend school'? The question pre-dates the university headscarf ban and pertains to wearing the headscarf at either the secondary (from 11 to 13 years) or high school level (14 to 18 years). Gülen's response was unequivocal:

> It is religiously impermissible for a woman to attend a school where she cannot practice her religion. *Whatever the cost, she must endeavor and cover her head.* If she considers attending school to be some kind of religious obligation, let me say that I do not know of any such obligation. If

---

[16] While there is no record of Gülen publicly calling for Hizmet's female participants to join Hizmet's workforce at the time, that was the message conveyed on behalf of Gülen, in private, by Hizmet's senior participants (*abis/ağabeys*) to the broader movement. That explains the overwhelming effort to mobilise this outcome through summer retreats where prospective teachers underwent fast-tracked teacher training courses to meet the demand of Hizmet's growing network of schools and *dershanes* for girls.

[17] See articles 10(a), 11(a), and 12(a) of the relevant regulation that pertains to the uniform of all primary, secondary, and high school female students (*Resmi Gazete* 1981).

she has arrived at a personal religious *ijtihad* that this is obligatory because she will proselytise to female students at school, that this will enable her to be useful to Islam, that she sees great benefit in this, that she is absolutely committed to preaching God's message to others by doing so even if that means going to hell, I do not find such rationalisations acceptable and she should re-think and condition herself to not compromise her religion at the outset of her life. Covering one's head is a religious obligation (*nas*) set by the Qur'an. A person commits a big sin for every minute she leaves a strand of her hair uncovered. Whatever reward and *jihad* she aims to achieve by uncovering her hair is conditional; its outcome is unknown. To whom will she preach, whom will she influence, it is all uncertain. *A person cannot justify an act which is a definitive sin for its conditional gain.... She should have resolve to say I will not compromise my religion even if that means that I will be expelled from school.* (My translation and emphasis) (Gülen 2013b, sec. 00:00–02:00)

This response is consistent with Gülen's broader views on this topic from the 1970s and 1980s as discussed earlier. Thus, we can treat it as being indicative of Gülen's well-established thinking on this topic at the time.

In 1997, the military orchestrated a bloodless intervention against the Islamist-led coalition government,[18] forcing them (and the willing state bodies) to pass a number of laws and directives on the pretext of countering the subversive Islamist threat (*irtica*) in Turkey (Aslan 2016; Mango 2004, 96–98; Yilmaz 2015a, 70–72). One of these measures was the banning of all single-sex schools in Turkey from 1997 onwards (Erarslan and Rankin 2013, 457; C. Koca et al. 2005, 367).[19] Another of these measures banned all students from wearing the headscarf on university campuses. This headscarf ban was achieved by a 1997 Council of Higher Education directive (Elver 2012, 19). Thus, the 'battle over the headscarf became a central symbol in the fight for Turkey's national identity between secular and religious factions' (Badruzzaman et al. 2017, 27), with almost all religious groups in Turkey opposing the ban in public, even if some of them conceded or compromised in private.

---

[18] Colloquially known as *28 Şubat süreci* in Turkish (literally, '28th February process'), that is, the date on which the National Security Council took place and the military generals 'convinced' the Islamist government to adopt the series of measures noted above.
[19] With the exception of the state-run vocational religious (Imam Hatip) schools (C. Koca et al. 2005, 367).

It is in this context that Gülen revisited the issue both before (1995 and 1997) and after (1998 and 2005) the university headscarf ban was introduced.[20] Gülen's renewed position was that while he opposed the headscarf ban and was in favour of freedom of religion, he recognised that the issue had become 'very sensitive' (Gülen 2013a). As a result, he drew attention to the categorical difference and hierarchical priority between matters pertaining to belief (*usul al-Din*) and matters pertaining to religiously sanctioned action (*furu al-Din*) in Islam. The headscarf, like all other forms of religiously sanctioned action, was a matter of *furu*, not *usul*, and was therefore secondary to *usul*. Having made this distinction, and after adding that he was 'saddened' for those 'forced to make a choice' between their right to education and their right to religious practice, Gülen encouraged headscarf-adorning Muslim women, including Hizmet's female participants, to 'make their choice on the side of education' (Mercan 2017, 124). That meant removing their headscarves to continue their university education.

This was a very controversial position to take and made Hizmet deeply unpopular with other Islamic groups in Turkey who chose to oppose the ban, at least publicly. This raises the question as to causality: why did Gülen change his mind when he had publicly advocated for a diametrically opposed view in the 1980s? One explanation is that Gülen sought to appease the secularist military establishment. While that may have played a role, it overlooks the processual nature of Hizmet's preceding practice and its substantive (if pre-reflexive) consequence. This leads us to another question: how is this issue relevant to the broader discussion of women's rights in Islam? After all, Gülen is not standing up for the freedom of religion or belief of Turkey's pious women by encouraging them to remove their headscarves to attend university. In response, I would point out that it is relevant insofar as it demonstrates how Hizmet's practice produced an emergent reinterpretation (*ijtihad*) on a widespread religious practice (i.e., the wearing of the headscarf), which allowed Turkey's pious Muslim women to access higher education. That, in turn, goes to the question of how practice can negotiate the boundaries of what is religiously permissible for pious Muslim women, with implications for their social, educational, and economic empowerment, through practice-based

---

[20] See Gülen's 1995 interview (Gülen 1995a), his book chapter first published in 1997 (Gülen 2011c), and the press release dated January 30, 1997 (Gülen 2013a). See also his following interviews dated March 13, 1997 with Orhan Yurtsever (Gülen 2013a); July 21, 1997 with Nevval Sevindi (Mercan 2017, 123); June 21, 1998 with Avni Özgürel (Mercan 2017, 124); and 2005 with Mehmet Gundem (Mercan 2017, 124).

X	Boys' schools	Girls' schools	Dissonance	Y
Practice	Hizmet opens secular schools and *dershanes* for boys from 1982 onwards	Hizmet opens secular schools and *dershanes* for girls from 1990 onwards, which requires a steady input of female staff	Hizmet's educational practice versus the headscarf ban	Gülen encourages women to choose education over the headscarf
	Internalisation		Externalisation	

Figure 4.4 The intervening process on education over the headscarf

knowledge production. This comes within the expansive notion of 'women's rights' as understood within (and stated at the outset of) this chapter.

We can now move on to elaborate the intervening process as shown in Figure 4.4. This will help us to differentiate between what caused Gülen to articulate a revised position at that *point in time* (i.e., 1995 and 1998) and what caused him to revise his position *to begin with* (i.e., Hizmet's opening of boys' schools in 1982 and girls' schools in 1990). The distinction is crucial to appreciating how and why this reinterpretation emerged.

This takes us back to the founding of Hizmet's boys' schools in Turkey in 1982. Turkey has a deeply centralised education system that binds all schools and educational outlets in the country, including private ones, under the umbrella and regulation of the Ministry of Education (Gündüz 2009). This goes back to the Law of Unification of Instruction (*Tevhid-i Tedrisat*) of 1924 and the aim to unify all forms of education in the country in order to ensure that it furthers the founding principles of the Republic of Turkey, which includes *laicism* (Gündüz 2009, 197). With the exception of recent changes, Turkish law required that all public and private schools in Turkey abide by its secularist laws and regulations relating to the substance and style of education, including matters pertaining to curriculum, pedagogy, ideological orientation, and uniform. In doing so, Hizmet had agreed, at least in principle, to become a proxy of the secularist state, which meant enforcing Turkey's secularist rules and regulations through its schools.[21] That included regulations relating to uniforms, which excluded any type of headgear by default,[22] at its

---

[21] For example, all Hizmet schools taught the approved national (secular) curriculum (Agai 2003, 51; Clement 2011, 76) and included '"Atatürk corners," in which [Mustafa Kemal] Atatürk's statues, pictures [also found in every classroom], sayings and other symbols of the secular Republic, were exhibited' (Turam 2007, 27). See also Kömeçoğlu 1997, 79.

[22] See footnote 17 above.

boys' (as it pertained to its teachers) and girls' schools (as it pertained to its teachers and students) from 1982 and 1990, respectively, onwards.[23]

This suggests that Hizmet had increasingly conceded the hierarchical priority of founding and running these schools above scrupulously upholding its values, principles, and adherence to religious rules as it had once practiced and advocated for in the 1970s and 1980s. That, in return, suggests that Gülen's revised position on the headscarf, as stated in 1995 and 1998, was rooted in Hizmet's practice of founding and running secular schools in Turkey from 1982 and 1990 onwards.

This raises another question: why had Gülen changed his mind about the value he ascribed to wearing the headscarf versus the value of continuing formal (and therefore, secular) education in Turkey? This question directs us toward Hizmet's educational practices since it was in the context of those practices that Gülen's counsel on the headscarf issue had changed. After all, when Gülen counselled against removing the headscarf to continue formal education, Hizmet was not running a single school in Turkey or abroad. When Gülen counselled the opposite, Hizmet was running hundreds of schools in Turkey. Thus, whatever his views on the headscarf, Gülen's views on the value ascribed to formal education had clearly changed in the context of Hizmet's educational efforts and practices. This transformation can be explained as taking place in three steps.

Step 1: Right versus Duty
As quoted in the earlier part of this chapter, Gülen's response to the question about removing the headscarf to attend school during a 'question and answer' sermon from the 1980s (Gülen 2013b), demonstrates that, at the time, Gülen considered education to be only conditionally valuable insofar as it allowed Muslim students to missionise to fellow students while in school. In other words, attending school was nominally valuable. According to Gülen, attending school while wearing the headscarf was *a right to religious manifestation and education against the state* (i.e., a right protected against state intervention),[24] whereas wearing the headscarf as a religious practice *was a*

---

[23] That said, anecdotal evidence suggests that some Hizmet schools and *dershanes* were more relaxed when it came to permitting students to wear the headscarf on school premises until 1997 but that even these schools fell into line after 1997.

[24] The human rights position on headscarf bans for higher education students is a deeply contested issue, with the European Court of Human Rights and the United Nations Human Rights Committee appearing to have come down on either side of the argument (Ssenyonjo 2007; C. Evans 2006; Elver 2012; McGoldrick 2006). These decisions pre-date Gülen's statements. Moreover, my focus here is on how these students construed their options and their rights versus duties, as opposed to how

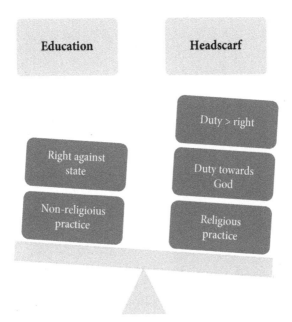

Figure 4.5 Step 1—duty towards God outweighs right against state

religious duty towards God. Conceptualised in this manner (see Figure 4.5), a Muslim could not commit a 'definitive sin' (by removing the headscarf) for a 'conditional gain' (e.g., the opportunity to missionise to fellow students).

Step 2: Duty versus Duty

By 1982, Gülen was advocating that Muslims had a responsibility to contribute to society and science. Muslims therefore had to be well educated in both the religious and secular (natural and social) sciences. Through this argument, Gülen reconceptualised the religious value of 'secular' education. Thus, founding, running, and attending secular schools was now an Islamic duty towards God (i.e., an Islamic practice) because it enabled pious Muslims to qualify as teachers, doctors, engineers, and scientists and thereby contribute to both society and science as required of them by God. This notion was increasingly extended to girls since 1990. As a result, the choice in the face of the headscarf ban was no longer between a secular right *against the state* (the right to education while wearing the headscarf) versus a religious

these human rights' courts and committees interpreted these rights in the face of such bans many years later.

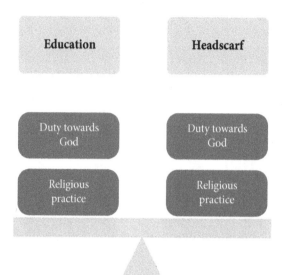

Figure 4.6 Step 2—education and headscarf equalised as duties towards God

duty *towards God* (the religious obligation to wear the headscarf), where religious duty always outweighed secular rights. Instead, the choice became one between the *duty towards God* (by attending school) versus the *duty towards God* (by wearing the headscarf). In this reconceptualised formula (see Figure 4.6), both the wearing of the headscarf and the founding/running/attending a secular school were equalised as religious *duties* (in the form of practices) *towards* God.

Step 3: Collective versus Personal
To equalise two or more elements (considerations, goals, principles, laws, etc.) often requires the adoption of a *deciding principle* by which one can determine which element supersedes the other when two or more of them conflict. Faced with the headscarf ban, Gülen explains that his deciding principle was the hierarchical priority between *usul* and *furu*. While articulated in this fashion, Hizmet's practice to date suggests that the hierarchical priority for Hizmet and Gülen is in fact between the perpetuation of Hizmet's social practices as opposed to its discontinuation; in other words, a bias for the pathway that maximises the potential to continue Hizmet's practices. This notion is not without foundation. After all, in *fiqh*, all things being equal, considerations pertaining to the collective (or *maslahah*) outweigh those

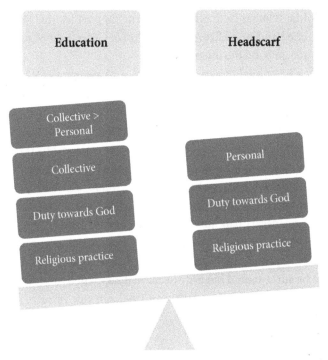

Figure 4.7 Step 3—collective considerations outweigh personal considerations

considerations pertaining to the individual (Abou El Fadl 2001, 82). Since Hizmet's social practices are, by and large, inclusive and extensive, they often pertain to the interests of the collective over the interest of any one individual (H. Yavuz 2013, 33). Either way, wearing the headscarf discharges a religious obligation that is personal, not collective, and it pertains to *furu*, not *usul*. Reconceptualised in this manner, education becomes loaded with religious significance in a way that the religious injunction on the headscarf is not (see Figure 4.7).

Thus, the founding and running of boys' schools led to the founding and running of girls' schools. That, in return, (i.e., the first two links of the intervening process) led to the internalisation of the reconceptualised value ascribed to formal secular education as a form of religious practice and duty towards God. While Gülen's counsel for founding boys' schools was of course vital to begin with, it was not his counsel per se but the application of it through practice that precipitated the internalisation of that reconceptualised value described above. That internalisation is evident from

Hizmet's initial reluctance to Hizmet's ardent support for this form of practice, on the one hand, and Hizmet's expansion of Gülen's advocacy on education to include girls, on the other.

Hizmet's educational practices for girls and women ran into conflict with the nationwide headscarf ban in 1997. This conflict precipitated an externalisation of Hizmet's internalised bias towards secular education for both substantive (i.e., the reconceptualised value ascribed to education as shown through Steps 1 to 3 above) and instrumental reasons (i.e., the need to staff Hizmet's growing network of schools in and beyond Turkey), which of course reinforced one another (e.g., the value ascribed to education translated into more schools, which demanded more teachers). Gülen's statement on the headscarf ban, justified by recourse to Islamic categorisations of belief and action, was an externalised *ijtihad*, which was rooted in this practice-based dynamic that had begun in 1982. In other words, the ban was a hurdle to be surmounted but only because it happened to be 'in the way' of Hizmet's ongoing practice since 1982 and 1990, not vice versa.

Alternative Explanation: Context

Before moving on, let us pause here to ask if we can attribute the aforementioned direct outcomes to an alternative explanation; that is, for example, the prevailing religious, social, cultural, political, economic conditions and the context of the time? This question would suggest that context was the primary force behind Hizmet's emergent reinterpretations, not practice.

In Chapter 1, I explained how practice-based epistemology conceptualises the relationship among practice, knowledge, and context. In accordance with that discussion, I am not denying that context influences practice, nor am I making an exclusivist claim that denies the possibility of the production of knowledge outside of the processes described in this book.

Rather, I am concerned with practice as a form of knowledge production here for two reasons—first, because it is the most plausible explanation for Hizmet's emergent reinterpretations as examined in this book and second, because my notion of practice-based knowledge production explains how religious knowledge is produced through the symbiotic relationship between internalised-tacit and externalised-explicit knowledge. That approach matters, because it allows us to go beyond the fragmented epistemological dualisms of religious knowledge (e.g., official/lived, theoretical/experiential) as problematised in relation to the rapprochement literature on Islam and human rights as discussed in Chapter 1. Simply put, practice allows us to account for a form of knowledge production that symbiotically connects with both the experiences of the faithful (lived religion) and the inherited tradition of religious epistemology (official or formal religion). Without practice, we are back to the conciliatorist approach of attempting to theologise a way forward through semiotic expositions, which was shown to be wanting. A context-based explanation for Hizmet's emergent reinterpretations not only fails to adequately account for how and why the observed epistemic outcomes ensued as they did (my first reason for choosing practice as a form of knowledge production in this instance) but also how and why those epistemic changes were internalised by Hizmet participants and supporters as they appear to have been (my second reason).

Furthermore, the challenge that this alternative explanation poses lies in its assumption that practice is not the context for the epistemic outcomes under consideration. To the contrary, '[s]tudying "context" from a practice perspective implies, in fact, studying analytically and processually how different practices are associates, and what are the practical implications of their relationships for the practice at hand' (Nicolini 2013, 234). In other words, according to a practice-based approach, the context of the epistemic outcomes under consideration are the practices that produced them (Cook and Wagenaar 2012, 15). Therefore, to offer *context* as an alternative explanation to *practice-based context* is to offer a form of context that is somehow beyond practice (i.e., a *non-practice context*), such as immutable conditions and settings.

For example, both this alternative explanation and I would argue that Gülen revised his opposition to girls' attending school because Hizmet's constituents continued to send their daughters to school, despite Gülen's counsel to the contrary. Up to this point, we would agree. From here onwards, however, this alternative explanation would account for the subsequent developments, not by reference to the success of Hizmet's schools from 1982 onwards (i.e., a practice-based context), but by the liberalisation, urbanisation, growing religious middle class, economic development, and rising trend of secular and Islamic notions of feminism during this period (i.e., *arguably*, non-practice-based contextual forces).

After all, we know that by 1975 a number of Imam Hatips (state-run religious schools) began admitting girls to their all-boys' schools (Aksoy 2005, 158). The mixing of boys and girls caused a backlash, which precipitated the founding of the first all-girls Imam Hatip school in 1977 (Aksoy 2005, 152). From 1983 to 1991, the Turkish military sought to legitimise the secular Turkish state by promoting 'the Turkish-Islamic synthesis,' an amalgam of (non-observant) Sunni Islam and Turkish nationalism (Eligür 2010). That entailed further concessions to public manifestations of religion. From 1970 to 1990, Turkey experienced a massive surge of urbanisation from the traditionally conservative rural regions. That, coupled with premier Turgut Özal's (1927–1993) economic reforms of 1983–1989, helped create a new religious middle class in Turkey (Öniş 2004; Turam 2007, 22–23, 51).

Nevertheless, the foregoing conditions were facilitative rather than determinative of Hizmet's practices and the changes it brought about. In other words, while these conditions made it easier for Hizmet to perform these practices, they do not explain how and why those practices came about to begin with, nor do they explain how and why those practices produced the type of epistemic outcomes that they did in a manner consistent with the historical account of what ensued. For example, why did Hizmet open girls' schools in Turkey from 1990 onwards, if not for the success of the boys' schools that began in 1982. Or why was Hizmet so keen to encourage its female participants to join Hizmet's workforce from 1990 onwards, if not to staff its growing network of schools? And, most importantly, how did Hizmet internalise its eventually externalised epistemic outcomes if not through practice? Here, context fails to adequately account for Hizmet's differential practices and the epistemic implications of doing so. This is why Nicolini warns against using context as an 'explanatory factor' as it plays an 'eliminativist role' in that it 'shortcut[s] and substitute[s] for a more detailed analysis of how the conditions for actions came about' (2013, 234).

Cumulative Outcomes: Segregation and the Role of Women

Unlike direct outcomes, practice-based *cumulative* knowledge production ensues over a longer period of time and terrain, through the contribution of multiple practices and practices bundles, which simultaneously intersect to corrode and mutually re-shape one another as well as the observed epistemic outcome under consideration. Simply put, no one practice or event explains the outcome under consideration in this type of knowledge production. Thus, the interplay within and between Gülen's sayings and Hizmet's doings often takes place in an unassuming, complex, incremental, latent, and long *dureé* manner. This overlaps with social movement outcome theory which encourages an evaluation of movement outcomes over a long period of time (Suh 2012, 3.5).

The intervening processes pertaining to Hizmet's evolving position and practice on gender-based segregation and on the diversified role of Hizmet's female participants within and beyond Hizmet are virtually the same, which is why I will examine them together. During Hizmet's formative period, Gülen preached that women were inferior to men, that they were best suited as homemakers, and that they corrupted men and society. As a result, he maintained, women should remain at home and be covered when outside, and the sexes should be strictly separated in the public space. Consequently, at that time, women had one role within Hizmet: to teach Islam to girls and women in informal settings. Beyond that, those who were married to Hizmet's male participants, were to support their husbands so that they, in return, could support Hizmet in the best way possible.

By 2016, Hizmet's attitude towards women and Hizmet's range of activities had dramatically changed and diversified, respectively. As a result, Hizmet's female participants were now becoming teachers, administrators, community organisers (*bölgeci*), dialogue practitioners, journalists, presenters, storytellers, writers, motivational speakers, health care professionals, and the like, within and outside Hizmet. This is what I mean by the diversification of roles for Hizmet's female participants within and beyond Hizmet. Furthermore, Hizmet's female participants were taking on leadership roles for projects run by and for women within Hizmet while also beginning to penetrate the decision-making boards of Hizmet's *formal* organisations, such as schools and dialogue organisations. As a result, Hizmet's female participants were becoming far more visible within Hizmet, and Hizmet's strict application of gender-based segregation was beginning to wane (Curtis 2015, 143). These developments were supported by Gülen's statements on these issues during the same period. This, of course, is not the same as claiming that men and women have equal opportunities within Hizmet; they do not. After all, while the trajectory of change is towards greater opportunity for women, Hizmet's male participants still dominate Hizmet's leadership roles and formal and informal decision-making bodies. By zooming in and out of Hizmet's practices, I have identified the following interconnected entities of the intervening process to explain how and why the trajectory of change is towards greater opportunity for women within Hizmet (see Figure 4.8).

X	Girls' schools	Hicret, education, and dialogue	Women's hizmet	Dissonance	Y
Practice	Hizmet's women graduate from university to work in Hizmet's girls' schools and dershanes	Hizmet's schools and dialogue practices abroad bring Hizmet into sustained social interaction with the other	Bayanlar hizmeti (women's hizmet) empowers Hizmet's women	Hizmet's dialogue creates and highlights dissonance	Gülen's statements
		Internalisation		Externalisation	

Figure 4.8 The intervening process on the role of women and segregation

According to Figure 4.8, three interconnected entities helped Hizmet internalise that which was then externalised as an emergent reinterpretation. These included the founding of girls' schools in the 1990s, which caused Hizmet to internalise the value of educating girls and encouraged women to join Hizmet's workforce; the expansion of Hizmet overseas through *hicret* (migration), education, and dialogue in the late 1990s, which caused Hizmet to internalise the acceptability of desegregating space to run coeducational schools and dialogue organisations and to discover new ways of experiencing faith and religious activism overseas free from the pressures and sensitivities of being a pious Muslim at home; and, the evolution of *bayanlar hizmeti* (literally, 'women's hizmet' or Hizmet's activities run by and for women) by the early 2000s into a practice that caused Hizmet to internalise the increasingly complexified notion of the role of women in Hizmet and society. Hizmet's dialogue in the West also precipitated a dissonance, which in turn, catalysed the externalisation of Hizmet's emergent reinterpretation. I will now explain how and why these entities interconnect with one another to produce the observed epistemic outcomes under consideration.

Internalisation

As with two of the previous issues discussed above, this intervening process also begins with the founding of schools for girls in 1990. As I have shown, among other things, the founding of girls' schools caused Hizmet to reverse its position on the role of women in Hizmet and to call upon its female participants to join Hizmet's workforce. Thus, the motivation to teach at Hizmet's schools and *dershanes* ensured that Hizmet's female participants were educated to at least a bachelor degree level. This was in addition to the extracurricular informal religious education that Hizmet provided its female participants through *sohbets* (religious discussion forums), religious retreats, and its emphasis on self-improvement (Cıngıllıoğlu 2017). According to Sunier, '[o]nce a member, [Hizmet participants] follow a trajectory of intense learning and reflecting on a wide variety of sources of knowledge' (2014, 2203). As Ayşe put it, '[w]e tried to sleep less in order to have more time left for reading. We read an enormous number of books. As a matter of fact, we read seventy books in five months'. Özdalga finds this testimony to be 'quite astonishing' and notes that it was obvious that Gülen had 'influenced Ayfle (sic) and her friends about the importance of reading extensively' (2003, 104). As a result, while some have questioned whether Hizmet's schools produce critical minds (H. Yavuz 2013, 104–6, 114), Hizmet's formal and informal educational practices have at least intellectually enabled and empowered its participants within the prevailing educational paradigms of the polities in which they operate (G. Çelik et al. 2015, 10).

Furthermore, Hizmet's schools, *dershanes*, and scholarships facilitated upward social mobility by empowering Hizmet's female participants with job security, economic independence from family, and innovative practice opportunities within and outside of Turkey (Turam 2007, 20–21; Curtis 2015, 150–51).[25] Turkey's religiously observant women 'had been reluctant to work among people who would not respect her Islamic identity. Because this identity entailed covering her head, [they] preferred to work in a milieu where women's and men's spheres truly were separated' (Özdalga 2003, 89). Hizmet schools provided not only segregated space and prayer facilities for its staff members, but also low-cost bus services, free lunch, on-site nurseries, and an hour's break between every two to three hours of work for teachers with children at the on-site staff nursery, especially those who were still breastfeeding (Özdalga 2003, 112; Gurbuz-Kucuksari 2008, 486). While this reinforced gender-based segregation in the short term, it also enabled and empowered Hizmet's female participants socially, economically, culturally, and intellectually, in both the medium and the long term. Furthermore,

---

[25] See also Sametoğlu 2015, 149, 152–53, 157.

these female participants were now prepared to partake in Hizmet's activities abroad, which began in earnest in the mid- to late 1990s.

This brings us to the second link in the intervening process, which comprises a practice bundle including *hicret* on the one hand and Hizmet's educational and dialogue-related practices abroad on the other. I have already discussed the theoretical and empirical basis of this link in Chapters 2 and 3, respectively. Accordingly, this practice bundle precipitated sustained social interaction with the other, which in turn, relativised and moderated the views, beliefs, and opinions of Hizmet participants through a process described as cognitive compromise. Thus, rather than repeat that theoretical and empirical discussion here, I will focus on how and why the same transformative process relates this time to Hizmet's evolving position and practice on gender-based segregation and the role of women.

Hizmet's practices in 160 countries worldwide, including those that relate to education, dialogue, relief work, grass roots religious activism, media, business networking and so on, complexified Hizmet's identity. After all, Hizmet began as a conservative religious congregation in 1966 in Izmir, Turkey, and until 1990 it was focused primarily on opening schools within its country of origin. It is only from the early to mid-1990s that Hizmet began to expand overseas, principally through coeducational schools and dialogue organisations. As Neslihan T. Kılıç notes, Hizmet gained the opportunity of 'engaging with different people' from '2000 onwards when it expanded its efforts to the European and American continent through education [and] dialogue'. This globalisation supported 'diversity and cultural pluralism' within the movement. According to Kılıç, among other things, 'engaging with others in new places' helped Hizmet to 'internalise global values, a human rights discourse' with implications for Hizmet's position and practice on women and women's rights (my translation) (2014).

Hizmet's activities overseas provided its participants with the occasion to question the origin of personal and collective precepts and practices, which served as a 'vehicle to change inherent misogynist gender ideals that can be ascribed more to culture than to Islam' (Hällzon 2008, 309). Given the foregoing, Sophia Pandya notes how several Hizmet participants 'spoke of ways in which gender roles have changed in the US. In particular, their movements' activities are less segregated than in Turkey, and women's degree of activism and sense of urgency and purpose is greater' (2009, 143). As one Hizmet participant explains, 'I've met lots of people. I'm more involved in the

US society now. If there were no movement, I would just go to school and not be very active' (Pandya 2009, 139). Curtis observes the same phenomenon among Hizmet's female participants both in Turkey and the United States. Based on 120 interviews with Hizmet's female participants (split evenly between Turkey and the United States) conducted from 2007 to 2013, she notes that '[a] shared characteristic that stands out overwhelmingly is their desire to engage in civic life and to participate beyond the boundaries of their own faith circles' (2015, 141).

Pandya's research on *hicret* and Hizmet's female participants in the United States suggests that Hizmet's practice of encouraging its participants to continue their participation in Hizmet outside of Turkey has empowered its female participants to reexplore, reexpress, and reevaluate their religion (2009, 133). She reports that '[w]omen spoke to me of feeling more "free" in the US from family, social, and political tension that some experienced in Turkey regarding their involvement'. She claims that 'independence from their native context' allowed these women to 'more effectively practice their religion' (2009, 133). This independence and freedom had a 'bearing' on these women and on their 'social lives, religious activities and practices, and on their *understandings of Gülen's message*' (my emphasis) (Pandya 2009, 133). That freedom, coupled with Hizmet's dialogue, which provided its female participants with an additional platform from which to explore and engage in wider society, amplified the influence to ensue from Hizmet's social interaction.

Free from social stigma and familial pressure, Hizmet's men have also been at greater liberty to explore and support greater equality at home. As one Hizmet participant notes, 'I've heard people making fun of Gülen men—that they are too gentle and not masculine enough! They tease our men', before noting how Gülen cries during his talks and sermons and how his well-known sensitivity is at odds with the Turkish sense of masculinity (Pandya 2009, 142; Özyürek 1997, 41). That 'freedom', coupled with an effort to interact and integrate, is likely to have influenced Hizmet's men and their traditional norms regarding the role of men and women. As Pandya noted, 'the roles that Gülen men play have also undergone transformation, and that men here are more willing to help with domestic tasks, and more family-focused than what they said was "typical" for the average Turkish man' (2009, 143). Today, it is not unusual to encounter Hizmet's men remaining at home to care for the children while the women are outside organising a Hizmet event or working to support the family.

Thus, Hizmet's goal of expanding its activities overseas, through primarily education and dialogue, resulted in sustained social interaction with the other. That, in return, complexified Hizmet's identity and relativised Hizmet's position and practice on a range of issues, including the role of women in Hizmet. As a result, Hizmet began to internalise the acceptability of de-segregating Hizmet space to run coeducational schools and dialogue organisations overseas and to discover new ways of *being* away from the pressures and sensitivities found at home.

The increased mixing of the sexes in Hizmet can be seen as dialogue with the *internal-other* (i.e., Hizmet's women), which in turn is likely to have precipitated the same processes associated with dialogue and sustained social interaction with the *external-other* as discussed in this chapter and in Chapters 2 and 3. Again, this draws our attention to how Hizmet's outward-looking practices produce inward-looking (internal) consequences.

This brings us to *bayanlar hizmeti*, that is, a bundle of interconnected Hizmet practices run by and for women (Curtis 2015, 144). The literature on Gülen, Hizmet, and women is silent on the origin of *bayanlar hizmeti*. Anecdotal accounts suggest that *bayanlar hizmeti* began in the 1980s with the singular focus of inculcating the insular, patriarchal, conservative, formulaic, and exclusionary notions of Islamic orthopraxy to Hizmet's female constituents. That objective was achieved through overtly religious, well-established Hizmet practices, including *sohbets* (religious talks), *kamps* (religious retreats), and *rehberlik* (religious mentoring). While anecdotal, this historical narrative is consistent with my appraisal of Hizmet's religiosity during its formative period (1966–1982), as discussed above. Given its focus on raising religious sensibility, hierarchically speaking, *bayanlar hizmeti* comes under *bölgecilik*, that is, the branch of Hizmet that is focused on grass roots religious activism as discussed in the Introduction chapter.

Thus, *bayanlar hizmeti* (the third link in the intervening process) historically predates the first two links in the intervening process (i.e., women joining Hizmet's workforce as teachers and Hizmet's expansion overseas). Nonetheless, it is shown as following as opposed to preceding them in the intervening process because it increasingly evolved into its present state, producing the type of outcomes in which I am interested, as a result of its encounter with those practices as represented by the first and second link in the intervening process. In that sense, *bayanlar hizmeti* represents a culmination of the broader changes experienced by women in Hizmet and Hizmet on women and women's rights. Furthermore, by continuing to enable and empower Hizmet's female participants, it continues to support Hizmet's activities overseas (the previous link), which is represented in the intervening process by a 'feedback loop' in the form of a reverse arrow (Beach and Pedersen 2019, 77).

The founding of girls' schools and *dershanes* from 1990 onwards (first link) was the first development that caused *bayanlar hizmeti* to change course. After all, this development provided *bayanlar hizmeti* with a new mission: to encourage their constituents (i.e., Hizmet participants and sympathisers who attended their events) to attend university to qualify as teachers in order to staff Hizmet's growing network of schools (Erken 1995, 68–69). Thus, this body of *hizmet* was now having to appeal to an educated class of women while also gaining a foothold on Turkey's university campuses up and down the country, which inevitably led to the recruitment of new supporters (Aydın 2016). The upshot of this development was that it helped to diversify the constituents and reach of *bayanlar hizmeti*, which in turn caused it to diversify the nature of its activities to ensure that it continued to appeal to its expanding base (Kılıç 2014). In other words, *bayanlar hizmeti* was no longer focused solely on religious counselling and guidance, which had inevitably become less formulaic and exclusionary to allow for the type of educational attainment and professional work that it was now encouraging its participants to pursue. It was also providing educational, moral, social, and professional support, as noted above (Curtis 2015, 144).

The expansion of Hizmet abroad, through *hicret* (second link), further complexified *bayanlar hizmeti* as it increasingly became exposed to the type of relativisation and moderation processes described above on account of *bayanlar hizmeti* being part and parcel of the broader body of Hizmet. In addition, the highly educated and ambitious nature of Hizmet's female participants abroad helped to further enrich *bayanlar hizmeti* as a form of practice. As Pandya notes, Hizmet's female participants in the United States are 'either studying or working, often in male-dominated fields such as technology or science. All of them led very active lives, fitting in their frenzied schedule of cultural and religious activities with work, school, and domestic duties' (2009, 142). Moreover, the challenge of appealing to Turkish Muslim women abroad, socialised by the socio-cultural context outside of Turkey, forced *bayanlar hizmeti* to once again adapt to their new-found constituents. For example, while *bayanlar hizmeti* was not particularly concerned with promoting social integration among its constituents in Turkey, that was a key objective for Golden Rose, a women's organisation run by Hizmet's female participants in Belgium (Kılıç 2012, 53).²⁶ These factors helped to shape the nature, input, and outlook of *bayanlar hizmeti* abroad.

Thus, prior to the Turkish government's crackdown in 2016, and despite its point of origin, *bayanlar hizmeti* had evolved into an interconnected bundle of Hizmet practices that supported women's educational attainment, upward social mobility, career development, economic independence, and experiential exposure through educational, social, professional, and religious practices and organisations (Kılıç 2014). By 2010, *bayanlar hizmeti* was 'so well established and developed' that they were running institutions and activities for women in Turkey from all careers, catering to every level of education, economic status, spiritual sensibility, and geographical region (Curtis 2015, 142). This helped Hizmet to internalise the complexified identity, competency, role, and function of women in Hizmet and society.

In sum, therefore, all of the practices represented in the first three links of the intervening process conspired with one another to change and transform themselves as they did their carriers, that is, Hizmet's female participants. All three practices in the links achieved this change by facilitating the cultivation of confident, reflexive, outgoing, ambitious, and well-educated women who were capable of competing with men in highly specialised fields *outside* of Hizmet, while also participating in practices and activities (as producers and not just consumers), alongside their male counterparts, *in* Hizmet (Kılıç 2012, 54). As a result, today there is 'no one role that women in the Gülen Movement play, rather, there are many'. As of 2015, these included, 'entrepreneurs, teachers, opera singers, TV personalities, . . . journalists, engineers . . . , stay-at-home mothers, doctors, pharmacists, nurses, AIDS and cancer researchers, forensic psychologists, . . . Qur'ān school teachers, dormitory managers and university professors' with a 'wide cadre of highly successful professional women who take part in Gülen communities' in Turkey alone (Curtis 2015, 142).²⁷ As noted earlier, this points to the diversification of roles for Hizmet's female participants in and beyond Hizmet.

Accordingly, Kılıç argues that '[a]mong women of Turkish origin, a new Islam type is rising in relation to [the] Hizmet Movement' and that this new type of Islam is being built on the shoulders of a 'new religious identity for women', where women strive to be both Muslim and modern (2012, 56).

---

²⁶ The diversity of *bayanlar hizmeti* in different parts of the world is also underscored in Curtis 2015, 149.
²⁷ See also Kılıç 2014.

According to Curtis, this change is not uncritical but rests on the shoulders of Hizmet's women whose critique extends from Kemalism and feminism on the one hand to notions of Islamic orthodoxy that claim that a 'women's place is in the home' or 'only men are spiritual authorities in the Islamic tradition', on the other (2012, 153).

Therefore, if Hizmet has transformed its participants through practice, then its transformed participants are transforming *it* (i.e., Hizmet) by reproducing those practices in a way and manner that is more suited to their complexified, enriched, and empowered identity, outlook, ambition, and goals (Curtis 2015, 138). In other words, the 'changing demographic of the rank and file of Hizmet [is] also transform[ing] Gülen's vision of Islam in the contemporary globalized world' (Sunier and Landman 2015, 93–94). While this process began with Hizmet's instrumentalisation of women in Hizmet (and thereby Hizmet's internalisation of that instrumentalised value), it has evolved to a point where Hizmet's transformed participants are able to reproduce Hizmet's practices in a manner that increasingly recognises the inherent value of women as well.

The religious legitimacy and/or desirability for this transformation of women and their relationship with men within Hizmet was achieved in and through Hizmet's practice. More specifically, Hizmet *internalised* the permissibility (and value) of educating girls, of opening the workforce to women, of increasingly desegregating Hizmet's space to run coeducational schools and dialogue organisations (especially in the West, where Hizmet is now primarily focused), and of diversifying the roles and positions of women within Hizmet in the process of actually doing so.

As a result, Hizmet's female participants draw on Gülen's more recent teachings that are more meaningful to them, while ignoring his earlier teachings from Hizmet's formative period, that are less meaningful to them. This is shown in the numerous studies conducted by a variety of researchers that include interviews with such participants and supporters, as cited in this chapter. The interviewees in those studies do not quote Gülen's earlier teachings, nor do they attempt to explain the apparent contradiction between the two sets of teachings (Özdalga 2003; Curtis 2005, 2012a, 2015; Andrea 2006; Gurbuz-Kucuksari 2008; Hällzon 2008; Pandya 2009; Rausch 2009, 2015; Kılıç 2012). Rather, and as one interviewee simply puts it, '[s]he said, "Mr. Gülen says women must get educated, work, and have power in society" as opposed to focusing on life as a stay-at-home mom or volunteer' (Stephenson 2007, 153).

Dissonance: 'Where Are the Women'?

Hizmet's dialogue overseas played a role in the internalisation process. However, the same practice also played an important role in the externalisation of that which had been, and was being, internalised as well. This underscores the multidirectional nature of practice, which can precipitate internalisation at one level and externalisation at another.

As discussed in Chapter 3, while Hizmet's first dialogue organisations were founded in 1999 to 2000, they did not begin to achieve traction until 2005. I know this from personal experience because I worked for the Centre for Intercultural Dialogue Studies, a Hizmet organisation that ran from 2004 to 2006 to supply Hizmet's dialogue organisations in Europe with material, know-how, and project-based support (Companies Database 2018). Hizmet's early day practices overseas focused primarily on interfaith dialogue through events such as performances by whirling dervishes, the celebration of Prophet Muhammad's birthday (*Mawlud al-Nabi*), interfaith fast-breaking dinners, the sharing of *Eid* meals and 'Noah's pudding' events,[28] women's interfaith circles, understanding world religions seminars, church visits and talks, Easter vigil events, interfaith picnics, and interfaith trips to Turkey.[29]

This was new territory for Hizmet outside of Turkey and brought with it greater scrutiny. Hizmet was increasingly challenged regarding the role of women and gender-based segregation in the context of its burgeoning number of dialogue events overseas, especially in the West. A typical dialogue event organised by Hizmet during this early period often featured a mixed group of non-Muslim male and female guests hosted by an all-male group of Hizmet participants. Hizmet's women were nowhere to be *seen*, and that, of course, was the point (Ebaugh 2010, 50, 120).[30] This invisibility extended to private dinner parties hosted by Hizmet supporting families where

---

[28] Noah's pudding (or *Ashura*) is a sweet dish that is traditionally prepared on the 10th day of the Islamic month of Muharram. According to Islamic tradition, Prophet Noah and his family prepared this pudding from the last bits of food remaining on the Ark (e.g., grains, nuts, and fresh and dried fruits) following the Great Flood. It is customary among Muslims in Turkey and the Balkans to prepare this dish in the month of Muharram and to share it with neighbours and friends. Hizmet co-opted this tradition to facilitate dialogue among different communities outside of Turkey (Dialogue Society 2011).

[29] For example, for a discussion of Hizmet's dialogue events in the UK from 1999 to 2015, see Weller 2015, 244–46. For Hizmet's dialogue events in Toronto from 2000 to 2015, see Intercultural Dialogue Institute GTA 2015.

[30] The issue of invisibility is also indirectly acknowledged by those pieces that attempt to explain or refute it. For example, see Kılıç 2012, 55; Curtis 2012, 120, 2015, 137.

the women served their guests from behind closed doors while the men of the household and Hizmet's male dialogue practitioners did the entertaining (Turam 2007, 117–19). While this arrangement was understandable for a strictly conservative Muslim group, it was far less so for those who were keen to engage in dialogue with the other. The irony was that the more dialogue events that Hizmet organised in this manner, the greater the number of challenges it received. In that sense, it was hostage to its own success.

This raised not only an issue of dissonance but also an issue of deep-rooted hypocrisy. After all, Hizmet's men could dialogue with 'outsider' women, but Hizmet's women could not dialogue with men from within or outside the movement (Turam 2007, 117–19). If Islam banned men and women from mixing, then how were Hizmet's men able to justify their interaction with non-Muslim women? If Hizmet's interpretation of the rules allowed for Hizmet's men to interact with non-Muslim women, then why did that flexibility not also apply to Hizmet's women? Why were they not permitted to mix and mingle with non-Muslim men? Thus, 'where are the women'? was one of the most repeated questions put to Hizmet's (male) participants during these dialogue events, which was eventually picked up by researchers examining the movement (Curtis 2012, 120–21, 2015, 155; Turam 2007, 118).

This question challenged both gender-based segregation in Hizmet, as it drew attention to the invisibility of Hizmet's female participants, and the role of women within Hizmet; it suggested that either women had no significant role to play or that their roles could be represented (usurped) by men *in lieu* of them in public. This challenge forced Hizmet to reflexively engage with an issue that had been, and was being, unassumingly complexified since the founding of Hizmet's first girls' school in 1990.

This dissonance, along with the questions it provoked, helped reduce Hizmet's emphasis on gender-based segregation, especially in the context of Hizmet's dialogue-based events and organisations overseas. Hizmet's female participants became increasingly visible at both its public and private functions, particularly in 'Europe and America' from '2010 onwards' (my translation) (Kılıç 2014). For example, for the first time, in 2007, the Brussels-based Intercultural Dialogue Platform appointed a woman to its board of trustees, which until then had consisted of four men. This person was also an active volunteer of the Platform's day-to-day work from 2007 to 2011 (Het Belgische Staatsblad 2008). Similarly, for the first time, in 2008, the London-based Dialogue Society appointed a woman as both a member of the board of trustees and an executive co-director of its day-to-day activities (LinkedIn

2020).³¹ By 2015, Hizmet's London-based mosque³² had appointed its first woman chief executive, 'making her one of only a handful of females in the same role across the country' (M. Smith 2016). Including women on the board of trustees and executive team led these organisations to desegregate their internal meetings and office space from this point onwards. A similar outcome ensued when Hizmet began to run coeducational schools in the United States and Western Europe beginning in the early 2000s (Steenbrink 2015, 211; Weller 2015, 242).

Thus, Hizmet became challengeable because it came forward as an Islamic actor with a dialogic message predicated on Islamic humanism that was at fundamental odds with the patriarchal interpretations of Islamic orthodoxy. In Turkey, that challenge translated into Gülen being pressed on this subject matter in the numerous interviews he gave, which will be discussed further below. Outside of Turkey, that translated into Hizmet being challenged, particularly in the West, for its patriarchal habits and reflexes that rendered its female participants invisible, as discussed above (Turam 2007, 118). Without Hizmet's dialogue practice, there would have been far less occasion and theological ground on which to press Hizmet. Being accessible and challengeable, however facilitated a recognition and gradual redress of the aforementioned dissonance (Hällzon 2008, 302).

Externalisation: Gülen on the Role of Women and Segregation

So far, we have examined how Hizmet has internalised the epistemic implications of its practice, *in practice*, which has thereby shaped its tacit knowledge on the issue under consideration. The internalisation of the epistemic implications of Hizmet's practice occurred at the pre-reflexive level of consciousness because it was gradual, unassuming, unintended, and without explicit explanation or justification by recourse to the body of Islamic knowledge or any other body of knowledge for that matter. We have also seen how conflict and dissonance caused Hizmet to reflexively engage with that which it had pre-reflexively internalised. It is at this juncture that Gülen's comments on these two issues (externalisation) comes into play.

---

[31] I was the executive director of this organisation at the time.
[32] http://www.rumimosque.org.uk

As already discussed, by launching Hizmet's dialogue in 1994, Gülen made himself and Hizmet accessible and challengeable on a range of issues from that point onwards. As discussed in Chapter 3, Gülen met ninety journalists and writers in 1995, but there is no record showing that he met any in 1993 (Mercan 2017, 135). That dramatic change of interaction with Turkey's media came about through the launch of Hizmet's dialogue practice in 1994. Gülen was challenged on the role of women in the media interviews he gave to the Turkish and foreign press from 1995 to 2004. In his first media interview, which he tellingly gave to a secular female journalist (Nuriye Akman) in 1995, he said that 'there is no problem with women leading. In fact, according to the Hanafi school of law, women can even be judges (*qadi*)' (my translation) (Gülen 1995c).

In his 2002 interview for the German daily *Frankfurter Allgemeine Zeitung* (Gülen 2012b), Gülen further elaborated his position by claiming that '[w]omen can assume different roles, including being magistrates and heads of state' (Mercan 2017, 127).[33] In his International Women's Day video message in 2017, Gülen said that there was no social, political, or legal role that women could not assume, including chief of military staff (Gülen 2017). Women could take up these positions because Gülen claimed there was no ontological inequality between men and women (Andrea 2006, 16). Rather, in his *Frankfurter Allgemeine Zeitung* interview, Gülen explained that 'a woman has no difference from a man in enjoying the rights of freedom of religion, freedom of expression, freedom to own and use property as they like, equality before the law, right to marry and establish a family, and confidentiality and immunity of their private lives' (Mercan 2017, 122).

In a 2004 interview (Gülen 2004), Gülen made the following comment on gender-based segregation: '[w]ithin the measures set forth by the religion, women and men can sit together and meet each other, as it is mostly the case', and he noted that women also visited the Prophet when '[t]hey had questions to ask'. Gülen went onto explain that 'women were praying [the prescribed prayers] with men' during the lifetime of the Prophet. While the women would stand behind men for the five daily prayers, without any barrier between them, 'everyone would participate in the supplications during a lunar or solar eclipse, or for rain.... They would be together' adding that 'women

---

[33] Mercan has translated a number of excerpts from Gülen's interviews during this period in his 2017 book. Thus, for demonstrable accuracy, I will use his translations where possible, while also referencing the original source.

and men can sit together side by side on sofas.... They can get into cars together, walk around in shopping malls, study at the same schools, and can be together while going to and from school. They can sit together when they convene for an important subject' (Mercan 2017, 125).

As is apparent, Gülen's response to questions on the role of women and gender-based segregation are diametrically opposed to what he so passionately sermonised from the 1970s and 1980s, as discussed in the first part of this chapter. Both his original and latter-day views on this issue were justified by recourse to Islam. For example, his reference to the Hanafi *madhhab* allowing women to work as judges (*qadis*) or his remarks on how men and women prayed together during the lifetime of the Prophet were provided to justify his revisionist comments during his interviews. As discussed in Chapter 2, Gülen's explicit articulation, aforementioned justification, and his (then-) recognised role as pious Islamic scholar, qualifies these practice-based revisions as religious reinterpretations (*ijtihad*).

Challenge: Pre-emptive Outcomes
This brings us to the causal link between the intervening process, as discussed so far, and Gülen's explicit articulation (externalisation) of Hizmet's emerging reinterpretation as discussed here. In the previous examples discussed in this book (the apostasy doctrine in Chapter 3 and the direct outcomes in the first half of this chapter), Gülen's articulation came at the 'end' of the intervening process. This allowed me to explain the epistemic outcome by the practice-based process that preceded it. What complicates matters in the present example is that Gülen's revisionist comments on the role (e.g., leadership) of women was first made during an interview in 1995, that is, *during* (not at the *end* of) the intervening process. This raises an important challenge: how can we attribute the substance of Gülen's response to the intervening process if that response was (pre-emptively) provided while the intervening process was still underway?

The broad point to make here is that it has been Hizmet's doings that have prodded, goaded, and guided the development of Gülen's sayings (i.e., views, teachings, positions) on women and women's rights. One practice-based revision demanded another, which in turn required a reinterpretation of the religious dictums that were said to underpin it. All of these developments began prior to Gülen's comments to the media in 1995. Thus, Gülen's comments to the media from 1995 onwards regarding the leadership of women was a logical extension of his previous revised opinions on girls attending school, women remaining at home, and Hizmet openings girls' schools from 1990 onwards (encapsulated by the first link of the intervening process). After all, if girls could attend school and university to study law, medicine, politics, and all other disciplines, why should they not be allowed to be lawyers, judges, doctors, and politicians with positions of authority over men? As a result, the substance of Gülen's said comments was in keeping with, and necessitated by, the general trajectory, if not present reality, of Hizmet's evolving practices at the time. In that sense, these comments amounted to a *pre-emptive articulation* of Hizmet's emergent reinterpretation, while still emerging.

This raises the following question: why did Gülen pre-emptively articulate a view on this but not on any of the other issues discussed so far in the present and previous chapters? The answer to this question brings us back to the intervening process. Hizmet was forced to reflexively grapple with the role of women within Hizmet in the context of running dialogue events abroad from 2000 and 2005 onwards. Gülen was forced to grapple with the same questions a decade earlier because he had adopted the practice of interfaith dialogue a decade prior (i.e., beginning in 1994) in an attempt to lead the way on this particular Hizmet practice. Thus, the same practice (dialogue) produced the same outcome (reflexivity) through the same process (challenging questions) for both Gülen and Hizmet, albeit at different points in time, for the reason just stated. This had not occurred in every other instance, in part, because Gülen had not been an early adopter of every other Hizmet practice (e.g., Gülen was late to migrate and has not run or taught in a Hizmet school). Therefore, the basis for Gülen's pre-emptive articulation on this issue reinforces (rather than undermines) the explanatory power of the intervening process in general and the dissonance-based entity of that intervening process in particular.

Finally, and as noted earlier, I am not making an exclusivist claim, which folds unless it holds in every instance. I am claiming that it holds in this instance because it provides us with the best possible explanation for the epistemic outcomes under consideration. If we remove practice, and attribute Gülen's pre-emptive articulation to context or agency, then we will fail to account not only for how and why the observed epistemic outcome historically ensued as it did but also how and why it was internalised as it was shown to be. Only with practice can we account for all of these dimensions of the knowledge production of the issues under consideration.

Conclusion

The theoretical-methodological focus on practice has allowed me to re-examine the relationship among Gülen, Hizmet, and knowledge production on issues pertaining to women and women's rights in Hizmet. This in turn has allowed me to focus on, and thereby credit, practice as opposed to the practitioner for these epistemic outcomes. The importance of this theoretical-methodological focus is vindicated by the literature that overlooks it. The discussion of the two groups of scholarly literature on Gülen and women's rights at the beginning of this chapter demonstrated the respective pitfalls of failing to appropriately contextualise Gülen's discourse within the wider framework of Hizmet's evolving practices. Here is another example, from a widely published scholar on the movement speaking to the issue of girls' education.

> A decade ago, this religious community was not even willing to allow their daughters to go to secondary or high schools. They preferred to send female students to the Qur'anic courses or the strictly female Imam Hatip schools. For years, Gülen publicly and privately encouraged the community to educate all their children regardless of gender. Today, there are many all-female schools and many of their graduates go on to universities. (H. Yavuz 1999, 125)

As I have shown, crediting Gülen for this change of practice is factually incorrect. However, the reason for Yavuz's misattribution is not simply an oversight of a historical backstory but an epistemological bias that privileges Cartesian epistemology, as discussed in Chapter 1, which in turn prioritises formal over informal, explicit over tacit forms of knowledge production, wherein the mind knows and the body enacts. This in return privileges the leader/follower paradigm wherein Gülen is the knowing, leading, and producing mind and Hizmet is the receiving, following, and implementing body. As the same author contended over a decade later, Gülen 'is always a step ahead of his community, but if necessary he would step back and wait in order to prepare the community to take a more progressive stand' (H. Yavuz 2013, 181). Thus, this epistemological bias creates an epistemological blind spot that overlooks the practice for the practitioner and requires conscious effort to overcome its resilient epistemological influence, which is what I have sought to achieve in this book.

In doing so, I have shown how the epistemic outcomes under consideration ensued through the symbiotic relationship between internalisation and externalisation. Thus, that which was externalised (Hizmet's emergent reinterpretations in the form of explicit knowledge) was rooted in, and an extension of, that which was internalised (cognitions, propositions, implications, dispositions, sensibilities, skills, and biases in the form of tacit knowledge) through practice. This combined the evolution, assimilation, legitimisation, and articulation of the emergent reinterpretation into a single process, where *knowing* arises from the *doing*-body to the reflexive mind, rather than vice versa. Overall, this means that a focus on practice allows us to account for the externalisation of Hizmet's internalised tacit knowledge through the symbiotic relationship between the two. Thus, this form of practice-based knowledge production eschews the duality problem as identified in the rapprochement literature on Islam and human rights in Chapter 1 by combining both facets of religious knowledge (formalised/experiential) as elements present in the performance of practice.

Furthermore, these direct and cumulative epistemic outcomes were *unforeseen* and *unintended*. After all, Gülen opposed girls attending school beyond the age of puberty, Hizmet founding girls' schools, and women leaving their homes to join Hizmet's workforce as teachers until the early 1990s, but that is what ensued as a result of the success of Hizmet's all-boys' schools founded from 1982 onwards. Similarly, there is no indication that Hizmet aimed to call upon its participants to remove their headscarves to attend university, to increasingly desegregate its activities and space, and to diversify the roles of its female participants (both within and outside of Hizmet), but those are the outcomes that ensued nonetheless, again, as a result of preceding practices in education, *hicret*, *bayanlar hizmeti*, and dialogue, as discussed above. Thus, in addition to being *unintended*, these outcomes were also the *organic* byproducts of Hizmet's practices (i.e., there was no external hand that deliberately intervened to bring them about in spite of the practices that shaped them).

As discussed in Chapter 2, this guards us against the twin limitations of Nonaka's model of knowledge conversion: *intentionality* (the deliberate intent to produce tacit-to-explicit knowledge conversion) and *externality* (the use of a process or tool that is external and artificial to the practice under examination to produce tacit-to-explicit knowledge conversion). That, in turn, ensures that we remain focused on examining the organically ensued epistemic consequences of social movement practice rather than the deliberately pursued epistemic products of corporate or formal entities (as discussed in organisational studies).

Case-centric process tracing stops when we have crafted a 'minimally sufficient explanation of an outcome' (Beach and Pedersen 2019, 282), which is achieved when we arrive at the conclusion that 'all the relevant facets of the outcome have adequately been accounted for and whether the evidence is best explained by the developed explanation rather than plausible alternatives' (Beach and Pedersen 2019, 286). I believe I have satisfied that criteria by demonstrating how and why Hizmet's emergent reinterpretations ensued in a manner that explains their relational conditions of internalisation and externalisation. In doing so, I have also discussed alternative explanations (e.g., appeasement, context, and agency) and challenges (e.g., pre-emptive articulation) that have reinforced and nuanced my appreciation for Hizmet's practice-based (direct and cumulative) knowledge production.

5
Conclusion

The Symbiotic Interplay between the Formalised and the Experiential

I began this book by asking whether social movement practice could produce Islamic knowledge on human rights in a manner that would allow us to call into question the assumed incompatibility between Islam and human rights. My reason for asking this question was formed both deductively and inductively. By appraising the scholarly approaches that focus on making *either* Islamic scripture or Muslim sensibility compatible with human rights together, I deductively problematised the epistemological duality that is inherent in both. In doing so, I demonstrated that a narrow focus on one or the other facet of religious knowledge impacts our ability to account for change within either. Thus, as shown in Chapter 1, the first approach fails to popularise its theoretical expositions among the faithful, whereas the second fails to account for religious legitimacy by, for example, locating itself within the inherited tradition of religious epistemology. I referred to this as the diametrical drawback of the two approaches. Hence, the motivation for exploring a single unit of analysis that can account for change within both facets of religious knowledge, by recognising the symbiotic interaction between the two.

It is at this juncture that I proposed focusing on practice as the locus of knowledge production wherein the formalised and experiential facets of religious knowledge are relationally present in the performance of practice as discussed in the latter half of Chapter 1. This allowed me to account for change in both facets of religious knowledge by avoiding a narrow focus on one or the other. As explained in the Introduction, I came to theorise about the relationship between knowledge production and practice, *in practice*, as a Hizmet participant. My research on practice, practice theories, practice-based epistemologies, practical theology, and lived religion complexified my appreciation for the epistemic dimension of practice along these lines, which suggested that *knowing* and *doing* were in fact combined in and through practice. Thus, armed with this plausible avenue for re-examining an age-old problem, I applied my *inductively theorised* notion of practice-based epistemology to my *deductively problematised* challenge of compatibility on two of the most contested issues in the context of Islam and human rights: apostasy and women's rights. I will now summarise the salient aspects of my findings, which will allow me to elucidate my original contribution to the literature on Islam and human rights.

I set out my theoretical and methodological framework in Chapters 1 and 2, respectively. I applied that theoretical-methodological framework to my examination of Hizmet's practices and its epistemic outcomes in relation to the Islamic doctrine on apostasy and women's rights in Chapters 3 and 4, respectively. I achieved that by tracing the interplay within and between Hizmet's doings and Gülen's sayings over an expansive temporospatial axis against a range of issues under consideration. I demonstrated that this form of knowledge production ensues through two basic movements: internalisation and externalisation. I used cognitive compromise and cognitive dissonance to organically link internalisation with externalisation. This allowed me to conceptualise the symbiotic relationship between the internalised-tacit and the externalised-explicit form of knowledge.

In the case of the apostasy doctrine, Hizmet's practices associated with *hicret* (migration), education, and dialogue precipitated cognitive compromise, which in turn caused Hizmet participants to relativise, moderate, and humanise their views and attitudes towards the other at the pre-reflexive level of consciousness. Externalisation occurred as and when Hizmet began to appreciate the cognitive dissonance between Islam's premodern apostasy doctrine and its dialogue practices and its efforts to achieve cognitive consonance by reinterpreting the former (i.e., apostasy doctrine) in accordance with the humanisation effect of its internalisation process that flowed from the latter (i.e., primarily, its dialogue practices).

I observed a similar pattern when tracing Hizmet in relation to women and women's rights, which included Hizmet's position and practice on girls' education, women joining Hizmet's workforce as teachers and administrators, the wearing of the headscarf, gender-based segregation, and the role of Hizmet's female participants within and beyond Hizmet. Hizmet's practices associated with education, *hicret*, dialogue, and *bayanlar hizmeti* (women's hizmet) caused Hizmet participants to internalise the value and religious permissibility of educating girls, encouraging women to join Hizmet's workforce, increasingly de-segregating the Hizmet space, and diversifying the role of women within and beyond Hizmet in the act of *doing*. Here, practice-based internalisation was aided by not just cognitive compromise but by the sensibilities to flow from upward social mobility, education, economic independence, and reexploring one's faith in foreign land. Once again, externalisation occurred as and when Hizmet began to appreciate the cognitive dissonance between its previously articulated position and practice in support of patriarchal interpretations of Islamic orthodoxy, on the one hand, and its increasingly discordant practices on the same issues going forward, on the other. This resulted in Hizmet revising the former in accordance with the internalised values, sensibilities, and tacit knowledge to accrue from its practices associated with the latter.

Thus, I found that these changes ensued *organically* and *unintentionally* (and, at times, counter-intentionally) from Hizmet's practice. For example, Gülen vehemently opposed the idea of girls attending school beyond the age of puberty, Hizmet opening girls' schools, women leaving their homes to join Hizmet's workforce, Hizmet's female participants removing their headscarves to continue their formal education, Hizmet increasingly desegregating its activities and diversifying the roles available and acceptable for its female participants, within and outside of Hizmet, respectively, until that is what ensued in and through Hizmet's practices, as shown in the intervening processes for each of these issues in Chapter 4. Similarly, there is no reason to believe that Gülen intended Hizmet's practices to precipitate its reinterpretation of the Islamic doctrine on apostasy when it began its dialogue efforts in 1994. Yet, once again, that is what accrued over a thirty-four-year period as shown in Chapter 3, demonstrating (as discussed in Chapter 1) that 'practices tend toward their own elaboration regardless of our explicit intentions' (Spinosa 2001, 210).

In the case of Hizmet, the *elaboration of those practices* had substantial implications for Hizmet's disposition and practice on matters pertaining to human rights. After all, Hizmet's revised position on apostasy and women's rights goes to the core of the human rights project, that is, the 'appreciation of the inherent dignity of each individual' (Klug 2000, 12)[1], which demands equality and non-discrimination, in all spheres of life, including religion and sex. Furthermore, Hizmet's revised provision on these two areas also pertains

---

[1] See the references to the 'dignity' and 'inherent dignity' of the human person in the UN Charter (Charter of the United Nations 1945) and the preamble to, and the articles of, the Universal Declaration of Human Rights 1948.

to more specific human rights provisions, such as the right to change religion and freedom of religion or belief in the case of the apostasy doctrine and the right to education and work, at the very least, in relation to women's rights. This reinforces the view that practice-based changes ensue at the pre-reflexive level of consciousness, which do not depend on our deliberate intent to come about.

Thus, that which was externalised (explicit knowledge) was rooted in the behaviors, sensibilities, dispositions, and skills that had been internalised (tacit knowledge) in and through practice. Furthermore, these explicit revisions were justified by recourse to Islamic sources, such as the Qur'an and Sunna, in a manner that is consistent with the criteria for formulating *ijtihads* (religious re/interpretation) as discussed at some length in Chapter 2. As a result, these revisions qualify as *ijtihads*. Therefore, this phenomenon combines production, assimilation, and legitimisation of the emergent reinterpretation into one relational process, where knowing arises from the *doing*-body to the *thinking*-mind, in and through practice, rather than vice versa. Overall, this means that a focus on practice allows us to account for the externalisation of Hizmet's internalised tacit knowledge through the interaction between the two.

Consequently, this form of practice-based Islamic knowledge production on, or as it relates to, human rights addresses the duality problem and the animating question of this study, as discussed in the Introduction and Chapter 1, by bringing together the formalised and experiential facets of religious knowledge, or *knowing* and *doing*, through a single unit of analysis, that is, social movement practice. It is in demonstrating *this*, that this book makes an original contribution to the literature on Islam and human rights. This complexifies, thickens, nuances, and enriches our understanding of how religious knowledge is re/produced, sustained, evoked, and evolved in practice. Altogether, this allows us to call into question the assumed incompatibility between Islam and human rights by drawing our attention to *practice* as the locus of socially transformative formalised Islamic knowledge production on human rights.

I compared this process to a water spring in Chapter 2, whereby water breaks the ground level (i.e., the level of reflexivity) owing to its own internally built-up pressure (i.e., the force of internalisation organically leading to a form of externalisation). I contrasted that with Nonaka's externalisation, which was more akin to a water well requiring deliberate intent and an external mechanism (i.e., the well) to draw up water (i.e., to extrapolate

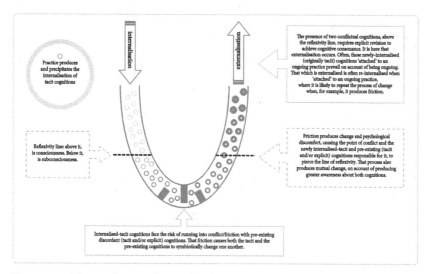

Figure 5.1 The symbiotic relationship between internalisation and externalisation

explicit knowledge from tacit knowledge). I demonstrated this (water spring-analogous) organic form of externalisation as intervening processes in Chapters 3 and 4. Having done that, with Figure 5.1, I will now lift the level of abstraction of the symbiotic relationship between internalisation and externalisation to the point of omitting all case specifics, which increases the scope for deriving generalisable insights from this research as discussed in Chapter 2.[2]

According to Figure 5.1, Hizmet's practice creates a *downward force* of internalisation, which—to use Festinger's terms—produces tacit cognitions in the form of sensibilities, dispositions, skills, habitus, culture, and mindset. This force is shown as the downward-facing arrow in Figure 5.1. If these internalised-tacit cognitions encounter no resistance (from pre-existing cognitions), then they are unlikely to produce observable change. However, internalised-tacit cognitions face the risk of running into conflict with

---

[2] There is always a risk of oversimplification when representing a social phenomenon in diagram form. Furthermore, it is often not possible to visually represent all aspects of a social phenomenon in a single diagram. For example, while this diagram is useful in demonstrating the interactive relationship between (the downward force of) internalisation and (the corresponding upward force of) externalisation, it is far less helpful in representing what happens as part of those two movements (i.e., the links of the intervening processes). For that, the intervening process-figures in Chapters 3 and 4 remain better suited.

pre-existing cognitions. Furthermore, an internalised-tacit cognition can cause a person to modify his or her pre-existing cognition(s). One of the ways that this can occur is through moderation (cognitive compromise). Modified pre-existing cognitions face the risk of running into conflict with unmodified ones. Where the resistance is greater than the downward force, it will create an equal counter-force to halt or minimise the downward pressure of internalisation from practice. However, if the practice continues, then the internalised-tacit cognitions are likely to build up pressure as they cause friction against pre-existing discordant cognitions (shown as rectangular blocks in the tube in Figure 5.1).

That friction (conflict) produces psychological discomfort, causing the point of conflict and the tacit cognitions responsible for it to pierce the line of reflexivity. This produces critical self-reflection. At times, this process of emergent realisation will be aided by an outsider's insightful questions, who has spotted another's conflictual beliefs or practices before the person in question has. Once a person becomes self-aware of this fact, they must decide if they want to hold onto their previous cognitions or revise them in accordance with those that they have internalised through practice. Often, there is a pre-reflexive bias in favor of the tacit cognition(s) that is being recursively reinforced through the practice in which it is embedded, which brought about a change of behavior on account of being actualised in the performance of practice, but the said person is yet to explicitly acknowledge this choice to themselves. Explicit revision usually requires some form of self-justification depending on the significance of the revised cognition. The externalised explicit revision is then re-internalised on account of being 'attached' to the ongoing practice(s) that produced it.

To bring this matter back to the case study. When the aforementioned process occurred in the context of Hizmet's practices, Gülen, and at times, other senior movement participants sought to justify the emergent revision. In doing so, (i) they affirmed the fact of its emergence, and (ii) they justified its revision by recourse to Islamic sources on account of the fact that the previous position was also justified by recourse to the same Islamic sources as well. This justification, in turn, converts the emergent revision into an emergent reinterpretation (*ijtihad*), and therefore, a form of explicit Islamic knowledge. This aspect of the process is shown as the upward-pointing arrow in Figure 5.1. That emergent reinterpretation is then reinternalised through the ongoing practices that produced them. Thus, this demonstrates how practice produces internalised-tacit cognition (which accounts for the change of disposition, sensibility, habitus, mindset, behavior, etc.), which in turn precipitates externalised-explicit cognition in a single process.

By tracing multiple issues in the context of numerous practices, I was able to complexify the nature of practice-based knowledge production to the point of differentiating between two types of the said process: direct and cumulative. In the case of the direct type, I found that a specific Hizmet doing influenced a correspondingly specific Gülen saying in a relatively prompt and linear manner. Hizmet's emergent reinterpretation of girls' education, Hizmet's female participants joining Hizmet's workforce as teachers, and the wearing of the headscarf during the 1997 university headscarf ban in Turkey all fall within this category. In the case of the cumulative type, I found that change did not proceed on the basis of a linear interaction; neither was it confined to the interaction between one form of practice and a corresponding set of teachings either. Instead, multiple doings and sayings collided to co-shape and co-influence one another and the epistemic outcomes under consideration in a far more cumulative, unassuming, incremental, and long *dureé* fashion. Thus, we need a far more comprehensive view to capture the ebb and flow of this form of knowledge production and the unexpected epistemic ripples it may cause elsewhere. Hizmet's emergent reinterpretation of the apostasy doctrine, gender-based segregation, and the diversified role of women within and beyond Hizmet falls within this category. I found that both forms of practice-based knowledge production produced unintended outcomes, as is the focus of my research.

This complexification is significant for a number of reasons. First, it alerts us to the fact that there can be more than one way that practice produces epistemic outcomes. This cautions us against being prescriptive when exploring the epistemic dimension of practice. Second, I was able to distil these two patterns of practice-based knowledge production by multiplying the issues and practices under consideration. A further multiplication of the issues and practices, therefore, is likely to further distil these two types of processes and/or help us to identify additional ways in which practice and knowledge interact. Third, this complexification alerts us to the dynamic, multidirectional, and multidimensional nature of practice. After all, we saw in Chapter 4 how a single practice (e.g., the opening of boys' schools) conspired with multiple practices, in different timelines, to produce different intervening processes that precipitated both direct (e.g., the opening of girls' schools) and cumulative outcomes (e.g., the increasingly desegregated Hizmet space). This suggests that practices that have since 'died' can continue to exist (in 'spirit') in terms of the continued effects they have through the practices that follow them. The 'spirit' of Hizmet's boys-only schools' practice appears to have lingered for a long time even after that practice was replaced with another.

Overall, the significance of this finding is further reinforced by the fact that this form of knowledge production was shown to ensue in relation to substantial explicit premodern Islamic dictums, doctrines, injunctions, and traditions with significant symbolic meaning (e.g., the headscarf). After all, the traditional Islamic position on apostasy from Islam, the headscarf, and the role and rights of women within society was broadly established by the juristic consensus (*ijma*) of the *madhhab*-founding premodern jurists, who in turn, anchored their views in the Qur'an and Sunna. Furthermore, pious Turkish Muslim men and women have been reproducing Islam's patriarchal teachings in modern society through their everyday lives. Thus, Hizmet's emergent reinterpretations were, for the most part, not just rhetorical but also practical. In other words, they had real-life implications for those involved. Nonetheless, I have shown how practice can produce change even on these robust Islamic teachings, which alerts us to the possibility of its ability to do so in relation to equally substantial Islamic doctrines in the context of other practices and issues as well.

Furthermore, while my main focus and contribution have been to the literature on Islam and human rights, my analyses and findings also relate and contribute to other scholarly discussions, fields, and disciplines. For example, in Chapter 1, I noted that 'thus far relatively few attempts have been made to theorize informal learning and knowledge production through involvement in social action' (Choudry 2009, 8). I echoed the view that this was rooted in how *movement practice* and *knowledge production* was conceptualised. Movement practice focuses on whether movements have met their stated objectives as vehicles for social and political change (Kelley 2002, IX), and knowledge production focuses on the original, single, and conventional authorship of scholars (Choudry and Kapoor 2010, 2). I also demonstrated that the social movement literature on knowledge production was dominated by a focus on adult education and movement intellectuals (akin to conventional forms of knowledge production), social learning (rather than knowledge production), and organisational knowledge (which, by and large, limits the substance of knowledge to organisational issues). Thus, in looking at social movement knowledge production, my research not only examines an understudied aspect of social movement studies but does so in a manner that contrasts with how knowledge production is often conceptualised in the context of social movement literature as well.

Second, this book contributes to the literature on Hizmet by reversing (or flattening) the leader/follower, producer/consumer, originator/disseminator, and mind/body paradigm that pervades the literature as shown in Chapter 1. Both 'critical' and 'sympathetic' scholars are joined in a Cartesian bias towards Hizmet's knowledge production, wherein Gülen is conceptualised as the *producing*-mind and Hizmet as the *disseminating*-body. This bias blinds us to the epistemic nature, role, and function of social movement practice, including the role of Gülen's practice which is integral to that of Hizmet's collective practice. That, in turn, causes us to conflate the dynamics that produce Hizmet's unintended emergent epistemic outcomes (i.e., Hizmet's practices) with the person who often verbalises it as indeed emerged (i.e., Gülen). This is an example of the *post hoc ergo propter hoc* fallacy, that is, the assumption that A causes B on account of B following A.[3] I have shown not only how this explanation is historically inaccurate but also how it fails to explain Hizmet's success in internalising, legitimising, and externalising its epistemic outcomes in the process of producing it.

This brings me to the limitations of my book and the potential avenues for further research. The first limitation relates to the issues and practices that have not been traced in this book. Deciding which issues and practices to include results in determining which issues and practices to exclude. My analyses, claims, and conclusions relate to the issues and practices discussed in this book. This, however, does not absolve Hizmet from performing other forms of practices that produce other types of (epistemic) outcomes in relation to human rights on issues not traced in this book. This also explains why I have maintained a qualified claim that stands by my findings in relation to the issues discussed in Chapters 3 and 4 rather than put forward a more general claim in relation to Hizmet's practices *in toto*. Subsequent research may want to explore how Hizmet's other practices fare in relation to other types of human rights issues that are not traced herein.

Conversely, the second limitation of my research relates to the issues and practices traced in this book. I explained the systematic basis by which I determined the issues and practices for this book in the Introduction. Simply

---

[3] I guarded against this fallacy by maintaining a methodical focus on how and why the entities of the intervening processes were causally linked to one another, which I tested against challenges and alternative explanations.

put, the discussion on Islam and human rights determined my two issues of concern: apostasy and women's rights. That, coupled with Nicolini's zooming in and out movements allowed me to determine those practices that appeared to have a causal connection with the issues under consideration. I narrowed the list of practices down in accordance with the methodological framework set out in Chapter 2. Accordingly, case-centric process tracing stops when we have crafted a *'minimally sufficient explanation* of an outcome' (my emphasis) (Beach and Pedersen 2019, 282), which is achieved when we arrive at the conclusion that 'all the relevant facets of the outcome have adequately been accounted for and whether the evidence is best explained by the developed explanation rather than plausible alternatives' (Beach and Pedersen 2019, 286). A focus on crafting a 'minimally sufficient explanation' (i.e., including those practices that were irreplaceable in the intervening process as opposed to those that were not; Beach and Pedersen 2013, 30–31) meant eliminating practices with tangential effect. As a result, my intervening processes in Chapters 3 and 4 focus on accounting for those entities (i.e., practices and events) that were critical to the outcomes under consideration for the issues of concern. They do not, for example, include practices that impinged upon the outcome in a non-critical manner by, for example, delaying it. Here, I am thinking of Hizmet's informal opaque decision-making processes in relation to Hizmet's informal activities, such as *bölgecilik* (i.e., grass roots religious activism).

Hizmet's *bölgeciler* (informal community organisers) discuss Hizmet's *bölgecilik* activities for men and women at private male-dominated meetings, which is then communicated to *bayanlar hizmeti* (i.e., Hizmet's women's activities run by and for women, as discussed in Chapter 4). In some places, a female representative of *bayanlar hizmeti* will be present at these meetings, but she will be vastly outnumbered by the men. The fact that these meetings are informal, private, and male-dominated has implications for women's access and representation, which in turn places Hizmet's female participants at a disadvantage in relation to those activities as well as Hizmet's ability to produce female leaders in relation to Hizmet's mixed grass roots activities and areas of practice.

This suggests that two or more Hizmet practices can be in competition or friction with one another (as shown in Figure 5.2), where one delays (or, theoretically, stalls or even reverses) the other. While this form of competition/friction does not appear to have altered the outcomes under consideration in this book, it is likely to have delayed them in relation to women's roles

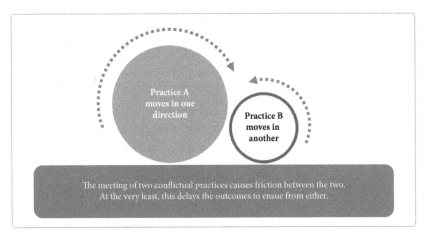

Figure 5.2 When two competing practices meet

within Hizmet. Subsequent research may further complexify my findings by introducing an additional level of analysis that includes those practices that produce latent resistance in the manner described.

This brings us to the third limitation of my research: the cross-case generalisability of my findings. This aspect of my research raises the following type of questions: are my findings generalizable to other (Islamic) social movements? If so, what are its conditions of generalisation? Furthermore, are my findings restricted to social movement practice, or can they ensue in relation to other forms of social practice or even personal practice?

The question of generalizability requires cross-case comparison, which I did not undertake for the reasons I explained in Chapter 2. One of those reasons was that comparative case studies are useful in isolating the conditions of generalisation, after the basic phenomenon, process, or event has been sufficiently explained or has been taken as granted; that was not the case here. Furthermore, establishing that basic phenomenon required in-depth research, analysis, and articulation of Hizmet's numerous practices against multiple issues across an expansive temporospatial axis spanning fifty years. That meant focusing on a single case in the present study, which can now be expanded through cross-case comparison in subsequent research. That would mean exploring whether or not the same or similar phenomenon occur, and under what conditions, with other (Islamic) social movements. That comparison can then be extended to other social groups and actors as well.

I noted in Chapter 2 that the general assumption in process tracing methodology was that case-centric process tracing was unlikely to produce cross-case generalisable insight because it often included case-specific entities (e.g., unique events, developments, or interventions) within its causal mechanism (or intervening process in my case) (Beach and Pedersen 2019, 283–84). However, I also countered that notion in Chapter 2 by reference to the patterned nature of practice (Pouliot 2015, 238), which lends itself to generalisable insights. Furthermore, I have not had to rely on case-specific entities as noted above when unpacking the intervening processes in the two preceding chapters. Instead, I found that the best possible explanations for the outcomes under consideration were rooted in the practices that contextualised them. I demonstrated this by focusing on how and why the activity-producing entities (i.e., the practices) were linked to one another in the intervening processes in Chapters 3 and 4, which involved the use of theoretical explanations (e.g., tacit/explicit knowledge, internalisation/externalisation, cognitive compromise, cognitive dissonance) to probe and elucidate the causal links and connections further. As discussed in Chapter 2, use of theoretical explanations allows us to make the intervening process 'more abstract by dropping details' from it (Beach and Pedersen 2019, 73). Therefore, the intervening processes of Chapters 3 and 4 raised the 'level of abstraction' by reducing their reliance on case specifics through the use of theoretical explanations (Beach and Pedersen 2019, 74). Figure 5.1 raises the level of abstraction even further by dropping all case-related details to show the interactive relationship between the internalised-tacit and the externalised-explicit forms of knowledge in practice-based knowledge production, as explored in this book.

My ability to raise the level of abstraction of the intervening processes has two implications for the generalisability of my findings. First, it demonstrates the *possibility* of generalisability. After all, these theoretical explanations are not unique to Hizmet. Second, it makes cross-case comparisons *easier* to achieve. For example, subsequent research can now focus on asking whether or not, and under what conditions, the practices of other (Islamic) social movements produce the two basic movements found in my research: the relational link between internalisation and externalisation in the context of knowledge production. Follow-up questions would include, whether or not, and under what conditions, the relational link between internalisation and externalisation involves the types of processes described in this book, such as cognitive compromise and cognitive dissonance. Are there other processes that have the same, similar, or different effect? What tacit knowledge does the movement's practice produce? What effect does this have? What happens when that tacit knowledge comes into conflict with the movement's pre-existing explicit knowledge? Do these processes lead to a change of tacit and/or explicit knowledge? Does that change of knowledge indicate a change of behavior and practice? In which direction does this change appear to be moving?

The key here is to apply a theoretical-methodological framework, such as the one described in the present study, which is attuned to the processual, provisional, relational, social, and interactive nature of practice, as discussed in Chapter 1. A theoretical-methodological framework that is attuned to the nature of the practice in the manner just described, will ensure that was is being traced in subsequent research is in fact a practice-based epistemic outcome, rather than something else. Furthermore, the aim should not be to pursue exact conformity (after all, even Hizmet's practices differed in their production of knowledge, which is described as 'direct' and 'cumulative' in Chapter 4), as this conformity would contravene the provisional nature of practice. Rather, the focus should be on exploring the epistemic dimensions of social movement practice and showing how it fares in relation to what I have set out in this book.

My work also brings to mind at least three areas of further research, independent of any limitations of my study. The first area relates to other forms of compatibility, notably, social movement practice and the compatibility of Islam, on the one hand, and democracy, secularism, freedom of speech, good governance, public accountability, and pluralism, on the other. Furthermore, it would be useful to consider flipping the analytical focus of this research onto practices that produce human rights knowledge (e.g., responses, reactions, assumptions, analyses, case law, reports) on, or in relation to, Islam as well. Flipping the analytical focus in that manner would involve determining which issues and practices to examine. One area of consideration could be those issues pertaining to religious manifestation in the public domain, that is, the contentious issues in relation to Muslim religious manifestation in Europe, such as, but certainly not limited to, wearing the headscarf in schools, wearing the face veil in public, and building mosques with minarets. Deciding the issues would determine the relevant practices to be pursued and reconstructed.

A second area of further research relates to the epistemic context in which practice-based knowledge production is explored. While

I theorised about this process in the context of the compatibility challenge vis-à-vis Islam and human rights, we do not need to be limited by considerations of compatibility alone. My theoretical-methodological framework could be used to explore the role of practice-based knowledge production in other contexts as well, such as extremism and counter-extremism. Today, a plethora of policies have been proposed around the world to counter the spread of violent extremist ideology claiming an Islamic justification (Kundnani and Hayes 2018, 2). Policy has tended to shift from supporting projects that directly engage with theological issues to those that do not (House of Commons 2010, 3; Home Office 2011, 2). Practice-based knowledge production could explicate how seemingly unrelated social practices are able to produce unintended epistemic outcomes that impinge upon the processes that relate to radicalisation and efforts to tackle it (Keles 2009).

A third area of research, as suggested by the present book, centers on exploring the ontological and epistemological affinity between Islam and practice theories. In Chapter 2, I discussed tacit and explicit knowledge from an Islamic (i.e., *emic*) point of view. I did so to demonstrate that an *emic* perspective did not allow us to theorise the process by which practice-based tacit knowledge externalised into explicit knowledge. This approach allowed me to justify the *etic* perspective of this study (i.e., a perspective from outside the Islamic framework) as a means of understanding how Islamic knowledge is produced in practice. In Chapter 2, I also looked at the role of practice in Islamic theology (i.e., the connection among practice, knowledge, and religious belief); epistemology (i.e., the nature of knowledge in Islam and its connection to practice); mysticism (i.e., the connection between practice and esoteric heart knowledge); and law/*fiqh* (i.e., practice and the characteristics of a *mujtahid*).

There are other areas of interesting overlap that I did not discuss because they were not within the parameters of my present focus. Subsequent research could explore these areas. For example, we encounter one of these areas in the classical Islamic theological discussions on creation and causality (Turner 2013, 95). According to the Sunni schools of *Ash'ari* theology, all creation is sustained, and all effects are brought about by God's continuous act of re-creation at all times (Turner 2013, 95–131; Esposito 1998, 73). This act is called *Sunnatullah*, that is, God's creative practice or divine behavior (Qur'an 17:77, 35:43).[4] In other words, it is God who rotates the planets around the

---

[4] This is also referred to as 'occasionalism' or 'Islamic occasionalism'. See Fakhry 2008.

sun (not the gravitational force of mass) as he continuously re-creates the planets and the sun while so doing. Similarly, it is God who moves my hands (in accordance with my will) as I type these words onto my keyboard, as he continuously re-creates me while doing. As a result, all human action, including human practice, is actualised by divine practice. According to this theological perspective, God is the ultimate practitioner of all practice that keeps everything afloat and connected at all time. This provides a practice-based ontology, which considers social and organisational phenomena to occur within and as a result of practice (Nicolini 2013, 13) with a theocentric underpinning, wherein all creation, not just social and organisational phenomena, persists through (divine) practice. According to this view, there is only practice. In some ways, to encounter the creating, ordering, and sustaining role of social practice in everyday life is in fact to encounter the hand of God.

Thus, in seeking to locate a single unit of analysis to explain stability and change in relation to the various facets of religious knowledge, we have, in fact, stumbled upon the foremost Islamic tenet of belief: *Tawheed*, the Unity of God or the point of singularity from which all originates and to which all inevitably returns. As a Muslim researcher, it therefore seems befitting to square the circle of this book by ending with reference to that beginning.

Bibliography

Abou El Fadl, Khaled. 2001. *Speaking in God's Name: Islamic Law, Authority and Women*. Oxford: Oneworld Publications.
Abou El Fadl, Khaled. 2004. *Islam and the Challenge of Democracy: A Boston Review Book*. Princeton, NJ: Princeton University Press.
Abou El Fadl, Khaled. 2007. *The Great Theft: Wrestling Islam from the Extremists*. New York: HarperOne.
Abou El Fadl, Khaled. 2009. "The Human Rights Commitment in Modern Islam." In *Wanted: Equality and Justice in the Muslim Family*, edited by Zainah Anwar, 113-78. Petaling Jaya: Musawah.
Acar, Ismail. 2011. "A Classical Scholar with a Modern Outlook: Fethullah Gülen and His Legal Thought." In *Mastering Knowledge in Modern Times: Fethullah Gülen as an Islamic Scholar*, edited by Ismail Albayrak, 65-84. Izmir: Blue Dome Press.
Afsaruddin, Asma. 2007. *The First Muslims: History and Memory*. Oxford: Oneworld Publications.
Agai, Bekim. 2002. "Fethullah Gülen and His Movement's Islamic Ethic of Education." *Critique: Critical Middle Eastern Studies* 11 (1): 27-47.
Agai, Bekim. 2003. "The Gülen Movement's Islamic Ethic of Education." In *Turkish Islam and the Secular State: The Gülen Movement*, edited by M. Hakan Yavuz and John L. Esposito, 48-68. New York: Syracuse University Press.
Ahmed, Leila. 1992. *Women and Gender in Islam: Historical Roots of a Modern Debate*. New Haven, CT: Yale University Press.
Akbarzadeh, Shahram, and Benjamin MacQueen. 2008a. "Framing the Debate on Islam and Human Rights." In *Islam and Human Rights in Practice: Perspectives across the Ummah*, edited by Akbarzadeh Shahram and MacQueen Benjamin, 1-11. New York: Routledge.
Akbarzadeh, Shahram, and Benjamin MacQueen, eds. 2008b. *Islam and Human Rights in Practice: Perspectives across the Ummah*. New York: Routledge.
Aksiyon. 2001. "İyi Bilirdik." September 1, 2001. https://tr.wikipedia.org/wiki/Aksiyon_(dergi)#/media/Dosya:Aksiyon_1_Eylül_2001.jpg. Accessed: 08/01/2021.
Aksoy, Murat. 2005. *Başörtüsü-Türban: Batılılaşma-Modernleşme, Laiklik ve Örtünme*. Istanbul: Kitap Yayinevi.
Albayrak, Ismail, ed. 2011. *Mastering Knowledge in Modern Times: Fethullah Gülen as an Islamic Scholar*. Izmir: Blue Dome Press.
Ali, Kecia. 2006. *Sexual Ethics and Islam: Feminist Reflections on Qur'an, Hadith and Jurisprudence*. London: Oneworld Publications.
Ali, Wajahat, Eli Clifton, Matthew Duss, Lee Fang, Scott Keyes, and Faiz Shakir. 2011. "Fear, Inc. The Roots of the Islamophobia Network in America." Washington, DC: Center for American Progress.
al-Sijistani, Abu Dawud Sulaiman bin Ash'ath. 2008. *English Translation of Sunan Abu Dawud*, Volume 4. Riyadh: Darussalam.

Ammerman, Nancy T. 2016. "Lived Religion as an Emerging Field: An Assessment of Its Contours and Frontiers." *Nordic Journal of Religion and Society* 29 (2): 83–99.

Ammerman, Nancy T, ed. 2007. *Everyday Religion: Observing Modern Religious Lives*. New York: Oxford University Press.

Amnesty International. 2019. "Turkey 2019." https://www.amnesty.org/en/countries/eur ope-and-central-asia/turkey/report-turkey. Accessed: 12/10/2020.

Andrea, Bernadette. 2006. "Women and Their Rights: Fethullah Gülen's Gloss on Lady Mary Wortley Montagu and Her Eighteenth-Century 'Embassy' to the Ottoman Empire." In *Islam in Contemporary World II: The Fethullah Gülen Movement in Thought and Practice, Conference Proceedings*, edited by Robert Hunt and Yüksel A Aslandoğan, 161–82. Houston, TX: The Light.

An-Na'im, Abdullahi A. 1992. *Human Rights in Cross-Cultural Perspectives: A Quest for Consensus*. Edited by Abdullahi A. An-Na'im. Philadelphia: University of Pennsylvania Press.

An-Na'im, Abdullahi A. 1995. "Toward an Islamic Hermeneutics for Human Rights." In *Human Rights and Religious Values: An Uneasy Relationship?*, edited by Abdullahi A. An-Na'im, Jerald D Gort, Henry Jansen, and Hendrik M Vroom, 229–42. Grand Rapids, MI: William B Eerdmans Publishing Co.

An-Na'im, Abdullahi A. 1996. *Toward an Islamic Reformation: Civil Liberties, Human Rights, and International Law*. New York: Syracuse University Press.

An-Na'im, Abdullahi A., and Louis Henkin. 2015. "Islam and Human Rights: Beyond the Universality Debate." *Proceedings of the Annual Meeting (American Society of International Law)* 94: 101–3.

Anthony, Andrew. 2015. "Losing Their Religion: The Hidden Crisis of Faith among Britain's Young Muslims." *The Guardian*, May 17, 2015. https://www.theguardian.com/global/2015/may/17/losing-their-religion-british-ex-muslims-non-believers-hidden-crisis-faith. Accessed: 03/06/2020.

Arat, Yeşim. 2010. "Religion, Politics and Gender Equality in Turkey: Implications of a Democratic Paradox?" *Third World Quarterly* 31 (6): 869–84.

Arik, Hulya. 2012. "Speaking of Women? Exploring Violence against Women through Political Discourses: A Case Study of Headscarf Debates in Turkey." *e-cadernos CES*, no. 16.

Asch, Solomon E. 1951. "Effects of Group Pressure upon the Modification and Distortion of Judgments." In *Groups, Leadership and Men: Research in Human Relations*, edited by Harold Guetzkow, 177–190, Pittsburgh: Carnegie Press.

Asch, Solomon E. 1955. "Opinions and Social Pressure." *Scientific American* 193 (5): 31–35.

Ashdown, Nick. 2018a. "Calls for Change Unlikely to Be Heard inside Turkey's Gülen Movement." *Ahval*, February 22, 2018. https://ahvalnews.com/turkey/calls-change-unlikely-be-heard-inside-turkeys-gulen-movement-0. Accessed: 08/09/2020.

Ashdown, Nick. 2018b. "Loathed, Hunted Down, Gülen Movement Finished in Turkey." *Ahval*, February 28, 2018. https://ahvalnews.com/turkey/loathed-hunted-down-gulen-movement-finished-turkey. Accessed: 08/09/2020.

Ashour, Omar. 2017. "Lions Tamed? An Inquiry into the Causes of De-Radicalization of Armed Islamist Movements: The Case of the Egyptian Islamic Group." *The Middle East Journal* 61 (4): 596–625.

Aslan, Ömer. 2016. "'Unarmed' We Intervene, Unnoticed We Remain: The Deviant Case of 'February 28th Coup' in Turkey." *British Journal of Middle Eastern Studies* 43 (3): 360–77.

Atay, Rifat. 2007. "Reviving the Suffa Tradition." In *Muslim World in Transition: Contributions of the Gülen Movement*, edited by Ihsan Yilmaz, Eileen Barker, Henri J. Barky et al., 459–72. London: Leeds Metropolitan University Press.

Austin, David. 2009. "Education and Liberation." *McGill Journal of Education* 44 (1): 107–18.

Awan, Imran, and Irene Zempi. 2017. "Impacts of Anti-Muslim Hate Crime." In *Islamophobia Still a Challenge for Us All*, edited by Farah Elahi and Omar Khan, 37–39. London: Runnymede.

Aydın, Gülden. 2016. "Cemaat'teki Kozmik Kadınların Görevi Neydi?" *Hürriyet*, August 18, 2016.https://www.hurriyet.com.tr/gundem/cemaatteki-kozmik-kadinlarin-gorevi-neydi-40192315. Accessed: 07/06/2020.

Baderin, Mashood A. 2003. *International Human Rights and Islamic Law*. New York: Oxford University Press.

Badruzzaman, Aeshna, Matthew Cohen, and Sidita Kushi. 2017. "Contending Images in Turkey's Headscarf Debate: Framings of Equality, Nationalism, and Religion." *Mediterranean Quarterly* 28 (3): 27–55.

Bakar, Osman. 2005. "Gülen on Religion and Science: A Theological Perspective." *The Muslim World* 95: 359–72.

Balcı, Bayram. 2003. "Fethullah Gulen's Missionary Schools in Central Asia and Their Role in the Spreading of Turkism and Islam." *Religion, State and Society* 31 (2): 151–77.

Balsiger, Philip, and Alexandre Lambelet. 2014. "Participant Observation." In *Methodological Practices in Social Movement Research*, edited by Donatella Della Porta, 144–72. Oxford: Oxford University Press.

Barlas, Asma. 2002. *"Believing Women" in Islam: Unreading Patriarchal Interpretations of the Qur'an*. Austin: University of Texas Press.

Barton, Greg. 2005. "Progressive Islamic Thought, Civil Society and the Gülen Movement in the National Context: Parallels with Indonesia." Paper presented at *Islam in the Contemporary World: The Fethullah Gülen Movement in Thought and Practice*. Rice University, Houston, Texas. November 12–13, 2005.

Başarı, Mustafa. 2019. "Memoir Draft Notes," Berlin, May 11, 2019.

Baxi, Upendra. 2002. *The Future of Human Rights*. New Delhi: Oxford University Press.

Bayat, Asef. 2007. *Making Islam Democratic: Social Movements and the Post-Islamist Turn*. Stanford, CA: Stanford University Press.

Beach, Derek, and Rasmus B. Pedersen. 2013. *Process-Tracing Methods: Foundations and Guidelines*. Grand Rapids: University of Michigan Press.

Beach, Derek, and Rasmus Brun Pedersen. 2019. *Process-Tracing Methods: Foundations and Guidelines*. Grand Rapdis: University of Michigan Press.

Beitz, Charles R. 2009. *The Idea of Human Rights*. Oxford: Oxford University Press.

Bell-Townsend, Erica. 2007. "Identities Matter: Identity Politics, Coalition Possibilities, and Feminist Organizing." Doctoral thesis. Washington University, St. Louis, Missouri.

Benard, Cheryl. 2003. "Civil Democratic Islam: Partners, Resources and Strategies." Santa Monica, CA: RAND.

Benard, Cheryl, and Lowell H Schwartz. 2007. "Building Moderate Muslim Networks." Santa Monica, CA: RAND.

Bennett, Andrew, and Jeffrey T. Checkel, eds. 2015. *Process Tracing: From Metaphor to Analytic Tool*. Cambridge: Cambridge University Press.

Berger, Peter, and Anton Zijderveld. 2010. *In Praise of Doubt: How to Have Convictions Without Becoming a Fanatic*. New York: HarperOne.

Beşer, Faruk. 2006. *Fethullah Gülen Hocaefendi'nin Fıkhını Anlamak*. Istanbul: Ufuk Kitap.

Bevington, Douglas, and Chris Dixon. 2005. "Movement-Relevant Theory: Rethinking Social Movement Scholarship and Activism." *Social Movement Studies* 4 (3): 185–208.
Bielefeldt, Heiner. 1995. "Muslim Voices in the Human Rights Debate." *Human Rights Quarterly* 17: 587–617.
Bielefeldt, Heiner. 2000. "'Western' versus 'Islamic' Human Rights Conceptions?: A Critique of Cultural Essentialism in the Discussion on Human Rights." *Political Theory* 28 (1): 90–121.
Biesterfeldt, Hinrich, Sebastian Günther, and Wadad Kadi, eds. 2016. *Accusations of Unbelief in Islam: A Diachronic Perspective on Takfir*. Leiden: Brill.
Bilici, Mucahit. 2006. "The Fethullah Gülen Movement and Its Politics of Representation in Turkey." *The Muslim World* 96: 1–20.
Bosi, Lorenzo, Marco Giugni, and Katrin Uba. 2016. "The Consequences of Social Movements: Taking Stock and Looking Forward." In *The Consequences of Social Movements*, edited by Lorenzo Bosi, Marco Giugni, and Katrin Uba, 3–37. Cambridge: Cambridge University Press.
Bourdieu, Pierre. 1977. *Outline of a Theory of Practice*. Cambridge: Cambridge University Press.
Bourdieu, Pierre. 1984. *Distinction: A Social Critique of the Judgement of Taste*. Cambridge, MA: Harvard University Press.
Bourdieu, Pierre. 1990. *The Logic of Practice*. Stanford, CA: Stanford University Press.
Bourdieu, Pierre, and Loic J. D. Wacquant. 1992. *An Invitation to Reflexive Sociology*. Cambridge: Polity Press.
Bowcott, Owen. 2019. "Turkey Seeks Extradition of UK Barrister over Twitter Activity." *The Guardian*, May 20, 2019. https://www.theguardian.com/law/2019/may/20/british-barrister-facing-extradition-to-turkey-over-tweets. Accessed: 07/09/2020.
Bowen, John R. 1993. *Muslims through Discourse: Religion and Ritual in Gayo Society*. Princeton, NJ: Princeton University Press.
Bowen, John R. 2007. *Why the French Don't Like Headscarves: Islam, the State, and Public Space*. Princeton, NJ: Princeton University Press.
Bratianu, Constantin. 2010. "A Critical Analysis of Nonaka's Model of Knowledge Dynamics." *Electronic Journal of Knowledge Management* 8 (2): 193–200.
Bratianu, Constantin. 2013. "The Triple Helix of the Organizational Knowledge Constantin." *Management Dynamics in the Knowledge Economy* 1 (2): 207–20.
Brems, Eva. 2004. "Reconciling Universality and Diversity in International Human Rights: A Theoretical and Methodological Framework and Its Application in the Context of Islam." *Human Rights Review* 5: 5–21.
Bruckmayr, Philipp. 2008. "Fethullah Gülen and Islamic Literary Tradition." In *Islam in the Age of Global Challenges: Alternative Perspectives of the Gülen Movement*, edited by Akbar Ahmad, John Borreli, Jill B. Carrol et al., 164–203. Georgetown University, Washington, DC, November 14–15, 2008.
Bruinessen, Martin Van. 2011. "Producing Islamic Knowledge in Western Europe: Disciplines, Authority and Personal Quest." In *Producing Islamic Knowledge: Transmission and Dissemination in Western Europe*, edited by Martin Van Bruinessen and Stefano Allievi, 1–21. Oxon, UK: Routledge.
Bruinessen, Martin Van, and Stefano Allievi, eds. 2011. *Producing Islamic Knowledge: Transmission and Dissemination in Western Europe*. Oxon, UK: Routledge.
Bulut, Şükrü. 2020. "Hayatımızı Risale-i Nur'a Vakfetme Meselesi." *Euro Nur*, February 18, 2020. http://www.saidnursi.de/hayatimizi-risale-i-nura-vakfetme-meselesi. Accessed: 27/07/2020.

Cagaptay, Soner. 2006. *Islam, Secularism and Nationalism in Modern Turkey: Who Is a Turk?* London: Routledge.
Can, Eyüp. 1996. *Fethullah Gülen Hocaefendi Ile Ufuk Turu.* 7th ed. Istanbul: AD Yayıncılık.
Çapan, Ergün. 2011. "Gülen's Teaching Methodology in His Private Circle." In *Mastering Knowledge in Modern Times: Fethullah Gülen as an Islamic Scholar*, edited by Ismail Albayrak, 127–56. Izmir: Blue Dome Press.
Capes, David. 2007. "Tolerance in the Theology and Thought of A. J. Conyers and F Gülen." In *Muslim World in Transition: Contributions of the Gülen Movement*, edited by Ihsan Yilmaz, Eileen Barker, Henri J. Barky et al., 428–29. London: Leeds Metropolitan University Press.
CDE News. 2020. "Orthodox Christians—300 Million Worldwide." April 19, 2020. https://cde.news/orthodox-christians-300-million-worldwide-today-are-observing-easter-their-biggest-holiday. Accessed: 03/01/2021.
Çelik, Emrah. 2012. *Renewal (Tajdid) in Islamic Thought: With Special Reference to Al-Ghazali and Abduh.* Saarbrucken, Germany: LAP LAMBERT Academic Publishing.
Çelik, Gürkan, Johan Leman, and Karel Steenbrink, eds. 2015. *Gülen-Inspired Hizmet in Europe: The Western Journey of a Turkish Muslim Movement.* Brussels: P.I.E. Peter Lang.
Certeau, Michel de. 1988. *The Practice of Everyday Life.* Berkeley, CA: University of California Press.
Césari, Jocelyne, Alexandre Caeiro, and Dilwar Hussain. 2004. "Islam and Fundamental Rights in Europe: Final Report." October 2004. Brussels: European Commission–DG Justice and Home Affairs.
Çetin, Muhammed. 2010. *The Gülen Movement: Civic Service without Borders.* New York: Blue Dome Press.
Charter of the United Nations and Statute of the International Court of Justice. 1945. San Francisco. https://treaties.un.org/doc/Publication/CTC/uncharter-all-lang.pdf. Accessed: 03/04/2018.
Chavez, Christina. 2008. "Conceptualizing from the Inside: Advantages, Complications, and Demands on Insider Positionality." *The Qualitative Report* 13 (3): 474–94.
Cherti, Myriam. 2010. "The Politics of Muslim Visibility in Europe: The Case of the Swiss Minaret Ban." *Public Policy Research* 17 (3): 157–61.
Choo, Chun Wei. 2006. *The Knowing Organization: How Organizations Use Information to Construct Meaning, Create Knowledge, and Make Decisions.* 2nd ed. New York: Oxford University Press.
Choudry, Aziz. 2009. "Editorial: Learning in Social Action: Knowledge Production in Social Movements." *McGill Journal of Education* 44 (1): 5–17.
Choudry, Aziz. 2010. "Global Justice? Contesting NGOization: Knowledge Politics and Containment in Antiglobalization Networks." In *Learning from the Ground Up: Global Perspectives on Social Movements and Knowledge Production*, edited by Aziz Choudry and Dip Kapoor, 17–34. New York: Palgrave Macmillan.
Choudry, Aziz, and Dip Kapoor. 2010. "Learning from the Ground Up: Global Perspectives on Social Movements and Knowledge Production." In *Learning from the Ground Up: Global Perspectives on Social Movements and Knowledge Production*, edited by Aziz Choudry and Dip Kapoor, 1–13. New York: Palgrave Macmillan.
Cıngıllıoğlu, Salih. 2017. *The Gülen Movement: Transformative Social Change.* New York: Palgrave Macmillan.
Clement, Victoria. 2011. "Faith-Based Schools in Post-Soviet Turkmenistan." *European Education* 43 (1): 76–92.

Çobanoğlu, Yavuz. 2012. "Asena'si Eksik Bir Hareket: Gülen Cemaati." *Birikim*, October 2012, 77–86.

Collier, David. 2011. "Understanding Process Tracing." *Political Science and Politics* 44 (4): 823–30.

Collins, Harry. 2001. "What Is Tacit Knowledge?" In *The Practice Turn in Contemporary Theory*, edited by Theodore R. Schatzki, Karin Knorr Cetina, and Eike von Savigny, 115–28. London: Routledge.

Companies Database. 2018. "Centre for Intercultural Dialogue Studies." August 15, 2018. https://www.companiesdb.org/company-centre-for-intercultural-dialogue-studies.html. Accessed: 21/08/2020.

Connell, Raewyn. 2007. *Southern Theory: The Global Dynamics of Knowledge in Social Science*. Cambridge: Polity Press.

Conway, Trudy D. 2014. *Cross-Cultural Dialogue on the Virtues: The Contribution of Fethullah Gülen*. New York: Springer.

Cook, S., D. Noam, and Hendrik Wagenaar. 2012. "Navigating the Eternally Unfolding Present: Toward an Epistemology of Practice." *The American Review of Public Administration* 42 (1): 3–38.

Cooper, Joel. 2007. *Cognitive Dissonance: Fifty Years of a Classic Theory*. Thousand Oaks, CA: SAGE.

Corradi, Gessica, Silvia Gherardi, and Luca Verzelloni. 2010. "Through the Practice Lens: Where Is the Bandwagon of Practice-Based Studies Heading?" *Management Learning* 41 (3): 265–83.

Cottee, Simon. 2015. *The Apostates: When Muslims Leave Islam*. London: Hurst.

Cox, Laurence, and Cristina Flesher Fominaya. 2009. "Movement Knowledge: What Do We Know, How Do We Create Knowledge and What Do We Do with It?" *Interface* 1 (1): 1–20.

Crossley, Nick. 1999a. "Fish, Field, Habitus and Madness: The First Wave Mental Health Users Movement in Great Britain." *British Journal of Sociology* 50 (4): 647–70.

Crossley, Nick. 1999b. "Working Utopias and Social Movements: An Investigation Using Case Study Materials from Radical Mental Health Movements in Britain." *Sociology* 33 (4): 809–30.

Crossley, Nick. 2001. *The Social Body: Habit, Identity and Desire*. London: SAGE.

Crossley, Nick. 2002. *Making Sense of Social Movements*. Buckingham, UK: Open University Press.

Curtis, Maria F. 2005. "The Women's Side of the Coin: The Gülen Movement in America, a New Turkish American Community Taking Root." Fethullah Gülen Website, https://fgulen.com/en/conference-papers-en/the-fethullah-gulen-movement-i/the-womens-side-of-the-coin-the-gulen-movement-in-america-a-new-turkish-american-community-taking-root. Accessed: 30/10/2020.

Curtis, Maria F. 2012. "Among the Heavenly Branches: Leadership and Authority Among Women in the Gülen Hizmet." In *The Gülen Hizmet Movement: Circumspect Activism in Faith-Based Reform*, edited by Tamer Balcı and Christopher L. Miller, 119–54. Newcastle upon Tyne, UK: Cambridge Scholars Publishing.

Curtis, Maria F. 2015. "Diasporic Faith, Faith in Diaspora Turkish Women's Public Spheres Yesterday, Today, and Tomorrow." In *Gülen-Inspired Hizmet in Europe: The Western Journey of a Turkish Muslim Movement*, edited by Gürkan Çelik, Johan Leman, and Karel Steenbrink, 137–55. Frankfurt am Main, Germany: P.I.E. Peter Lang.

Della Porta, Donatella, and Michael Keating, eds. 2008a. *Approaches and Methodologies in the Social Sciences: A Pluralist Perspective*. New York: Cambridge University Press.

Della Porta, Donatella. 2008b. "Introduction." In *Approaches and Methodologies in the Social Sciences: A Pluralist Perspective*, edited by Donatella Porta Della and Michael Keating, 1–15. New York: Cambridge University Press.

Della Porta, Donatella. 2014. "Social Movement Studies and Methodological Pluralism: An Introduction." In *Methodological Practices in Social Movement Research*, edited by Donatella Della Porta, 1–20. Oxford: Oxford University Press.

Dembour, Maire-Benedicte. 2006. *Who Believes in Human Rights: Reflections on the European Convention*. New York: Cambridge University Press.

Dialogue Society. 2011. *Connecting Communities: Noah's Pudding*. London: Dialogue Society.

Dialogue Society. 2019. "About Us" Webpage. http://www.dialoguesociety.org/about-us.html. Accessed: 01/02/2021.

Diamond, Larry. 2021. "Democratic Regression in Comparative Perspective: Scope, Methods, and Causes." *Democratization* 28 (1): 22–42.

Doi, Abdur Rahman I. 1997. *Shari'ah: The Islamic Law*. Ta Ha Publishers.

Donnelly, Jack. 2007. "The Relative Universality of Human Rights." *Human Rights Quarterly* 29 (2): 281–306.

Doorn-Harder, Nelly Van. 2005. "Gender and Religion: Gender and Islam." In *Encyclopedia of Religion*. 2nd ed. Edited by Lindsay Jones, 5: 3364–71. Detroit: Macmillan Reference USA.

Droogers, Andre. 1989. "Syncretism: The Problem of Definition, the Definition of the Problem." In *Dialogue and Syncretism: An Interdisciplinary Approach*, edited by Jerald D. Gort, Hendrik M. Vroom, Rein Fernhout, and Anton Wessels, 7–25. Grand Rapids, MI: William B. Eerdmans Publishing Co.

Dudai, Ron. 2019. "The Study of Human Rights Practice: State of the Art." *Journal of Human Rights Practice* 11 (2): 273–95.

Dunn, Shannon. 2015. "Islamic Law and Human Rights." *The Oxford Handbook of Islamic Law*, October 2015: 1–26.

DW. 2014. "Gülen Movement under Fire in Germany." February 27, 2014. http://www.dw.com/en/gülen-movement-under-fire-in-germany/av-17464038. Accessed: 29/12/2017.

Dwyer, Sonya Corbin, and Jennifer L. Buckle. 2009. "The Space Between: On Being an Insider-Outsider in Qualitative Research." *International Journal of Qualitative Methods* 8 (1): 54–63.

Ebadi, Shirin, and Moaveni Azadeh. 2006. *Iran Awakening: A Memoir of Revolution and Hope*. New York: Random House.

Ebaugh, Helen Rose. 2010. *The Gülen Movement: A Sociological Analysis of a Civic Movement Rooted in Moderate Islam*. New York: Springer.

Eickelman, Dale F. 2013. "Foreword." In Colin Turner, *The Qur'an Revealed: A Critical Analysis of Said Nursi's Epistles of Light*, xi–xii. Berlin: Gerlach Press.

El-Banna, Sanaa. 2013. *Resource Mobilization in Gülen-Inspired Hizmet: A New Type of Social Movement*. New York: Blue Dome Press.

Elahi, Farah, and Omar Khan, eds. 2017. *Islamophobia Still a Challenge for Us All*. London: Runnymede.

Eligür, Banu. 2010. "The Turkish-Islamic Synthesis and the Islamist Social Movement." In *The Mobilization of Political Islam in Turkey*, 81–135. Cambridge: Cambridge University Press.

Elver, Hilal. 2012. *The Headscarf Controversy: Secularism and Freedom of Religion*. New York: Oxford University Press.

Erarslan, Ayse Burcin, and Bruce Rankin. 2013. "Gender Role Attitudes of Female Students in Single-Sex and Coeducational High Schools in Istanbul." *Sex Roles* 69: 455–68.
Erdoğan, Latif. 2006. *Küçük Dünyam*. Istanbul: Doğan Kitap.
Erdoğan, Latif. 2015. "Gülen ve Tesettür Kavramı." *Tevhid Haber*, February 10, 2015. http://www.tevhidhaber.com/gulen-ve-tesettur-kavrami-109514h.htm. Accessed: 01/03/2017.
Ergene, Mehmet Enes. 2008. *Tradition Witnessing the Modern Age: An Analysis of the Gülen Movement*. Clifton, NJ: Tughra Books.
Erken, Sevim. 1995. "Toplumsal Değişmeler Karşisinda Tavir Belirlemede Dini Gruplar: Fethullah Gülen Cemaati." Yüksek Lisans Tezi. Ondukuz Mayis University.
Esposito, John L. 1998. *Islam: The Straight Path*. 3rd ed. New York: Oxford University Press.
Esposito, John L. 2010. *The Future of Islam*. New York: Oxford University Press.
Esposito, John L. 2019. "Islamophobia and Radicalization: Roots, Impact and Implications." In *Islamophobia and Radicalization: Breeding Intolerance and Violence*, edited by John L. Esposito and Derya Iner, 15–33. Cham. Germany: Palgrave Macmillan.
Esposito, John L., and Ihsan Yilmaz. 2010. "Transnational Muslim Faith-Based Peacebuilding: Initiatives of the Gülen Movement." *European Journal of Economic and Political Studies* 3: 87–102.
Evans, Carolyn. 2006. "The Islamic Scarf in the European Court of Human Rights." *Melbourne Journal of International Law* 7: 52–73.
Evans, Malcolm. 1997. *Religious Liberty and International Law in Europe*. Cambridge: Cambridge University Press.
Evans, Malcolm. 2011. "Review of 'Collected Essays in Law: Abdullahi An-Na'im: Islam and Human Rights. Edited by Mashood A Baderin.'" *Ecclesiastical Law Journal* 13 (01): 111–15.
Evans, Tony. 1996. *US Hegemony and the Project of Universal Human Rights*. Basingstoke, UK: Macmillan.
Evans, Tony. 2005. *The Politics of Human Rights: A Global Perspective*. 2nd ed. London: Pluto Press.
Eyerman, Ron, and Andrew Jamison. 1991. *Social Movements: A Cognitive Approach*. Cambridge: Polity Press.
Fakhry, Majid. 2008. *Islamic Occasionalism: And Its Critique by Averroes and Aquinas*. New York: Routledge.
Falk, Richard A. 2000a. "The Geopolitics of Exclusion: The Case of Islam." In *Human Rights Horizons: The Pursuit of Justice in a Globalizing World*, 147–64. New York: Routledge.
Falk, Richard A. 2000b. *Human Rights Horizons: The Pursuit of Justice in a Globalizing World*. New York: Routledge.
Farley, Edward. 1987. "Interpreting Situations: An Inquiry into the Nature of Practical Theology." In *Formation and Reflection: The Promise of Practical Theology*, edited by Lewis S. Mudge and James N. Poling, 1–26. Philadelphia: Fortress Press.
Festinger, Leon. 1957. *A Theory Cognitive Dissonance*. Stanford, CA: Stanford University Press.
Flaskerud, Ingvild. 2018. "'Street Theology': Vernacular Theology and Muslim Youth in Norway." *Islam and Christian–Muslim Relations* 29 (4): 485–507.
Flaskerud, Ingvild, and Oddbjørn Leirvik. 2018. "The Study of Islam between University Theology and Lived Religion: Introductory Reflections." *Islam and Christian–Muslim Relations* 29 (4): 413–27.

Flood, Alison. 2019. "Turkish Government Destroys More than 300,000 Books." *The Guardian*, August 6, 2019. https://www.theguardian.com/books/2019/aug/06/turkish-government-destroys-more-than-300000-books. Accessed: 12/02/2021.

Foley, Griff. 2004. *Learning in Social Action: A Contribution to Understanding Informal Education*. Leicester, UK: NIACE.

Foucault, Michel. 1980. *Power/Knowledge: Selected Interviews and Other Writings 1972–1977*. Edited by Colin Gordon. New York: Pantheon Books.

Fougner, Tore. 2017. "Fethullah Gülen's Understanding of Women's Rights in Islam: A Critical Reappraisal." *Turkish Studies* 18 (2): 251–77.

Friedman, Yohanan. 2003. *Tolerance and Coercion in Islam: Interfaith Relations in the Muslim Tradition*. Cambridge Studies in the Islamic Civilization. New York: Cambridge University Press.

Garfinkel, Harold. 1967. *Studies in Ethnomethodology*. Upper Saddle River, NJ: Prentice Hall.

Gazeteciler ve Yazarlar Vakfı. 2014. "Gazeteciler ve Yazarlar Vakfı" (Organizational brochure). Istanbul.

George, Alexander L., and Andrew Bennett. 2005. *Case Studies and Theory Development in the Social Sciences*. Cambridge, MA: MIT Press.

Ghanea-Hercock, Nazila, Alan Andrew Stephens, and Raphael Walden, eds. 2007. *Does God Believe in Human Rights?* Leiden: Martinus Nijhoff Publishers.

Gherardi, Silvia. 2000. "Practice-Based Theorizing on Learning and Knowing in Organizations." *Organization* 7 (2): 211–23.

Gherardi, Silvia. 2003. "Knowing as Desiring. Mythic Knowledge and the Knowledge Journey in Communities of Practitioners." *Journal of Workplace Learning* 15 (7/8): 352–58.

Gherardi, Silvia. 2006. *Organizational Knowledge: The Texture of Workplace Learning*. Oxford: Blackwell Publishing.

Gherardi, Silvia. 2009. "Introduction: The Critical Power of the 'Practice Lens.'" *Management Learning* 40 (2): 115–28.

Gherardi, Silvia, and Davide Nicolini. 2003. "To Transfer Is to Transform." In *Knowing in Organizations: A Practice-Based Approach*, edited by Davide Nicolini, Silvia Gherardi, and Dvora Yanow, 204–24. Armonk, NY: M. E. Sharpe.

Giddens, Anthony. 1979. *Central Problems in Social Theory: Action, Structure and Contradiction in Social Analysis*. London: Palgrave.

Gilsenan, Michael. 1982. *Recognizing Islam: An Anthropologist's Introduction*. Oxon, UK: Routledge.

Giugni, Marco. 1999. "How Social Movements Matter: Past Research, Present Problems, Future Developments." In *How Social Movements Matter*, edited by Marco Giugni, Doug McAdam, and Charles Tilly, xiii–xxxiii. Minneapolis: University of Minnesota Press.

Giusti, Serena, and Elisa Piras. 2020. *Democracy and Fake News: Information Manipulation and Post-Truth Politics*. New York: Routledge.

Global Legal Research Centre. 2014. "Laws Criminalizing Apostasy in Selected Jurisdictions." May 2014. Washington, DC: The Law Library of Congress.

Göle, Nilüfer. 1996. *The Forbidden Modern: Civilization and Veiling*. Ann Arbor: University of Michigan Press.

Goodale, Mark. 2007. "Locating Rights, Envisioning Law between the Global and the Local." In *The Practice of Human Rights: Tracking Law between the Global and the Local*, edited by Mark Goodale and Sally Engle Merry, 1–38. New York: Cambridge University Press.

Goodale, Mark, and Sally Engle Merry, eds. 2007. *The Practice of Human Rights: Tracking Law Between the Global and the Local*. New York: Cambridge University Press.

Gourlay, Stephen. 2006. "Conceptualizing Knowledge Creation: A Critique of Nonaka's Theory." *Journal of Management Studies* 43 (7): 1415–36.

Gözaydın, İştar B. 2009. "The Fethullah Gülen Movement and Politics in Turkey: A Chance for Democratization or a Trojan Horse?" *Democratization* 16 (6): 1214–36.

Graham, Elaine. 2009. *Words Made Flesh: Writings in Pastoral and Practical Theology*. London: SCM Press.

Graham, Elaine, Heather Walton, and Francis Ward. 2005. *Theological Reflections: Methods*. London: SCM Press.

Greene, Melanie J. 2014. "On the Inside Looking in: Methodological Insights and Challenges in Conducting Qualitative Insider Research." *The Qualitative Report* 19 (29): 1–13.

Grierson, Jamie, and Dan Sabbagh. 2020. "Largest Number of Prevent Referrals Related to Far-Right Extremism." *The Guardian*, November 26, 2020. https://www.theguardian.com/uk-news/2020/nov/26/just-one-in-10-prevent-referrals-found-at-risk-of-radicalisation. Accessed: 20/12/2020.

Griffin, James. 2008. *On Human Rights*. New York: Oxford University Press.

Grinell, Klas. 2007. "Beyond East and West: Fethullah Gülen and 'Border' Thinking." In *Peaceful Coexistence: Fethullah Gülen's Initiatives in the Contemporary World*, edited by Ihsan Yilmaz, Khaled Abou El Fadl, and Jean-Michel M. Cros, 203–13. Rotterdam: Leeds, UK Metropolitan University Press.

Grinell, Klas. 2015. *Reflections on Reason, Religion and Tolerance: Engaging with Fethullah Gulen's Ideas*. New York: Blue Dome Press.

Guemuesay, Ali Aslan. 2012. "Boundaries and Knowledge in a Sufi Dhikr Circle." *Journal of Management Development* 31 (10): 1077–89.

Gül, Songül Sallan, and Hüseyin Gül. April 2000. "The Question of Women in Islamic Revivalism in Turkey: A Review of the Islamic Press." *Current Sociology* 48(2): 1–26.

Gulay, Erol N. 2007. "The Gülen Phenomenon: A Neo-Sufi Challenge to Turkey's Rival Elite?" *Middle East Critique* 16 (1): 37–61.

Gülen, Fethullah M. 1993a. "Hoşgörü." Fethullah Gülen Website, https://fgulen.com/tr/fethullah-gulenin-butun-eserleri/cag-ve-nesil-serisi/fethullah-gulen-yeseren-dusunceler/200-fethullah-gulen-hosgoru. Accessed: 01/01/2016.

Gülen, Fethullah M. 1993b. *Questions: This Modern Age Puts Islam*. London: Truestar.

Gülen, Fethullah M. 1995a. "Cennet Ancak Kadınla Cennettir." Fethullah Gülen Website, https://fgulen.com/tr/turk-basininda-fethullah-gulen/fethullah-gulenle-gazete-roportajlari/hurriyette-ertugrul-ozkokle/7872-Hurriyet-Cennet-Ancak-Kadinla-Cennettir. Accessed: 11/09/2018.

Gülen, Fethullah M. 1995b. "Hoca'nın Hedefi Amerika İle Almanya" (Interview by Nuriye Akman). Fethullah Gülen Website, https://fgulen.com/tr/turk-basininda-fethullah-gulen/fethullah-gulenle-gazete-roportajlari/149-Sabahta-Nuriye-Akmanla/7853-Sabah-Hocanin-Hedefi-Amerika-Ile-Almanya-. Accessed: 01/01/2018.

Gülen, Fethullah M. 1995c. "Çiller Saygıyla Dinledi" (Interview by Nuriye Akman). *Sabah*, January 23, 1995.

Gülen, Fethullah M. 1995d. " NMO Hollanda televizyonu ile." Fethullah Gülen Website, October 19, 1995. https://fgulen.com/tr/basindan-tr/televizyon-roportajlari/NMO-NMO-Hollanda-televizyonu-ile. Accessed: 01/11/2021.

Gülen, Fethullah M. 1996. *Fatiha Üzerine Mülahazalar*. İzmir: Nil Yayınları.

Gülen, Fethullah M. 1998. Ozcan Keles's Translation of Gülen's FKM Talk on How Yamanlar Was Founded, October 11, 1998.

Gülen, Fethullah M. 1999. "1977 Yılı Vaaz ve Konferansları." Fethullah Gülen Website, https://fgulen.com/tr/ses-ve-video/fethullah-gulen-hitabet/fethullah-gulen-hocaefendinin-vaizligi/3588-fgulen-com-1977-Yili-Vaaz-ve-Konferanslari. Accessed: 01/10/2018.

Gülen, Fethullah M. 2000a. *Advocate of Dialogue: Fethullah Gülen*. Edited by Ali Ünal and Alphonse Williams. Fairfax: The Fountain.

Gülen, Fethullah M. 2000b. "The Necessity of Interfaith Dialogue: A Muslim Perspective." *The Fountain* 3 (31): 4–9.

Gülen, Fethullah M. 2001. "The Qur'an Says: There Is No Compulsion in Religion (2:256) What Does This Mean?" Fethullah Gülen Website, https://fgulen.com/en/fethullah-gulens-works/faith/questions-and-answers/24500-the-quran-says-there-is-no-compulsion-in-religion-2256-what-does-this-mean. Accessed: 01/03/2016.

Gülen, Fethullah M. 2002. "People of Service." Fethullah Gülen Website, December 16, 2002. https://fgulen.com/en/fethullah-gulens-works/pearls-of-wisdom-en/people-of-service. Accessed: 28/07/2020.

Gülen, Fethullah M. 2004. "Hükümetin AB Gayretini Samimi Buluyorum" (Interview by Nuriye Akman). *Zaman*, March 24, 2004.

Gülen, Fethullah M. 2005. *The Essentials of the Islamic Faith*. New Jersey: The Light, Inc.

Gülen, Fethullah M. 2006a. "'Dinde Zorlama Yoktur' Âyetini İzah Eder Misiniz?" Fethullah Gülen Website, https://fgulen.com/tr/fethullah-gulenin-butun-eserleri/iman/fethullah-gulen-asrin-getirdigi-tereddutler/470-fethullah-gulen-dinde-zorlama-yoktur-ayetini-izah-eder-misiniz. Accessed: 01/01/2016.

Gülen, Fethullah M. 2006b. *Key Concepts in the Practice of Sufism 1*. New Jersey: The Light, Inc.

Gülen, Fethullah M. 2006c. *M. Fethullah Gülen: Essays, Perspectives, Opinions*. 3rd ed. Izmir: The Light, Inc.

Gülen, Fethullah M. 2006d. "Ikindi Sohbetleri: Dialogue Is Dynamic." *Ahmet Kurucan Lecture Notes*, Pennsylvania, March 16, 2006.

Gülen, Fethullah M. 2006e. "Hizmet." Fethullah Gülen Website, May 13, 2006. https://fgulen.com/tr/eserleri/fasildan-fasila-2/hizmet. Accessed: 12/10/2020.

Gülen, Fethullah M. 2007. "Fethullah Gülen Hocaefendi: Dinde Zorlama Yoktur." YouTube, October 10, 2007. https://www.youtube.com/watch?v=k9RhVfkia28. Accessed: 05/01/2016.

Gülen, Fethullah M. 2009a. "Ikindi Sohbetleri: What Is Important in Dialogue." *Ahmet Kurucan Lecture Notes*, Pennsylvania, February 23, 2009.

Gülen, Fethullah M. 2009b. "Ikindi Sohbetleri: Dialogue Is a Give and Take." *Ahmet Kurucan Lecture Notes*, Pennsylvania, May 1, 2009.

Gülen, Fethullah M. 2010a. "Ikindi Sohbetleri: The Risk of over-Determination." *Ahmet Kurucan Lecture Notes*, Pennsylvania, March 11, 2010.

Gülen, Fethullah M. 2010b. "Aksiyon Öncelikli Düşünce." *Herkül*, May 24, 2010. http://www.herkul.org/bamteli/aksiyon-oncelikli-dusunce. Accessed: 10/10/2020.

Gülen, Fethullah M. 2010c. "Düşünce-Aksiyon İç İçeliği." *Özgür Herkül*, October 13, 2010. http://www.herkul.org/kirik-testi/dusunce-aksiyon-ic-iceligi. Accessed: 12/10/2020.

Gülen, Fethullah M. 2011a. *Asrın Getirdiği Tereddütler 3*. İzmir: Nil Yayınları.

Gülen, Fethullah M. 2011b. *Çekirdekten Çınara*. İzmir: Nil Yayınları.

Gülen, Fethullah M. 2011c. "Usul, Furu ve Tesettur." In *Prizma 2*, 175–78. İzmir: Nil Yayınları.
Gülen, Fethullah M. 2012a. "Fethullah Gülen Bir Reformist Midir?" Fethullah Gülen Website, January 26, 2012. http://fgulen.com/tr/hayati-tr/sorularla-fethullah-gulen/fethullah-gulen-bir-reformist-midir. Accessed: 14/10/2020.
Gülen, Fethullah M. 2012b. "Prediger Fethullah Gülen: Tue Gutes, Und Lasse Es Wirken" (Interview by Rainer Hermann). *Frankfurter Allgemeine Zeitung*. December 6, 2012.
Gülen, Fethullah M. 2013a. "Fethullah Gülen Hocaefendi, Tesettür ve Başörtüsü İçin 'Farz Değil' / 'Olmasa Da Olur' Dedi Mi?" Fethullah Gülen Website, https://fgulen.com/tr/fethullah-gulen-kimdir/gulen-hakkinda/sorularla-fethullah-gulen/37634-fethullah-gulen-hocaefendi-tesettur-ve-basortusu-icin-farz-degil-olmasa-da-olur-dedi-mi. Accessed: 11/09/2018.
Gülen, Fethullah M. 2013b. "Fetullah Gülen ve Başörtüsü Konusunda Yaptığı Dönüş." YouTube, December 23, 2013. https://www.youtube.com/watch?v=LU_aMLA6Ng4&ab_channel=yuka79m. Accessed: 01/06/2018.
Gülen, Fethullah M. 2014. "Almanya Mulakati. Nisan 2014." DocPlayer, April 2014. http://docplayer.biz.tr/8884211-Almanya-mulakati-nisan-2014.html. Accessed: 27/05/2020. For the German translation of the said interview, see https://sdub.de/guelen-sdub-interview/. Accessed: 07/07/2022.
Gülen, Fethullah M. 2017. "Islamic Scholar Fethullah Gulen's Video Message for International Women's Day." YouTube, March 7, 2017. https://www.youtube.com/watch?v=kgVB_DVcEnc&feature=youtu.be. Accessed: 13/09/2018.
Gülen, Fethullah M. 2020. "Sorular ve Çıkış Yolları." Fethullah Gülen Website, https://fgulen.com/tr/ses-ve-video-tr/sorular-ve-cikis-yollari?start=25. Accessed: 01/08/2018.
Gündüz, Mustafa. 2009. "Sociocultural Origins of Turkish Educational Reforms and Ideological Origins of Late Ottoman Intellectuals (1908–1930)." *History of Education* 38 (2): 191–216.
Gurbuz-Kucuksari, Gulsum. 2008. "Unresolved Concerns of Women in the Modern Age: How Does the Gülen Movement Contribute to the Women Question?" In *Islam in the Age of Global Challenges: Alternative Perspectives of the Gülen Movement*, edited by Akbar Ahmad, John Borreli, Jill B. Carrol et al., 474–90. Georgetown University, Washington, DC, November 14–15, 2008.
Gürbüz, Mustafa E., and Mary Bernstein. 2012. "'Thou Shall Not Protest!': Multi-Institutional Politics, Strategic Nonconfrontation and Islamic Mobilizations in Turkey." Edited by Sharon Erickson Nepstad and Lester R. Kurtz. *Nonviolent Conflict and Civil Resistance* 34: 63–91.
Haddad, Yvonne Yazbeck. 2011. "Muslims, Human Rights, and Women's Rights." In *Religion and the Global Politics of Human Rights*, edited by Thomas Banchoff and Robert Wuthnow, 71–97. New York: Oxford University Press.
Hall, Budd L. 2009. "A River of Life: Learning and Environmental Social Movements." *Interface* 1 (1): 46–78.
Hall, David D. 1997. "Introduction." In *Lived Religion in America: Toward a History of Practice*, edited by David D. Hall, vii–xiii. Princeton, NJ: Princeton University Press.
Hallaq, Wael B. 1997. *A History of Islamic Legal Theories: An Introduction to Sunni Usul Al-Fiqh*. Cambridge: Cambridge University Press.
Hallaq, Wael B. 2009. *An Introduction to Islamic Law*. Cambridge: Cambridge University Press.

Hällzon, Patrick. 2008. "The Gülen Movement: Gender and Practice." In *Islam in the Age of Global Challenges: Alternative Perspectives of the Gülen Movement*, edited by Akbar Ahmad, John Borreli, Jill B. Carrol et al., 288–316. Georgetown University, Washington, DC. November 14–15, 2008.

Haluza-DeLay, Randolph. 2008. "A Theory of Practice for Social Movements: Environmentalism and Ecological Habitus." *Mobilization: The International Quarterly* 13 (2): 205–18.

Harmon-Jones, Eddie, and Judson Mills. 1999. "An Introduction to Cognitive Dissonance Theory and an Overview of Current Perspectives on the Theory." In *Science Conference Series. Cognitive Dissonance: Progress on a Pivotal Theory in Social Psychology*, edited by Eddie Harmon-Jones and Judson Mills, 3–21. Washington, DC: American Psychological Association.

Hassencahl, Fran. 2009. "Framing Women's Issues in The Fountain Magazine." In *East and West Encounters: The Gülen Movement*, edited by Varun Soni, Andrew Achenbaum, and Reza Aslan, 33–44. University of Southern California, Los Angeles. December 5–6, 2009.

Hauerwas, Stanley. 2005. "Homiletics Interview: Stanley Hauerwas." *Homiletics Online*, https://www.homileticsonline.com/subscriber/interviews/hauerwas.asp. Accessed: 29/03/2021.

Hellyer, Hisham A., ed. 2018. *The Islamic Tradition and The Human Rights Discourse*. Washington, DC: Atlantic Council.

Hendrick, Joshua D. 2013. *Gülen: The Ambiguous Politics of Market Islam in Turkey and the World*. New York: New York University Press.

Het Belgische Staatsblad. 2008. "Wijziging Statuten." March 14, 2008. http://www.ejustice.just.fgov.be/tsv/tsvf.htm. Accessed: 06/08/2020.

Hilsdon, Anne Marie, and Santi Rozario. 2006. "Special Issue on Islam, Gender and Human Rights." *Women's Studies International Forum* 29: 331–38.

Hinchman, Lewis P. 1984. "The Origins of Human Rights: A Hegelian Perspective." *The Western Political Quarterly* 37 (1): 7–31.

Hiro, Dilip. 1986. "The Islamic Wave Hits Turkey." *The Nation*. June 28, 1986.

Holford, John. 1995. "Why Social Movements Matter: Adult Education Theory, Cognitive Praxis, And the Creation of Knowledge." *Adult Education Quarterly* 45 (2): 95–111.

Hollenbach, David. 2010. "Comparative Ethic, Islam and Human Rights: Internal Pluralism and the Possible Development of Tradition." *Journal of Religious Ethics* 38 (3): 580–87.

Holst, John D. 2002. *Social Movements, Civil Society, and Radical Adult Education*. Westport, CT: Bergin and Garvey.

Home Office. 2011. "Prevent Strategy." June 2011. London. https://assets.publishing.service.gov.uk/government/uploads/system/uploads/attachment_data/file/97976/prevent-strategy-review.pdf Accessed: 05/10/2020.

Home Office. 2017. "Country Policy and Information Note. Turkey: Gülenism (Version 1.0, April 2017)." London.

House of Commons Communities and Local Government Committee. 2010. "Preventing Violent Extremism Sixth Report of Session 2009–2010." March 16, 2010. London.

House of Commons Foreign Affairs Committee. 2016. "'Political Islam', and the Muslim Brotherhood Review." November 1, 2016. London.

House of Commons Foreign Affairs Committee. 2017. "The UK's Relations with Turkey: Tenth Report of Session 2016–17." March 21, 2017. London.

Howley, Kevin. 2008. "Through an Activist Lens: Social Movement Theory and Practice." *Social Movement Studies* 7 (1): 97–100.
Human Rights Watch. 2017. "In Custody: Police Torture and Abductions in Turkey," October 2017. https://www.hrw.org/sites/default/files/report_pdf/turkey1017_web_0.pdf. Accessed: 03/04/2018.
Humphrey, John P. 1983. *Human Rights and the United Nations: A Great Adventure*. New York: Transnational Publishers.
Hunter, Shireen T. 2009. "Conclusions and Prospects." In *Reformist Voices of Islam: Mediating Islam and Modernity*, edited by Shireen T. Hunter, 287–98. Armonk, NY: M. E. Sharpe.
Huntington, Samuel. 1993. "The Clash of Civilizations?" *Foreign Affairs* (Summer) 72 (3): 22–49.
Ibrahim, Joseph. 2015. *Bourdieu and Social Movements: Ideological Struggles in the British Anti-Capitalist Movement*. Basingstoke. UK: Palgrave Macmillan.
İddianame No: 2017/325. 2017. Aksaray Cumhuriyet Başsavcılığı, September 28, 2017. Aksaray, Turkey.
Ignatieff, Michael. 2001. "The Attack on Human Rights." *Foreign Affairs* 80 (6): 102–16.
Intercultural Dialogue Institute GTA. 2015. "Newsletter." Toronto.
International Humanist and Ethical Union. 2017. "Freedom of Thought 2017: A Global Report on the Rights, Legal Status and Discrimination against Humanists, Atheists and the Non-religious." London.
Ishay, Michelin R. 2004. *The History of Human Rights: From Ancient Times to the Globalization Era*. Oakland: University of California Press.
Jacobs, Alan M. 2015. "Process Tracing the Effects of Ideas." In *Process Tracing: From Metaphor to Analytic Tool*, edited by Andrew Bennett and Jeffrey T. Checkel, 41–73. Cambridge: Cambridge University Press.
Jahanbakhsh, Forough. 2010. "Review of Making Islam Democratic: Social Movements and the Post-Islamist Turn by Asef Bayat. Stanford, CA: Stanford University Press, 2007, Xxi+291 Pp." *Comparative Studies of South Asia, Africa and the Middle East* 30 (1): 152–53.
Janis, Irving L. 1982. *GroupThink*. Boston: Houghton Mifflin.
Johnston, David L. 2015. "Islam and Human Rights: A Growing Rapprochement?" *American Journal of Economics and Sociology* 74 (1): 113–48.
Jouili, Jeanette S, and Schirin Amir-moazami. 2006. "Knowledge, Empowerment and Religious Authority Among Pious Muslim Women in France and Germany." *The Muslim World* 96: 617–42.
Kadıoğlu, A. 1994. "Women's Subordination in Turkey: Is Islam Really the Villain?" *Middle East Journal* 48 (4): 645–60.
Kamali, Mohammad Hashim. 2008. *Shari'ah Law: An Introduction*. Oxford: Oneworld Publications.
Kandiyoti, Deniz. 1991a. "End of Empire: Islam, Nationalism and Women in Turkey." In *Women, Islam and the State*, edited by Deniz Kandiyoti, 22–47. London: Macmillan.
Kandiyoti, Deniz. 1991b. "Introduction." In *Women, Islam and the State*, edited by Deniz Kandiyoti, 1–21. London: Macmillan.
Karp, David Jason. 2013. "The Location of International Practices: What Is Human Rights Practice?" *Review of International Studies* 39 (4): 969–92.
Kaya, Serdar. 2011. "Review of Cumhuriyet'in Dindar Kadınları [The religious women of the Republic] Fatma K. Barbarosoğlu. İstanbul: Profil, 2009. 231 pp. ISBN 978-975-996-229-6." *Contemporary Islam* 5: 211–12.

Kayaoglu, Turan. 2010. "Preachers of Dialogue: International Relations and Interfaith Theology." In *Islam and Peacebuilding: Gülen Movement Initiatives*, edited by John L. Esposito and Ihsan Yilmaz, 147–68. Izmir: Blue Dome Press.

Kayaoglu, Turan. 2014. "Trying Islam: Muslims before the European Court of Human Rights." *Journal of Muslim Minority Affairs* 34 (4): 345–64.

Keles, Ozcan. 2007. "Promoting Human Rights Values in the Muslim World: The Case of the Gülen Movement." In *Muslim World in Transition: Contributions of the Gülen Movement*, edited by Ihsan Yilmaz, Eileen Barker, Henri J. Barky et al., 683–708. London: Leeds Metropolitan University Press.

Keles, Ozcan. 2009. *Deradicalisation by Default: The 'Dialogue' Approach to Rooting out Violent Extremism*. London: Dialogue Society.

Keles, Ozcan. 2013. "The Gülen Movement and Promoting Human Rights Values." In *The Muslim World and Politics in Transition: Creative Contributions of the Gülen Movement*, edited by Greg Barton, Paul Weller, and Ihsan Yilmaz, 192–208. London: Bloomsbury.

Keles, Ozcan. 2016a. "Written Evidence to Foreign Affairs Committee on UK's Relations with Turkey." Ozcan Keles Website, December 1, 2016. http://i.ozcankeles.org/uploads/2016/12/Written-Evidence_FAC_Oct-2016.pdf. Accessed: 05/09/2020.

Keles, Ozcan. 2016b. "Islamic Knowledge: Divine versus Human (Turkish)." Ozcan Keles Website, February 14, 2016. https://www.ozcankeles.org/islamic-knowledge-divine-versus-human-55. Accessed: 07/09/2020.

Keles, Ozcan. 2016c. "Press Release: Özcan Keleş [ENGLISH]." Ozcan Keles Website, October 25, 2016. https://www.ozcankeles.org/press-release-ozcan-keles-english-84. Accessed: 07/09/2020.

Keles, Ozcan. 2017. "Additional Written Evidence to Foreign Affairs Committee on UK's Relations with Turkey." Ozcan Keles Website, February 3, 2017. http://i.ozcankeles.org/uploads/2017/04/Additional-Written-Evidence-from-AFSV-and-DP.pdf. Accessed: 06/09/2020.

Keles, Ozcan. 2018a. "İçeriden ve Dışarıdan Eleştiri." Ozcan Keles Website, February 22, 2018. https://www.ozcankeles.org/iceriden-ve-disaridan-elestiri-169. Accessed: 07/09/2020.

Keles, Ozcan. 2018b. "İçtihat Heyetleri ve Hizmet Hareketi'ne Yöneltilecek En Temel Eleştiri." Ozcan Keles Website, March 5, 2018. https://www.ozcankeles.org/ictihat-heyetleri-ve-hizmet-hareketine-yonetilecek-en-temel-elestiri-172. Accessed: 10/09/2020.

Keles, Ozcan. 2018c. "İnkisar ve Hizmet Hareketinin Sadeleştirilmesi." Ozcan Keles Website, December 6, 2018. https://www.ozcankeles.org/inkisar-ve-hizmet-hareketinin-sadelestirilmesi-200. Accessed: 07/10/2020.

Keles, Ozcan. 2018d. "Hamteli: Analoji Manaloji ve Şaşkın Küheylan." Ozcan Keles Website, December 12, 2018. https://www.ozcankeles.org/hamteli-analoji-manaloji-ve-saskin-kuheylan-221. Accessed: 03/04/2020.

Keles, Ozcan. 2019. "Twitter Nağme: Çağlayan Dergisi ve 'Eleştiri Çıkmazı' Yazısı." Ozcan Keles Website, February 8, 2019. https://www.ozcankeles.org/caglayan-dergisi-ve-elestiri-cikmazi-yazisi-236. Accessed: 10/10/2020.

Keles, Ozcan. 2020. "UK Court Rejects Turkey's Extradition Request for Ozcan Keles." Ozcan Keles Website, London. December 10, 2020. https://www.ozcankeles.org/extradition_request_outcome-339. Accessed 21/12/2020.

Keles, Ozcan. 2021. "Why Hizmet Needs Self-Criticism | M Behzad Fatmi." YouTube, June 26, 2021. https://www.youtube.com/watch?v=HOD6RMXs9lg&ab_channel=MBehzadFatmi. Accessed: 07/07/2022.

Keles, Ozcan, and Yüksel Alp Aslandoğan. 2016. "Foreign Affairs Committee Hearing, Tuesday 15 November 2016." Parliamentlive.TV, November 15, 2016. https://parliamentlive.tv/Event/Index/be2e73ba-1edd-4c32-a86f-f2ad347596c2. Accessed 07/09/2020.

Keles, Ozcan, Ismail M. Sezgin, and Ihsan Yilmaz. 2019. "Tackling the Twin Threats of Islamophobia and Puritanical Islamist Extremism: Case Study of the Hizmet Movement." In *Islamophobia and Radicalization: Breeding Intolerance and Violence*, edited by John L Esposito and Derya Iner, 265–83. Cham, Germany: Palgrave Macmillan.

Kelley, Robin D. G. 2002. *Freedom Dreams: The Black Radical Imagination*. New York: Beacon Press.

Kelman, Herbert C. 1958. "Compliance, Identification, and Internalization: Three Processes of Attitude Change." *Journal of Conflict Resolution* 2 (1): 51–60.

Kelman, Herbert C. 2005. "Interests, Relationships, Identities: Three Central Issues for Individuals and Groups in Negotiating Their Social Environment." *Annual Review of Psychology* 57 (1): 1–26.

Kermani, Secunder. 2018. "Acquitted of Blasphemy and Living in Fear in Pakistan." *BBC News*, December 9, 2018. https://www.bbc.co.uk/news/world-asia-46465247. Accessed 20/05/2020.

Keskin, Tugrul. 2009. "A Comparative Analysis of Islamist Movements in the Neoliberalization Process: Jama'at-e-Islami in Pakistan and the Fethullah Gülen Movement in Turkey – Reactions to Capitalism, Modernity and Secularism." Doctoral thesis. Virginia Polytechnic Institute and State University, Blacksburg, VA.

Kılıç, Neslihan Tekin. 2012. "Sociality and Visibility of the Women of Turkish Origin in Europe: The Case of the Golden Rose Association." *Ozean Journal of Social Science* 5 (2): 49–58.

Kılıç, Neslihan Tekin. 2014. "Hizmet Hareketi'nde Kadın ve Kamusal Alan." Fethullah Gülen Website, November 26, 2014. https://fgulen.com/tr/turk-basininda-fethullah-gulen/fethullah-gulen-hakkinda-kose-yazilari/2014-kose-yazilari/46614-neslihan-tekin-kilic-zaman-hizmet-hareketinde-kadin-ve-kamusal-alan. Accessed: 01/07/2018.

Kim, Heon Choul. 2008. "The Nature and Role of Sufism in Contemporary Islam: A Case Study of the Life, Thought and Teachings of Fethullah Gülen." Doctoral thesis. The Temple University.

Kim, Jihyun. 2016. "The Nature of Adult Learning in Social Movements." *Journal of Lifelong Learning* 25: 29–50.

King, Anthony. 2000. "Thinking with Bourdieu against Bourdieu: A 'Practical' Critique of the Habitus." *Sociological Theory* 18 (3): 417–33.

Klaas, Brian. 2016. *The Despot's Accomplice: How the West Is Aiding and Abetting the Decline of Democracy*. London: Hurst.

Klug, Francesca. 2000. *Values for a Godless Age: The Story of the United Kingdom's New Bill of Rights*. London: Penguin Group.

Koca, Canan, F. Hülya Aşçi, and Giyasettin Demirhan. 2005. "Attitudes toward Physical Education and Class Preferences of Turkish Adolescents in Terms of School Gender Composition." *Adolescence* 40 (158): 365–75.

Koca, Özgür. 2015. "The Principles of the Construction of the 'Other' in Fethullah Gülen's Thought." *Journal of Dialogue Studies* 3 (2): 73–85.

Koç, Doğan. 2012. *Strategic Defamation of Fethullah Gülen: English vs. Turkish*. Lanham, MD: University Press of America.

Kömeçoğlu, Uğur. 1997. "A Sociologically Interpretative Approach to the Fethullah Gülen Community Movement." MA thesis. Boğaziçi University, Istanbul, Turkey.
Kömeçoğlu, Uğur. 2008. "Concordance between Asceticism and Activism: The Numinous Dimension of an Islamic Community Movement." In *Groups, Ideologies and Discourses: Glimpses of the Turkish Speaking World*, edited by Christoph Herzog and Barbara Pusch, 61–81. Würzburg: Ergon Verlag.
Kösebalaban, Hasan. 2003. "The Making of Enemy and Friend." In *Turkish Islam and the Secular State: The Gülen Movement*, edited by M. Hakan Yavuz and John L. Esposito, 170–83. New York: Syracuse University Press.
Kundnani, Arun. 2014. *The Muslims Are Coming!: Islamophobia, Extremism, and the Domestic War on Terror*. London: Verso.
Kundnani, Arun, and Ben Hayes. 2018. "The Globalisation of Countering Violent Extremism Policies: Undermining Human Rights, Instrumentalising Civil Society." Amsterdam: The Transnational Institute.
Kurtz, Lester R. 2005. "Gülen's Paradox: Combining Commitment and Tolerance." *The Muslim World* 95 (July): 373–84.
Kuru, Ahmet T. 2003. "Fethullah Gülen's Search for a Middle Way between Modernity and Muslim Tradition." In *Turkish Islam and the Secular State: The Gülen Movement*, edited by M. Hakan Yavuz and John L. Esposito, 115–30. New York: Syracuse University Press.
Kuru, Ahmet T. 2005. "Globalization and Diversification of Islamic Movements: Three Turkish Cases." *Political Science Quarterly* 120 (2): 253–74.
Kuru, Ahmet T. 2007. "Changing Perspectives on Islamism and Secularism in Turkey: The Gülen Movement and the Ak Party." In *Muslim World in Transition: Contributions of the Gülen Movement*, edited by Ihsan Yilmaz, Eileen Barker, Henri J. Barky et al., 140–51. London: Leeds Metropolitan University Press.
Kuru, Ahmet T. 2019. *Islam, Authoritarianism and Underdevelopment: A Global and Historical Comparison*. New York: Cambridge University Press.
Kurucan, Ahmet. 2006a. "İslam Hukukunda Düşünce Özgürlüğü." Doktora Tezi. Atatürk University, Erzurum Turkey.
Kurucan, Ahmet. 2006b. *Niçin Diyalog*. İzmir: Işık Yayınları.
Kurucan, Ahmet. 2007. *İslâm'da Düşünce Özgürlüğü*. Istanbul: Zaman Kitap.
Kurucan, Ahmet. 2008. "Kocanın Karısını Dövmesi Zalimce Bir Davranıştır." Fethullah Gülen Website, October 24, 2008. https://fgulen.com/tr/basindan-tr/kose-yazilari/Ahmet-Kurucan-Zaman-Kocanin-Karisini-Dovmesi-Zalimce-Bir-Davranistir. Accessed: 03/02/2016.
Kurucan, Ahmet. 2021. *Din Özgürlüğü Kapsamında Irtidat*. Süreyya Yayınları.
Kurucan, Ahmet, and Mustafa Kasim Erol. 2012. *Dialogue in Islam: Qur'an, Sunnah, History*. London: Dialogue Society.
Kurzman, Charles. 2004. "Conclusion: Social Movement Theory and Islamic Studies." In *Islamic Activism: A Social Movement Theory Approach*, edited by Quintan Wiktorowicz, 289–303. Bloomington: Indiana University Press.
Lacey, Jonathan. 2014. "'Turkish Islam' as 'Good Islam': How the Gülen Movement Exploits Discursive Opportunities in a Post-9/11 Milieu." *Journal of Muslim Minority Affairs* 34 (2): 95–110.
Lambek, Michael. 1993. *Knowledge and Practice in Mayotte: Local Discourses of Islam, Sorcery and Spirit Possession*. Toronto: University of Toronto Press.
Lambek, Michael. 1997. "Knowledge and Practice in Mayotte." *Cultural Dynamics* 9(2): 131–48.

Langdon, Jonathan. 2009. "Learning to Sleep without Perching: Reflections by Activist-Educators on Learning in Social Action in Ghanaian Social Movements." *McGill Journal of Education* 44 (1): 79–105.

Leaman, Oliver. 2007. "Towards an Understanding of Gülen's Methodology." In *Muslim World in Transition: Contributions of the Gülen Movement*, edited by Ihsan Yilmaz, Eileen Barker, Henri J. Barky et al., 503–10. London: Leeds Metropolitan University Press.

Lemberg-Pedersen, Martin. 2015. "The Rise and Fall of the ERPUM Pilot: Tracing the European Policy Drive to Deport Unaccompanied Minors." *RSC Working Paper Series*. No. 108.

Lewin, Kurt. 1947. "Group Decision and Social Change." In *Readings in Social Psychology*, edited by Newcomb Theodore and Hartley Eugene, 330–44. New York: Henry Holt.

LinkedIn. 2020. "Ilknur Kahraman." https://www.linkedin.com/in/ilknur-kahraman-11108426. Accessed: 02/08/2020.

Loeffler, Reinhold. 1988. *Islam in Practice: Religious Beliefs in a Persian Village*. Albany: State University of New York Press.

Lorenzen, Thorwald. 2000. "Towards a Theology of Human Rights." *Review and Expositor* 97: 49–67.

Lötüs, Musa. 1989. *Ve Tesettür Meselesi*. İzmir: Nil.

Maddison, Sarah, and Sean Scalmer. 2006. *Activist Wisdom: Practical Knowledge and Creative Tension in Social Movements*. Sydney: UNSW Press.

Mahoney, James. 2010. "After KKV: The New Methodology of Qualitative Research." *World Politics* 62 (1): 120–47.

Mahoney, James. 2015. "Process Tracing and Historical Explanation." *Security Studies* 24 (2): 200–218.

Malaurie, Claire Bazy, Sarah Cleveland, Regina Kiener, Hanna Suchocka, Kaarlo Tuori, and Jan Velaers. 2016. "Opinion on Emergency Decree Laws No.s 667-676 Adopted Following the Failed Coup of 15 July 2016." Adopted by the Venice Commission at its 109th Plenary Session, Venice, 9–10 December 2016.

Malaurie, Claire Bazy, Sarah Cleveland, Regina Kiener, Hanna Suchocka, Kaarlo Tuori, and Jan Velaers. 2016. "Opinion on Emergency Decree Laws No.s 667-676 Adopted Following the Failed Coup of 15 July 2016." *Adopted by the Venice Commission at its 109th Plenary Session*, Venice, December 9–10, 2016.http://www.venice.coe.int/webforms/documents/default.aspx?pdffile=CDL-AD(2016)037-e. Accessed: 01/03/2018.

Mango, Andrew. 2004. *The Turks Today*. London: John Murray.

Martensson, Ulrika, and Eli-Anne Vongraven Eriksen. 2018. "Accurate Knowledge: Implications of 'Lived Islamic Theology' for the Academic Study of Islamic Disciplines." *Islam and Christian–Muslim Relations* 29 (4): 465–83.

Mawdudi, Abdul A'la. 1977. *Human Rights in Islam*. Lahore: Islamic Publications Ltd.

Mayer, Ann Elizabeth. 1994. "Universal versus Islamic Human Rights: A Clash of Cultures or Clash with a Construct." *Michigan Journal of International Law* 15 (2): 307–404.

Mayer, Ann Elizabeth. 1995. *Islam and Human Rights: Tradition and Politics*. 2nd ed. London: Westview Press.

Mayer, Ann Elizabeth. 2003. "The Refah Case: Did Islam and Islamism Distract the European Court of Human Rights from Appraising the Merits of the Case?" Paper presented at *The Turkish Welfare Party Case: Implications for Human Rights in Europe*. Central European University, Budapest, Hungary. June 14, 2003.

Mayer, Ann Elizabeth. 2018. *Islam and Human Rights: Tradition and Politics*. 5th ed. New York: Routledge.
McAdam, Doug. 1999. "The Biographical Impact of Activism." In *How Social Movements Matter*, edited by Marco Giugni, Doug McAdam, and Charles Tilly, 117–46. Minneapolis: University of Minnesota Press.
McGoldrick, Dominic. 2006. *Human Rights and Religion: The Islamic Headscarf Debate in Europe*. Oxford: Hart Publishing.
McGuire, Meredith B. 2008. *Lived Religion: Faith and Practice in Everyday Life*. New York: Oxford University Press.
Mercan, Faruk. 2008. *Fethullah Gülen. Gülen'in Sıradışı Hayatı, ABD'de Geçirdiği Dokuz Yılın Hikâyesi*. Istanbul: Doğan Kitap.
Mercan, Faruk. 2017. *No Return from Democracy: A Survey of Interviews with Fethullah Gülen*. Izmir: Blue Dome Press.
Merleau-Ponty, Maurice. 1962. *Phenomenology of Perception*. London: Routledge.
Mernissi, Fatima. 1991. *The Veil and the Male Elite: A Feminist Interpretation of Women's Rights in Islam*. New York: Addison-Wesley.
Merton, Robert K. 1936. "The Unanticipated Consequences of Purposive Social Action." *American Sociological Review* 1 (6): 894–904.
Meyer, David S., and Nancy Whittier. 1994. "Social Movement Spillover." *Society for the Study of Social Problems* 41 (2): 277–98.
Michel, Thomas. 2002. "Turkish Experience for Muslim-Christian Dialogue: A Thinker: B. S. Nursi & an Activist: M. F. Gülen." In *Conference on: Peace and Dialogue in a Plural Society: Common Values and Responsibilities*. Sydney, Australia. March 3, 2002.
Michel, Thomas S. J. 2005. "Sufism and Modernity in the Thought of Fethullah Gülen." *The Muslim World* 95 (July): 341–58.
Miller, Hannah. 2010. "From 'Rights-Based' to 'Rights-Framed' Approaches: A Social Constructionist View of Human Rights Practice." *International Journal of Human Rights* 14 (6): 915–31.
Morsink, Johannes. 1999. *The Universal Declaration of Human Rights: Origins, Drafting, and Intent*. Philadelphia: University of Pennsylvania Press.
Motta, Sara C., and Ana Margarida Esteves, eds. 2014. "Journal Issue: The Pedagogical Practices of Social Movements [Special Issue]." *Interface* 6 (1).
Mueller, Jason C. 2016. "The Evolution of Political Violence: The Case of Somalia's Al-Shabaab." *Terrorism and Political Violence*, 1–26. DOI: 10.1080/09546553.2016.1165213.
Nadir Kitap. 2020. "Gazeteciler ve Yazarlar Vakfı Yayınları Kitapları." https://www.nadirkitap.com/kitapara.php?ara=kitap&kategori=0&kitap_Adi=&yazar=&ceviren=&hazirlayan=&siralama=fiyatartan&satici=0&ortakkargo=0&yayin_Evi=GAZETEC%DDLER VE YAZARLAR VAKFI YAYINLARI&yayin_Yeri=&isbn=&fiyat1=&fiyat2=&tarih1=0&tarih2=0&guzelcilt. Accessed: 30/10/2020.
Najjaj. April L. 2009. "Using the Gülen Movement to Broaden Discussions in the West Concerning Muslim Women." Paper presented at *Conference Proceedings. East and West Encounters: The Gülen Movement*, edited by Varun Soni, Andrew Achenbaum, Reza Aslan, et al., 125–31. University of Southern California, Los Angeles, CA. December 5–6, 2009.
Nasr, Seyyed Hossein. 2003. *Islam: Religion, History, and Civilization*. New York: HarperOne.

Nassauer, Anne. 2016. "From Peaceful Marches to Violent Clashes: A Micro-Situational Analysis." *Social Movement Studies* 15 (5): 515–30.

Navin, Mark. 2011. "The Authority of Human Rights Practice." *Jurisprudence* 2 (1): 239–47.

Neitz, Mary Jo. 2012. "Lived Religion: Signposts of Where We Have Been and Where We Can Go from Here." In *Religion, Spirituality and Everyday Practice*, edited by Giuseppe Giordan and Jr William H Swatos, 45–55. New York: Springer.

Neslen, Arthur. 2020. "EU States Can Ban Kosher and Halal Ritual Slaughter, Court Rules." *Politico*, December 17, 2020. https://www.politico.eu/article/eu-states-can-ban-kosher-and-halal-ritual-slaughter-court-rules/#:~:text=The EU's highest court has,the rights of religious groups.&text=The proposed ban in Flanders,produced elsewhere%2C the court added. Accessed: 22/12/2020.

Nicolini, Davide. 2013. *Practice Theory, Work and Organization: An Introduction*. Oxford: Oxford University Press.

Nicolini, Davide, Silvia Gherardi, and Dvora Yanow. 2003. "Introduction." In *Knowing in Organizations: A Practice-Based Approach*, edited by Davide Nicolini, Silvia Gherardi, and Dvora Yanow, 3–31. New York: Routledge.

Nina, Khouri. 2007. "Human Rights and Islam: Lessons from Amina Lawal and Mukhtar Mai." *The Georgetown Journal of Gender and the Law* 8 (93): 93–109.

Nonaka, Ikujiro. 1991. "The Knowledge-Creating Company." *Harvard Business Review*, November-December, 69 (6): 96–104.

Nonaka, Ikujiro. 2007. "The Knowledge-Creating Company." *Harvard Business Review*, July–August, 85: 162–71.

Nonaka, Ikujiro, and Hirotaka Takeuchi. 1995. *The Knowledge-Creating Company: How Japanese Companies Create the Dynamics of Innovation*. New York: Oxford University Press.

Nurser, John. 2003. "The 'Ecumenical Movement' Churches, 'Global Order,' and Human Rights: 1938–1948." *Human Rights Quarterly* 25: 841–81.

Nurser, John. 2005. *For All Peoples and All Nations: Christian Churches and Human Rights*. Geneva: WCC Publications.

Nyhagen, Line. 2017. "The Lived Religion Approach in the Sociology of Religion and Its Implications for Secular Feminist Analyses of Religion." *Social Compass* 64 (4): 495–511.

Nzinga, Kalonji, David N. Rapp, Christopher Leatherwood, Matthew Easterday, Leoandra Onnie Rogers, Natalie Gallagher, and Douglas L. Medin. 2018. "Should Social Scientists Be Distanced from or Engaged with the People They Study?" *Proceedings of the National Academy of Sciences of the United States of America* 115 (45): 11435–41.

Oda TV. 2013. "Cemaat Dershaneleri Hangi İsimleri Alıyor." December 16, 2013. https://odatv4.com/cemaat-dershaneleri-hangi-isimleri-aliyor-1612131200.html. Accessed: 01/01/2021.

Oh, Irene. 2007. *The Rights of God: Islam, Human Rights, and Comparative Ethics*. Washington, DC: Georgetown University Press.

Oh, Irene. 2008. "Approaching Islam: Comparative Ethics through Human Rights." *Journal of Religious Ethics* 36 (3): 405–23.

Okuyan, Mukadder, and Nicola Curtin. 2018. "'You Don't Belong Anywhere, "You're in-between"': Pious Muslim Women's Intersectional Experiences and Ideas about Social Change in Contemporary Turkey." *Feminism and Psychology* 28 (4): 488–508.

Oliver, Pamela. 1993. "Reviewed Work(s): Social Movements: A Cognitive Approach by Ron Eyerman and Andrew Jamison." *Social Science Quarterly* 74 (1): 234–35.
O'Neil, Mary Lou, and Sule Toktas. 2014. "Women's Property Rights in Turkey." *Turkish Studies* 15 (1): 29–44.
Öniş, Ziya. 2004. "Turgut Özal and His Economic Legacy: Turkish Neo-Liberalism in Critical Perspective." *Middle Eastern Studies* 40 (4): 113–34.
Orlikowski, Wanda J. 2002. "Knowing in Practice: Enacting a Collective Capability in Distributed Organizing." *Organization Science* 13 (3): 249–73.
Orsi, Robert A. 1985. *The Madonna of 115th Street: Faith and Community in Italian Harlem, 1880–1950*. New Haven, CT: Yale University Press.
Ozcetin, Hilal. 2009. "'Breaking the Silence': The Religious Muslim Women's Movement in Turkey." *Journal of International Women's Studies* 11 (1): 106–19.
Özdalga, Elisabeth. 2003. "Following in the Footsteps of Fethullah Gülen: Three Women Teachers Tell Their Stories." In *Turkish Islam and the Secular State: The Gülen Movement*, edited by M. Hakan Yavuz and John L. Esposito, 85–114. Syracuse, NY: Syracuse University Press.
Özdalga, Elisabeth. 2005. "Redeemer or Outsider? The Gülen Community in the Civilizing Process." *Muslim World* 95 (3): 429–46.
Özyürek, Esra G. 1997. "Feeling Tells Better Than Language: Emotional Expression and Gender Hierarchy in the Sermons of Fethullah Gülen Hocaefendi." *New Perspectives on Turkey* 16 (Spring): 41–51.
Pahl, Jon. 2019. *Fethullah Gülen: A Life of Hizmet*. Izmir: Blue Dome Press.
Pamir, Balçiçek. 2008. "Gülen Türkiye'ye Neden Dönmek İstemiyor?" *HaberTürk*, October 2, 2008. https://www.haberturk.com/yasam/haber/100543-gulen-turkiyeye-neden-donmek-istemiyor. Accessed: 25/08/2020.
Pandya, Sophia. 2009. "Creating Peace on Earth through Hicret: Female Gülen Followers in America." In *East and West Encounters: The Gülen Movement*, edited by Varun Soni, Andrew Achenbaum, and Reza Aslan, 134–45. Los Angeles: University of Southern California.
Park, Bill. 2007. "The Fethullah Gülen Movement as a Transnational Phenomenon." In *Muslim World in Transition: Contributions of the Gülen Movement*, edited by Ihsan Yilmaz, Eileen Barker, Henri J. Barky et al., 46–59. London: Leeds Metropolitan University Press.
Park, Bill. 2012. *Modern Turkey: People, State and Foreign Policy in a Globalized World*. New York: Routledge.
Pattison, Stephen, and James Woodward. 2010. *Introduction to Pastoral and Practical Theology*. Oxford: Blackwell.
Peters, Rudolph, and Gert J.J. De Vries. 1976. "Apostasy in Islam." *Die Welt Des Islams* 17 (1/4): 1–25.
Petito, Fabio. 2009. "Dialogue of Civilizations as an Alternative Model for World Order." In *Civilizational Dialogue and World Order: The Other Politics of Cultures, Religions, and Civilizations in International Relations*, edited by Michalis S. Michael and Fabio Petito, 47–68. New York: Palgrave.
Pew Research Center. 2013. "The World's Muslims: Religion, Politics and Society." April 30, 2013. https://www.pewforum.org/2013/04/30/the-worlds-muslims-religion-politics-society-overview. Accessed 05/10/2016.

Pew Research Center. 2016. "The Divide over Islam and National Laws in the Muslim World." April 27, 2016. http://www.pewglobal.org/2016/04/27/the-divide-over-islam-and-national-laws-in-the-muslim-world. Accessed: 03/12/2018.

Pew Research Center. 2017a. "6. Religious Beliefs and Practices." July 26, 2017. http://www.pewforum.org/2017/07/26/religious-beliefs-and-practices. Accessed 03/12/2018.

Pew Research Center. 2017b. "Why Muslims Are the World's Fastest-Growing Religious Group." April 6, 2017. http://www.pewresearch.org/fact-tank/2017/04/06/why-muslims-are-the-worlds-fastest-growing-religious-group. Accessed: 03/12/2018.

Polanyi, Michael. 1962. *Personal Knowledge: Towards a Post-Critical Philosophy*. London: Routledge and Kegan Paul.

Polanyi, Michael. 2009. *The Tacit Dimension*. Chicago: University of Chicago Press.

Popp, Maximilian. 2012. "Altruistic Society or Sect? The Shadowy World of the Islamic Gülen Movement." *Spiegel Online*, August 8, 2012. http://www.spiegel.de/internatio nal/germany/guelen-movement-accused-of-being-a-sect-a-848763.html. Accessed 29/12/2017.

Pouliot, Vincent. 2015. "Practice Tracing." In *Process Tracing: From Metaphor to Analytic Tool*, edited by Andrew Bennett and Jeffrey T. Checkel, 237–59. Cambridge: Cambridge University Press.

Prasant, Kumar, and Dip Kapoor. 2010. "Learning and Knowledge Production in Dalit Social Movements in Rural India." In *Learning from the Ground Up: Global Perspectives on Social Movements and Knowledge Production*, edited by Aziz Choudry and Dip Kapoor, 193–210. New York: Palgrave Macmillan.

Preis, Ann-Belinda S. 1996. "Human Rights as Cultural Practice: An Anthropological Critique." *Human Rights Quarterly* 18: 286–315.

Pruce, Joel R. 2015a. "The Practice Turn in Human Rights Research." In *The Social Practice of Human Rights*, edited by Joel R. Pruce, 1–20. New York: Palgrave Macmillan.

Pruce, Joel R., ed. 2015b. The Social Practice of Human Rights. New York: Palgrave Macmillan.

Punton, Melanie, and Katharina Welle. 2015. "Applying Process Tracing in Five Steps." Annexe to CDI Practice Paper 10, Brighton: Institute of Development Studies, April 10, 2015.

Ramadan, Tariq. 2001. *Islam, the West and the Challenges of Modernity*. Leicester, UK: The Islamic Foundation.

Ramadan, Tariq. 2009. *Radical Reform: Islam Ethics and Liberation*. New York: Oxford University Press.

Rausch, Margaret J. 2008. "Progress through Piety: *Sohbetler* (Spiritual Gatherings) of the Women Participants in the Gülen Movement." In In *Islam in the Age of Global Challenges: Alternative Perspectives of the Gülen Movement*, edited by Akbar Ahmad, John Borreli, Jill B. Carrol et al., 610–34. Georgetown University, Washington, DC, November 14–15, 2008.

Rausch, Margaret J. 2009. "Gender and Leadership in the Gülen Movement: Women Followers' Contributions to East-West Encounters." In *East and West Encounters: The Gülen Movement*, edited by Varun Soni, Andrew Achenbaum, and Reza Aslan, 175–93. Los Angeles: University of Southern California.

Rausch, Margaret J. 2015. "Women and the Hizmet Movement." In *Hizmet Means Service: Perspectives on an Alternative Path Within Islam*, edited by Martin E. Marty, 123–44. Los Angeles: University of California Press.

Refah Partisi v. Turkey. 2003. 41340/98, 41342/98, 41343/98 and 41344/98, ECHR.

Rehin, George. 1993. "Reviewed Work(s): Social Movements: A Cognitive Approach by Ron Eyerman and Andrew Jamison." *The British Journal of Sociology* 44 (3): 552–53.

Resmi Gazete. 1981. "Millî Eğitim Bakanliği Ile Diğer Bakanliklara Bağli Okullardaki Görevlilerle Öğrencilerin Kılık Kıyafetlerine Ilişkin Yönetmelik." July 22, 1981. No: 17537.

Resmi Gazete. 2016. "Kanun Hükmünde Karaname. Olağanüstü Hal Kapsamında Alınan Tedbirlere Ilişkin Kanun Hükmünde Kararname. Karar Sayısı: KHK/667." July 23, 2016. No. 29779.

Risse, Thomas, and Kathryn Sikkink. 1997. "The Socialization of International Human Rights Norms into Domestic Practices: Introduction." In *The Power of Human Rights: International Norms and Domestic Change*, edited by Thomas Risse, Stephen C. Ropp, and Kathryn Sikkink, 1–38. New York: Cambridge University Press.

Ritter, Daniel P. 2014. "Comparative Historical Analysis." In *Methodological Practices in Social Movement Research*, edited by Donatella Della Porta, 97–116. Oxford: Oxford University Press.

Robinson, Firdevs. 2018. "Gülənçilər Özlərini Tənqid Etməyə Başlayıb." *BBC Azerbaijan*, March 6, 2018. https://www.bbc.com/azeri/amp/region-43302283?__twitter_impression=true. Accessed 08/09/2020.

Rosenthal, Franz. 2007. *Knowledge Triumphant: The Concept of Knowledge in Medieval Islam.* Leiden: Brill.

Rudolph, Peters. 2005. *Crime and Punishment in Islamic Law: Theory and Practice from the Sixteenth to the Twenty-First Century.* New York: Cambridge University Press.

Sabah. 2014. "Tarihimizin En Büyük İhaneti." February 28, 2014. http://gazete.netgazete.com/gazeteler_arsiv.php. Accessed 28/12/2017.

Sachedina, Abdulaziz. 1993. "Review of Abdullahi Ahmed An-Na'im, Toward an Islamic Reformation: Civil Liberties, Human Rights, and International Law (Syracuse, NY: Syracuse University Press, 1990), pp. 270." *International Journal of Middle East Studies* 25 (1): 155–57.

Sachedina, Abdulaziz. 2009. *Islam and the Challenge of Human Rights.* New York: Oxford University Press.

Sadri, Mahmoud. 2001. "Sacral Defense of Secularism: The Political Theologies of Soroush, Shabestari, and Kadivar." *International Journal of Politics, Culture, and Society* 15 (2): 257–70.

Saeed, Abdullah. 2018. *Human Rights and Islam: An Introduction to Key Debates between Islamic Law and International Human Rights Law.* Cheltenham, UK: Edward Elgar.

Saeed, Abdullah, and Hassan Saeed. 2004. *Freedom of Religion, Apostasy and Islam.* Aldershot, UK: Ashgate Publishing.

Şahin, M. Abdülfettah. 1985. *Asrın Getirdiği Tereddütler.* T.Ö.V. Yayınevi.

Salih, Zeinab Mohammed. 2015. "Sudan Threatens 25 Muslims with Death on Charges of Apostasy." *The Guardian*, December 16, 2015. https://www.theguardian.com/world/2015/dec/16/sudan-charges-25-death-penalty-apostasy-sharia-law. Accessed: 27/05/2020.

Salime, Zakia. 2011. *Between Feminism and Islam: Human Rights and Sharia Law in Morocco.* Minneapolis: University of Minnesota Press.

Sametoğlu, Sümeyye Ulu. 2015. "Halalscapes: Leisure, Fun and Aesthetic Spaces Created by Young Muslim Women of the Gülen Movement in France and Germany." In *Everyday Life Practices of Muslim in Europe*, edited by Erkan Toguslu, 143–61. Leuven: Leuven University Press.

Santos, Boaventura de Sousa. 2009. "If God Were a Human Rights Activist: Human Rights and the Challenge of Political Theologies Is Humanity Enough? The Secular Theology of Human Rights." *Law, Social, Justice Global Development* 1 (March): 1–42.

Santos, Boaventura de Sousa, Jodo Arriscado Nunes, and Maria Paula Meneses. 2008. *Another Knowledge Is Possible: Beyond Northern Epistemologies*. London: Verso.

Saritoprak, Zeki. 2003. "A Sufi in His Own Way." In *Turkish Islam and the Secular State: The Gülen Movement*, edited by M. Hakan Yavuz and John L. Esposito, 156–69. New York: Syracuse University Press.

Saritoprak, Zeki. 2005. "An Islamic Approach to Peace and Nonviolence: A Turkish Experience." *The Muslim World* 95 (July): 413–27.

Saritoprak, Zeki. 2011. "Fethullah Gülen and His Theology of Social Responsibility." In *Mastering Knowledge in Modern Times: Fethullah Gülen as an Islamic Scholar*, edited by Ismail Albayrak, 85–96. Izmir: Blue Dome Press.

Schacht, Joseph. 1982. *An Introduction to Islamic Law*. Oxford: Clarendon Press.

Schatzki, Theodore R. 2001a. "Introduction: Practice Theory." In *The Practice Turn in Contemporary Theory*, edited by Theodore R. Schatzki, Karin Knorr Cetina, and Eike von Savigny, 10–23. London: Routledge.

Schatzki, Theodore R. 2001b. "Practice Mind-Ed Orders." In *Scandinavian Journal of Management*, edited by Theodore R. Schatzki, Karin Knorr Cetina, and Eike von Savigny, 50–63. London: Routledge.

Schatzki, Theodore R., Karin Knorr Cetina, and Eike von Savigny, eds. 2001. *The Practice Turn in Contemporary Theory*. London: Routledge.

Schenkkan, Nate. 2018. "The Remarkable Scale of Turkey's 'Global Purge.'" *Foreign Affairs*, January 29, 2018.

Schielke, Samuli, and Liza Debevec. 2012. *Ordinary Lives and Grand Schemes: An Anthropology of Everyday Religion*. New York: Berghahn Books.

Schillinger, Jamie. 2011. "Book Review: Islam and the Challenge of Human Rights by Sachedina, Abdulaziz Review by Jamie Schillinger." *The Journal of Religion* 91 (4): 576–78.

Schindler, Sebastian, and Tobias Wille. 2015. "Change in and through Practice: Pierre Bourdieu, Vincent Pouliot, and the End of the Cold War." *International Theory* 7 (2): 330–59.

Schmidt, Robert. 2016. "The Methodological Challenges of Practising Praxeology." In *Practice Theory and Research: Exploring the Dynamics of Social Life*, edited by Gert Spaargaren, Don Weenink, and Machiel Lamers, 43–59. London: Routledge.

Schwedler, Jillian. 2011. "Can Islamists Become Moderates?: Rethinking the Inclusion-Moderation Hypothesis." *World Politics* 63 (2): 347–76.

Scott, Joan Wallach. 2007. *The Politics of the Veil*. Princeton, NJ: Princeton University Press.

Shabana, Ayman. 2010. *Custom in Islamic Law and Legal Theory: The Development of the Concepts of 'Urf and 'Adah in the Islamic Legal Tradition*. New York: Palgrave Macmillan.

Shah, Niaz A. 2006a. *Women, the Koran and International Human Rights Law: The Experience of Pakistan*. Leiden: Martinus Nijhoff Publishers.

Shah, Niaz A. 2006b. "Women's Human Rights in the Koran: An Interpretive Approach." *Human Rights Quarterly* 28 (4): 868–903.

Shove, Elizabeth, Mika Pantzar, and Matt Watson. 2012. *The Dynamics of Social Practice: Everyday Life and How It Changes*. London: SAGE.

Sleap, Frances, and Omer Sener. 2013. *Dialogue Theories*. London: Dialogue Society.

Smith, Christian. 1996. "Correcting a Curious Neglect, or Bringing Religion Back In." In *Disruptive Religion: The Force of Faith in Social-Movement Activism*, edited by Christian Smith, 1–25. New York: Routledge.

Smith, Matthew. 2016. "Mosque Confirms First Female Chief on International Women's Day." *Enfield Independent*, March 8, 2016. https://www.enfieldindependent.co.uk/news/14328485.mosque-confirms-first-female-chief-on-international-womens-day/. Accessed: 22/07/2020.

Sole, Deborah, and Amy Edmondson. 2002. "Situated Knowledge and Learning in Dispersed Teams." *British Journal of Management* 13 (S2): 17–34.

Soroush, Abdolkarim. 2002. *Reason, Freedom, and Democracy in Islam: Essential Writings of Abdolkarim Soroush, Translated from the Persian, Edited and with a Critical Introduction by Mahmoud Sadri and Ahmad Sadri*. New York: Oxford University Press.

Souto, Patrícia Cristina Do Nascimento. 2013. "Beyond Knowledge, Towards Knowing: The Practice-Based Approach to Support Knowledge Creation, Communication, and Use for Innovation." *Review of Administration and Innovation* 10 (1): 51–79.

Sözcü. 2014. "AKP'den Dersane Hamlesi!" February 6, 2014. https://web.archive.org/web/20140305063229/http://sozcu.com.tr/2014/genel/akpden-dersane-hamlesi-453349. Accessed 01/01/2021.

Spinosa, Charles. 2001. "Derridian Dispersion and Heideggerian Articulation: General Tendencies in the Practices That Govern Intelligibility." In *The Practice Turn in Contemporary Theory*, edited by Theodore R. Schatzki, Karin Knorr Cetina, and Eike von Savigny, 209–22. London: Routledge.

Ssenyonjo, Manisuli. 2007. "The Islamic Veil and Freedom of Religion, the Rights to Education and Work: A Survey of Recent International and National Cases." *Chinese Journal of International Law* 6 (3): 653–710.

Stammers, Neil. 2009. *Human Rights and Social Movements*. London: Pluto Press.

Star. 2014. "Moleküllerine Kadar Ayırırız." May 12, 2014. https://twitter.com/mahmutakpinar1/status/465868682673938433/photo/1. Accessed: 20/05/2020.

Steenbrink, Karel. 2015. "Gülen in the Netherlands between Pious Circles and Social Emancipation." In *Gülen-Inspired Hizmet in Europe: The Western Journey of a Turkish Muslim Movement*, edited by Gürkan Çelik, Johan Leman, and Karel Steenbrink, 197–223. Brussels: P.I.E. Peter Lang.

Stefanovski, Ivan. 2016. "Tracing Causal Mechanisms in Social Movement Research in Southeast Europe: The Cases of Bosnia and Herzegovina and Macedonia – Evidence from the 'Bosnian Spring' and the 'Citizens for Macedonia' Movements." *SEEU Review* 12 (1): 27–51.

Stephenson, Anna J. 2007. "Leaving Footprints in Houston: Answers to Questions on Women and the Gülen Movement." In *Muslim Citizens of the Globalized World: Contributions of the Gülen Movement*, edited by Robert Hunt and Yüksel Alp Aslandoğan, 145–60. New Jersey: IID & The Light, Inc.

Stiftung Dialog und Bildung. 2020. "About Us" Webpage. http://sdub.de/stiftung. Accessed: 12/10/2020.

Suh, Doowon. 2012. "Intricacies of Social Movement Outcome Research and Beyond: 'How Can You Tell' Social Movement Prompt Changes?" *Sociological Review Online* 17 (4): 1–11.

Sunier, Thijl. 2014. "Cosmopolitan Theology: Fethullah Gülen and the Making of a 'Golden Generation.'" *Ethnic and Racial Studies* 37 (12): 2193–208.

Sunier, Thijl. 2015. "Everyday Experiences, Moral Dilemmas and the Making of Muslim Life Worlds: Introductory Reflections." In *Everyday Life Practices of Muslims in Europe*, edited by Erkan Toguslu, 9–15. Leuven: Leuven University Press.

Sunier, Thijl, and Nico Landman. 2015. *Transnational Turkish Islam: Shifting Geographies of Religious Activism and Community Building in Turkey and Europe*. New York: Palgrave Macmillan.

Sutton, Philip W., and Stephen Vertigans. 2006. "Islamic 'New Social Movements'? Radical Islam, Al-Qa'ida and Social Movement Theory." *Mobilization: An International Journal* 11 (1): 101–15.

Swinton, John, and Harriet Mowat. 2006. *Practical Theology and Qualitative Research*. London: SCM Press.

Sykiainen, Leonid R., Paul L. Heck, Victoria Clement, Mohamed Nawab Osman, Yasien Mohamed, and Ozcan Keles. 2013. "Part Three: The Contexts of the Muslim World." In *The Muslim World and Politics in Transition: Creative Contributions of the Gülen Movement*, edited by Greg Barton, Paul Weller, and Ihsan Yilmaz, 127–216. New York: Bloomsbury.

Taha, Mahmoud M. 1987. *The Second Message of Islam*. New York: Syracuse University Press.

Tarabay, Jamie. 2013. "A Rare Meeting with Reclusive Turkish Spiritual Leader Fethullah Gulen." *The Atlantic*, August 14, 2013. https://www.theatlantic.com/international/arch ive/2013/08/a-rare-meeting-with-reclusive-turkish-spiritual-leader-fethullah-gulen/ 278662. Accessed: 10/07/2017.

Tarnas, Richard. 2010. *The Passion of the Western Mind: Understanding the Ideas That Shaped Our World View*. London: Pimlico.

Tasioulas, John. 2012. "On the Nature of Human Rights." In *The Philosophy of Human Rights: Contemporary Controversies*, edited by Gerhard Ernst and Jan-Christoph Heilinger, 17–59. Berlin, Boston.

Taylor, Charles. 1995. *Philosophical Arguments*. 2nd ed. Cambridge, MA: Harvard University Press.

Taylor, Paul M. 2005. *Freedom of Religion: UN and European Human Rights Law and Practice*. Cambridge: Cambridge University Press.

Tee, Caroline. 2016. *The Gülen Movement in Turkey: The Politics of Islam and Modernity*. London: I. B. Tauris.

Tee, Caroline. 2018. "The Gülen Movement in London and the Politics of Public Engagement: Producing 'Good Islam' before and after 15 July." *Politics, Religion and Ideology* 19 (1): 109–22.

The Netherlands Scientific Council for Government Policy (WRR). 2006. "Dynamism in Islamic Activism: Reference Points for Democratization and Human Rights." Amsterdam: Amsterdam University Press.

Tibi, Bassam. 1994. "Islamic Law/Shari'a, Human Rights, Universal Morality and International Relations." *Human Rights Quarterly* 16 (2): 277–99.

Tibi, Bassam. 2009. *Islam's Predicament with Modernity: Religious Reform and Cultural Change*. New York: Routledge.

Tibi, Bassam. 2014. *Political Islam, World Politics and Europe: From Jihadist to Institutional Islam*. 2nd ed. New York: Routledge.

Tilly, Charles. 1999. "From Interactions to Outcomes in Social Movements." In *How Social Movements Matter*, edited by Marco Giugni, Doug McAdam, and Charles Tilly, 253–70. Minneapolis: University of Minnesota Press.

Tittensor, David. 2014. *The House of Service: The Gülen Movement and Islam's Third Way*. New York: Oxford University Press.
Tittensor, David. 2015. "Islam's Modern Day Ibn Battutas: Gülen Teachers Journeying Towards the Divine." *British Journal of Middle Eastern Studies* 42 (2): 163–78.
Topal, Semiha. 2014. "Thoughts on Islam, Gender, and the Hizmet Movement." *Consensus* 35 (1): 4.
Turam, Berna. 2004. "The Politics of Engagement between Islam and the Secular State: Ambivalences of 'Civil Society.'" *British Journal of Sociology* 55 (2): 259–81.
Turam, Berna. 2007. *Between Islam and the State: The Politics of Engagement*. Stanford: Stanford University Press.
Turner, Colin. 2013. *The Qur'an Revealed: A Critical Analysis of Said Nursi's Epistles of Light*. Berlin: Gerlach Press.
U.S. Commission on International Religious Freedom. 2018. "Legislation Fact Sheet: Blasphemy." November 2018. Washington, DC.
United States Department of State. 2019. "Turkey 2018 Human Rights Report." Washington, DC. https://www.state.gov/documents/organization/289241.pdf%0Ahttps://mv.usmission.gov/wp-content/uploads/sites/212/HR-report-2018-Maldives-English.pdf. Accessed: 05/10/2020.
Uğur, Etga. 2004. "Intellectual Roots of 'Turkish Islam' and Approaches to the 'Turkish Model.'" *Journal of Muslim Minority Affairs* 24 (2): 327–45.
Uğur, Etga. 2013. "Organizing Civil Society: The Gülen Movement's Abant Platform." In *Muslim World and Politics in Transition: Creative Contributions of the Gülen Movement*, edited by Greg Barton, Paul Weller, and Ihsan Yilmaz, 47–64. London: Bloomsbury.
Universal Declaration of Human Rights. 1948. The United Nations, General Assembly. December 10, 1948.
Vahdat, Farzin. 2000a. "Post-Revolutionary Discourses of Mohammad Mojtahed Shabestari and Mohsen Kadivar: Reconciling the Terms of Mediated Subjectivity. Part I: Mojtahed Shabestari." *Critique: Critical Middle Eastern Studies* 9 (16): 31–54.
Vahdat, Farzin. 2000b. "Post-Revolutionary Discourses of Mohammad Mojtahed Shabestari and Mohsen Kadivar: Reconciling the Terms of Mediated Subjectivity. Part II: Mohsen Kadivar." *Critique: Critical Middle Eastern Studies* 9 (17): 135–57.
Valkenberg, Pim. 2015. "The Intellectual Format of the Hizmet Movement: A Discourse Analysis." In *Gülen-Inspired Hizmet in Europe: The Western Journey of a Turkish Muslim Movement*, edited by Gürkan Çelik, Johan Leman, and Karel Steenbrink, 49–65. Brussels: P.I.E. Peter Lang.
Ven, Johannes A. van der. 2006. "A Chapter in Public Theology from the Perspective of Human Rights: Interreligious Interaction and Dialogue in an Intercivilizational Context." *The Journal of Religion* 86 (3): 412–41.
Vennesson, Pascal. 2008. "Case Studies and Process Tracing: Theories and Practices." In *Approaches and Methodologies in the Social Sciences: A Pluralist Perspective*, edited by Porta Della Donatella and Michael Keating, 223–39. New York: Cambridge University Press.
Voices in Britain. 2018. "Green Paper 01: British Hizmet on Identity-Based Transparency." July 2018. http://www.voicesinbritain.org/assets/docs/green-papers/Green-Paper-01-British-Hizmet-on-Identity-Based-Transparency.pdf. Accessed: 01/01/2020.
Voll, John O. 2003. "Fethullah Gülen: Transcending Modernity in the New Islamic Discourse." In *Turkish Islam and the Secular State: The Gülen Movement*, edited by M. Hakan Yavuz and John L. Esposito, 238–48. New York: Syracuse University Press.

Wadud, Amina. 1999. *Qur'an and Woman: Rereading the Sacred Text from a Woman's Perspective*. New York: Oxford University Press.
Wagoner, Brady. 2008. "Making the Familiar Unfamiliar." *Culture and Psychology* 14 (4): 467–74.
Waltz, Susan. 2004. "Universal Human Rights: The Contribution of Muslim States." *Human Rights Quarterly* 26: 799–844.
Warsi, Sayeeda. 2017. *The Enemy Within: A Tale of Muslim Britain*. London: Penguin UK.
Weller, Paul. 2008. "Religious Freedom in the Baptist Vision and in Fethullah Gülen: Resources for Muslims and Christians." In *Islam in the Age of Global Challenges: Alternative Perspectives of the Gülen Movement*, edited by Akbar Ahmad, John Borreli, Jill B. Carrol et al., 754–81. Georgetown University, Washington, DC November 14–15, 2008.
Weller, Paul. 2015. "The Gülen Movement in the United Kingdom." In *Gülen-Inspired Hizmet in Europe: The Western Journey of a Turkish Muslim Movement*, edited by Gürkan Çelik, Johan Leman, and Karel Steenbrink, 239–51. Brussels: P.I.E. Peter Lang.
Weller, Paul. 2022a. *Fethullah Gülen's Teaching and Practice: Inheritance, Context and Interactive Development*. Cham, Germany: Palgrave Macmillan.
Weller, Paul. 2022b. *Hizmet in Transitions: European Developments of a Turkish Muslim-Inspired Movement*. Cham, Germany: Palgrave Macmillan.
West, W. Jefferson, II. 2006. "Religion as Dissident Geopolitics? Geopolitical Discussions within the Recent Publications of Fethullah Gülen." *Geopolitics* 11 (2): 280–99.
White, Jenny B. 2002. "Islamist Elitism and Women's Choices." In *Islamist Mobilization in Turkey: A Study in Vernacular Politics*. Seattle: University of Washington Press.
Wiktorowicz, Quintan. 2004. "Introduction: Islamic Activism and Social Movement Theory." In *Islamic Activism: A Social Movement Theory Approach*, edited by Quintan Wiktorowicz, 1–33. Bloomington: Indiana University Press.
Woolf, Harry, Jeffrey Jowell, Edward Garnier, and Sarah Palin. 2015. "A Report on the Rule of Law and Respect for Human Rights in Turkey Since December 2013." July 2015.
Yakutcan, Ahmet, and Cuma Ömür. 1991. *İslâm'da Resim, Heykel ve Mûsikî*. İzmir: Nil.
Yates, Luke. 2015. "Everyday Politics, Social Practices and Movement Networks: Daily Life in Barcelona's Social Centres." *British Journal of Sociology* 66 (2): 236–58.
Yavuz, İsmail, 2009. "Hâin Tuzak!" (This article includes an image of Aksiyon's cover story titled, "Patrik 'çizme'yi Aştı," dated July 1, 1995). *Hakikat*, https://www.hakikat.com/hakikat-dergisi/190/hain-tuzak. Accessed: 08/01/2021.
Yavuz, M. Hakan. 1999. "Search for a New Social Contract in Turkey: Fethullah Gulen, the Virtue Party and the Kurds." *SAIS Review* 19 (1): 114–43.
Yavuz, M. Hakan. 2003a. "Islam in the Public Sphere: The Case of the Nur Movement." In *Turkish Islam and the Secular State: The Gülen Movement*, edited by M. Hakan Yavuz and John L. Esposito, 1–18. New York: Syracuse University Press.
Yavuz, M. Hakan. 2003b. "The Gülen Movement: The Turkish Puritans." In *Turkish Islam and the Secular State: The Gülen Movement*, edited by M. Hakan Yavuz and John L. Esposito, 19–47. New York: Syracuse University Press.
Yavuz, M. Hakan. 2013. *Toward an Islamic Enlightenment: The Gülen Movement*. New York: Oxford University Press.
Yavuz, M. Hakan, and John L. Esposito. 2003a. "Introduction: Islam in Turkey: Retreat from the Secular Path?" In *Turkish Islam and the Secular State: The Gülen Movement*, edited by M. Hakan Yavuz and John L. Esposito, xiii–xxxiii. New York: Syracuse University Press.

Yavuz, M. Hakan, and John L. Esposito, eds. 2003b. *Turkish Islam and the Secular State: The Gülen Movement*. New York: Syracuse University Press.

Yavuz, M. Sait. 2008. "Women in Islam: Muslim Perspectives and Fethullah Gülen." In *Islam in the Age of Global Challenges: Alternative Perspectives of the Gülen Movement*, edited by Akbar Ahmad, John Borreli, Jill B. Carrol et al., 835–58. Georgetown University, Washington, DC. November 14–15, 2008.

Yilmaz, Ihsan. 2000. "Changing Turkish-Muslim Discourses on Modernity, West and Dialogue." Paper presented at the *Congress of the International Association of Middle East Studies*. Freie Universitat, Berlin, Germany. 5–7 October, 2000.

Yilmaz, Ihsan. 2003. "Ijtihad and Tajdid by Conduct: The Gülen Movement." In *Turkish Islam and the Secular State: The Gülen Movement*, edited by M. Hakan Yavuz and John L. Esposito, 208–37. New York: Syracuse University Press.

Yilmaz, Ihsan. 2005a. "Inter-Madhab Surfing, Neo-Ijtihad, and Faith-Based Movement Leaders." In *The Islamic School of Law: Evolution, Devolution, and Progress*, edited by Peri Bearman, Rudolph Peter, and Frank E Vogel, 191–206. Cambridge, MA: Harvard University Press.

Yilmaz, Ihsan. 2005b. *Muslim Laws, Politics and Society in Modern Nation States: Dynamic Legal Pluralisms in England, Turkey and Pakistan*. Aldershot, UK: Ashgate.

Yilmaz, Ihsan. 2005c. "State, Law, Civil Society and Islam in Contemporary Turkey." *The Muslim World* 95 (July): 385–411.

Yilmaz, Ihsan. 2008. "Beyond Post-Islamism: A Critical Analysis of the Turkish Islamism's Transformation toward Fethullah Gülen's Stateless Cosmopolitan Islam." In *Islam in the Age of Global Challenges: Alternative Perspectives of the Gülen Movement*, edited by Akbar Ahmad, John Borreli, Jill B. Carrol et al., 859–925. Georgetown University, Washington, DC, November 14–15, 2008.

Yilmaz, Ihsan. 2012. "Towards a Muslim Secularism? An Islamic 'Twin Tolerations' Understanding of Religion in the Public Sphere." *TJP Turkish Journal of Politics* 3 (2): 41–52.

Yilmaz, Ihsan. 2013. "Homo LASTus and Lausannian Muslim: Two Paradoxical Social-Engineering Projects to Construct the Best and the Good Citizen in the Kemalist Panopticon." *TJP Turkish Journal of Politics* 4 (2): 107–26.

Yilmaz, Ihsan. 2015a. *Kemalizm'den Erdoganizm'e*. Istanbul: Ufuk Yayınları.

Yilmaz, Ihsan. 2015b. "AKP's 'Book Burning' Stage." *Hizmet Movement Blogspot*, December 25, 2015. http://hizmetmovement.blogspot.com/2015/12/akps-book-burning-stage.html. Accessed: 12/01/2021.

Yilmaz, Ihsan. 2018. " Unofficial Islamic Legal Knowledge Production." SSRN, November 30, 2018, 1–19. Also available at Yilmaz, Ihsan. 2018. " Unofficial Islamic Legal Knowledge Production." SSRN, November 30, 2018, 1–19. Also available at https://ssrn.com/abstract=3326322.

YouTube. 2013. "The Fruit of Dialogue 1." (Uploaded to YouTube by account named Habib Mokhtar). April 1, 2013. https://www.youtube.com/watch?v=BNqobeZb8GM. Accessed: 01/08/2018.

Yucel, Salih. 2010. "Fethullah Gülen: Spiritual Leader in a Global Islamic Context." *Journal of Religion and Society* 12: 1–12.

Yukleyen, Ahmet. 2009. "Localizing Islam in Europe: Religious Activism among Turkish Islamic Organizations in the Netherlands." *Journal of Muslim Minority Affairs* 29 (3): 291–309.

Zhu, Zhichang. 2006. "Nonaka Meets Giddens: A Critique." *Knowledge Management Research and Practice* 4: 106–15.

Ziadah, Rafeef, and Adam Hanieh. 2010. "Collective Approaches to Activist Knowledge: Experiences of the New Anti-Apartheid Movement in Toronto." In *Learning from the Ground Up: Global Perspectives on Social Movements and Knowledge Production*, edited by Aziz Choudry and Dip Kapoor, 85–99. New York: Palgrave Macmillan.

Zigler, Ronald Lee. 2007. "Tacit Knowledge and Spiritual Pedagogy." *Journal of Beliefs and Values* 20 (2): 162–72.

Index

For the benefit of digital users, indexed terms that span two pages (e.g., 52–53) may, on occasion, appear on only one of those pages

Figures are indicated by *f* following the page number

abodes, 101
abstraction, 88*f*
act of doing, 88
adanmışlık (devotion to cause), 143, 144
adl (justice), 32–33
adultery, 100
adult learning, 55
Africa, 102–3
Ahmed, Leyla, 138
Akgül, Ahmet, 122
Ali, Ayaan Hirsi, 137
Alkan, Banu, 116
Allievi, Stefano, 48–49
amal. See practice
analogical reasoning (*qiyas*), 91–92, 92n.15
Anatolian Sufi Muslimness, 13–14
An-Na'im, Abudllahi, Ahmed, 35–36, 39
apostasy
   alternative explanations for, 126–27, 130–32
   challenges to, 119–22, 130–32
   dialogue and, 113–22
   dissonance from, 122–27
   doctrine, 100–3
   Gülen on, 106–10, 127–32
   hicret and, 110–11
   internalisation and, 110–11
   in Islam, 99, 132–34
   overview of, 103–6
apostate others, 110–11
appeasement, 130–32
applied Christianity, 47
Arab-Israeli War, 1
Ash'ari theology, 196–97
Asia, 102–3, 111–12
Aydın, Mehmet, 116

ban, of headscarfs, 154–62
Barazngi, Nimat Hafiz, 138
Barlas, Asma, 138
Bartholomeos (patriarch), 114–15, 116
Başarı, Mustafa, 150–53
bayanlar hizmeti (women's hizmet), 166, 166*f*, 170–72, 181, 184–85, 192
Bayat, Asef, 34, 36–42
Beach, Derek, 69–70, 71–74, 73*f*, 76
beliefs, 40–42, 41*f*, 42*f*, 160–62
Benard, Cheryl, 34–35
Bennet, Andrew, 67–68, 69
Berger, Peter, 82
Bielefeldt, Heiner, 26, 29–30
Bilen, Alber, 116
bin Laden, Osama, 37–38
bölgecilik (grass roots religious activism), 12–13, 15–16, 191–92
Bourdieu, Pierre, 55–56
Bowen, John R., 48
Brems, Eva, 33–34
Bruinessen, Martin Van, 48–49
Buber, Martin, 118
burkas, 2–3, 147. *See also* headscarfs

Caeiro, Alexandre, 26
Cairo Declaration of Human Rights (1990), 29–30
Çandar, Cengiz, 115
capital, 55–56
çarşaf. See headscarfs
Cartesianism, 45, 191
categorical rejection, 27–30
Catholicism, 114
causality, 130–32
causal mechanisms, 64, 66–67, 69–74, 73*f*, 75, 99, 194

Central Asia, 111–12
Centre for Intercultural Dialogue Studies, 174, 175–76
certainty (*yaqeen*), 96–97
Césari, Jocelyne, 26–27, 27n.1
Çetinkaya, Hikmet, 122
Choudry, Aziz, 53–54
Christianity
　applied, 47
　human rights in, 29
　Judaism and, 86–87, 119
　to Muslims, 115
　performance in, 40–42, 41*f*, 42*f*
　theology of, 7, 91
　in Western Civilization, 33–34
Çiller, Tansu, 114–15
coalition governments, 155, 155n.18
Coca-Cola, 17–18, 18n.16, 109–10
cognitive compromise, 82–84, 86–90, 194–95
cognitive dissonance, 84–90, 194–95
collective beliefs, 160–62
combination, 78–79
competition, in practice, 192–93, 193*f*
compromise, 82–84, 86–90, 194–95
concepts, of epistemic outcomes, 77–90
conceptualised intervening process, 90–98
conciliatorist approach, 30–35, 40–42
conflict, 148–64, 188
consequences, 121, 132–34
constructed *fiqh*, 35–36
context, 50–51, 86–90, 91–98, 99, 100–3, 137–40, 162–64
Corradi. Gessica, 57
cosmopolitan Islam, 113
crime, in Islam, 100–3, 109
culture
　cultural capital, 55–56
　cultural imperialism, 122
　in *dershanes*, 153–62
　education and, 159*f*, 160*f*, 161*f*
　globalisation of, 6
　of Hizmet movement, 143–44, 172
　intercultural dialogue, 109
　of movements, 52–53
　of Muslims, 6–7
　non-Muslims in, 87*f*

philosophy and, 1–3
　of Turkey, 10–11, 15–16, 21
cumulative outcomes
　cumulative epistemic outcomes, 181
　dissonance, 174–76
　externalisation, 176–79
　internalisation as, 166–73
　knowledge production and, 164–79
　for Muslims, 140–43
　pre-emptive outcomes, 178–79

Daesh, 27
dar al harb/dar al Islam (abodes), 101
deductive reasoning, 18, 183–84
Della Porta, Donatella, 67–68, 69
democracy, 2–3, 31
dershanes (university preparatory centres)
　culture in, 153–62
　education in, 135, 148, 150–51, 152–53, 166–68, 166*f*, 171
　intentions of, 10–11, 111–12
　in Turkey, 149, 149n.14
devotion to cause (*adanmışlık*), 143, 144
dialogue
　apostasy and, 113–22
　Centre for Intercultural Dialogue Studies, 174, 175–76
　education and, 110–11
　in Hizmet movement, 113–14, 119–22
　intercultural, 109
　practitioners of, 126
Dialogue Society, 19–20
direct outcomes, 140–43, 148–64, 182
discontent, 149–53
discourse, 60
dispositions (*habitus*), 55–56
dissonance, 84–90, 122–27, 174–76, 194–95
divine behavior (*Sunnatullah*), 196–97
doing
　act of, 88
　in Hizmet movement, 135–36, 140–43, 142*f*
　knowing and, 80, 181, 183–84, 186
　reflexivity and, 132–33
　sayings and, 66–67, 105*f*
　women's rights and, 142*f*
Donnelly, Jack, 28

Doron, Eliyahu Bakshi, 114
Dunn, Shannon, 26
duties, 158–60

Ebadi, Shirin, 138
Ecevit, Bülent, 114–15
education
  adult, 55
  culture and, 159f, 160f, 161f
  in *dershanes*, 135, 148, 150–51, 152–53, 166–68, 166f, 171
  dialogue and, 110–11
  direct outcomes from, 148–64
  girls', 149–53
  hicret and, 111–13, 122
  intervening process in, 157f
  media and, 109
  of Muslim women, 149–53
  stereotypes in, 146
  in Turkey, 111–13, 154–62
  in Western Civilization, 30
Egypt, 83
Eid, 174
Eid al Adha (Feast of Sacrifice), 48–49
embracive approach, 26–27, 27n.1
emerging dissonance, 122–27
empirical evidence, 72–73
entitlement (*haqq*), 32–33
epistemic outcomes
  case studies of, 67–76
  cognitive compromise in, 82–84, 86–90
  cognitive dissonance with, 84–90
  concepts of, 77–90
  conceptualized intervening process and, 90–98
  cumulative epistemic outcomes, 181
  explicit knowledge and, 77–78
  of *fiqh*, 64, 91–95
  of Hizmet movement, 64–67
  human rights and, 191
  internalisation and, 86–90
  of knowledge conversion, 95–98
  organisational studies of, 78–81
  of practice, 64, 67–76, 98, 178
  in practice-based epistemology, 81–86
  unintended internal, 51–53, 80–81, 121
epistemology
  conformity with, 129–30

duality, 183
epistemic context, 91–98
epistemic effects, 76
  of Hizmet movement, 53
  ontology and, 196
  practice-based, 47, 81–86
  religious, 133–34
  in scholarship, 42–43
Epistles of Light (Risale-i Nur), 13n.13
Erdoğan, Recep Tayyip, 127–28
Erken, Sevim, 144–45
Esposito, John L., 14
Europe
  European Commission on Islam and Fundamental Rights in Europe, 26
  European Court of Human Rights, 30–31
  European Union, 12
  Hizmet movement in, 112–13, 124, 128
  Muslims in, 130, 138–39
  United States and, 175–76
Evans, Malcolm, 25–26
excommunication, 127–28
ex-Muslims, 5–6, 103
experiential knowledge, 68, 183–97, 187f, 193f
explicit knowledge, 77–78, 89, 95–98
externalisation
  communication of, 178
  externalised *ijtihad*, 162
  Gülen and, 127
  internalisation and, 86–90, 87f, 88f, 99, 106f, 132–33, 149, 150f, 157f, 186–87, 187f
  by Muslim women, 176–79
  practice-based, 89
  psychology of, 176
  of reinterpretation, 127–32
  of tacit knowledge, 78–84
externality, 99, 133, 181–82
Eygi, Mehmet Şevket, 122

face veil (*niqab*), 109–10
Fadl, Khaled Abou El, 27–28, 35–36, 93
faith, 91, 96
Falk, Richard A., 29
faqih (Islamic jurist), 8
fast-breaking (*iftar*), 48–49

Feast of Sacrifice (*Eid al Adha*), 48–49
feminism, 137, 138, 172–73. *See also* women's rights
Festinger, Leon, 84–87, 87n.13, 187–88
fields (spheres of life), 55–56
fiqh (Islamic law)
  constructed, 35–36
  epistemic outcomes of, 64, 91–95
  human rights in, 30–31
  ijtihad and, 92–95, 92n.16, 97
  Islamic knowledge and, 90
  knowledge production and, 129–30
  to Muslims, 7–8
  premodern, 16–17, 33–34
  religion and, 32
  usul al-fiqh, 7–8, 32–33, 91–92
fitra (human nature), 32–33
Flaskerud, Ingvild, 48
formalised knowledge, 45, 183–97, 187*f*, 193*f*
fornication, 100
Foucault, Michel, 43–44
fuqaha (Islamic jurists), 91

Garfinkel, Harold, 43–44
Garih, Üzeyir, 116
gender-based segregation, 145–47, 157*f*, 174–76, 184–85
generalisability, 193–95
general others, 110–11
George, Alexander L., 67–68, 69
Germany, 177
Gherardi, Silvia, 57, 89
Giddens, Anthony, 43–44, 57
girls' education, 149–53
God. *See specific topics*
grassroots religious activism, 15–16, 42–43
Gülen, Muhammed Fethullah
  on apostasy, 106–10, 127–32
  Başarı and, 151–53
  challenges to, 101–2
  externalisation and, 127
  followers of, 62
  as founder, 10–12, 13–14
  on headscarfs, 158–62
  Hizmet movement and, 103–4, 178–79, 188–89

  intentions of, 185
  knowledge production and, 180–82
  on Muslim women, 135, 143–47
  Nursi and, 61, 143–44
  on Qur'an, 106–10
  reputation of, 23–24, 113–22, 135–36, 153–62, 154n.16
  sayings of, 140–43, 142*f*
  scholarship on, 60, 60n.29
  on segregation, 176–79
  teachings of, 59
  Turkey and, 149–50
  views of, 106, 138
  Weller on, 59n.26
  Western Civilization to, 14
  women's rights to, 143–47
Gülen movement. *See* Hizmet movement
Gulf War, 1

habitus (dispositions), 55–56
hadith (Prophetic sayings), 37, 100–1, 123
Hallaq, Wael B., 7
haqq (entitlement), 32–33
haraba (rebellion), 100
haram (sin), 143
Hassan, Riffat, 138
Hauerwas, Stanley, 40–42, 41*f*, 42*f*
headscarfs
  ban of, 154–62
  conflict with, 148–64
  in culture, 139, 148–64, 195
  gender-based segregation and, 184–85
  Gülen on, 158–62
  in Hizmet movement, 135
  in media, 2–3
  to Muslim women, 154–62
  women's rights and, 147
hegemony, 29, 42
Hendrik, Joshua D., 14–15, 59n.27
hicret (migration), 104, 106*f*, 110–13, 122, 184–85
Hizmet movement (aka Gülen movement). *See also specific topics*
  challenges to, 130–32
  consequences of, 132–34
  context for, 99
  culture of, 143–44, 172
  dialogue in, 113–14, 119–22

doing in, 135–36, 140–43, 142*f*
emergent reinterpretation in, 178–79, 181, 182
epistemic outcomes of, 64–67
epistemology of, 53
in Europe, 112–13, 124, 128
gender-based segregation in, 174–76
Gülen and, 103–4, 178–79, 188–89
Gülen movement and, 5, 15–17, 21–22n.18, 22, 67, 67n.1, 139–40, 146–47, 149–53, 150*f*, 157*f*
headscarfs in, 135
history of, 9, 10–12, 24, 109–10, 111–13
Hizmet movement and, 5, 15–17, 21–22n.18, 22, 67, 67n.1, 139–40, 146–47, 149–53, 150*f*, 157*f*
identity politics in, 18–24
ijtihad in, 16–17, 24, 60, 95
knowledge production and, 58, 59–62, 68, 90, 162–64
in media, 144–45
mujtahid (practitioner of *ijtihad*) in, 95
Muslim women in, 153–54
non-human rights practice in, 9–10
participants of, 75
politics of, 148–64, 157*f*
practice in, 6, 8–9, 20–21, 56–57, 88, 99, 106*f*, 136, 139, 176–79, 184
public self-criticism in, 21
reputation of, 22–23
sayings in, 135–36
scholarship on, 5–6, 10–18, 77, 180–82
Sunni Hanafi Maturidi orthodoxy in, 13–14
surveys from, 140
in United Kingdom, 19–20, 117, 175–76
hudud (God-ordained penal law), 100–3, 131
humanistic tradition
approaches to, 3–6, 24
in European Court of Human Rights, 30–31
to Muslims, 25–34, 63
politics of, 1–2
scholarship on, 6–10
human nature (*fitra*), 32–33
human rights. *See specific topics*

Human Rights in Islam (Mawdudi), 1
Huntington, Samuel, 28
Hussain, Dilwar, 26
hypocrisy, 175

identity politics, 2–4, 18–24
ideology, in modernity, 6
iftar (fast-breaking dinner), 48–49
IG. *See* Islamic Group
ijma (juristic consensus), 91–92, 91n.14, 100–1, 103, 190
ijtihad (religious reinterpretation)
apostasy and, 123–26
criteria for, 186
externalised, 162
fiqh and, 92–95, 92n.16, 97
in Hizmet movement, 16–17, 24, 60, 95
Islamic scholarship on, 178
mujtahid, 93–95, 96–97
organisational revisions in, 135
premodern *fiqh* and, 16–17
production of, 124, 129–30
Qur'an and, 130
theology and, 99
Imam Hatips, 163–64
iman. *See* faith
imperialism, 122
inductive reasoning, 18, 183–84
informal practice, 12–13
innovation (*bida*), 27–28
insider/outsider identity, 19–24
intentionality, 83–84, 99, 121, 133, 181–82, 185
intercultural dialogue, 109
internalisation
apostasy and, 110–11
context for, 86–90
downward force of, 187–88
epistemic outcomes and, 86–90
externalisation and, 86–90, 87*f*, 88*f*, 99, 106*f*, 132–33, 149, 150*f*, 157*f*, 186–87, 187*f*
by Muslim women, 166–73
through practice, 188
practice-based, 81, 89, 122
psychology of, 78–79
interpretative methodology, 65–66, 69

intervening process
   in education, 157*f*
   in girls' education, 149, 150*f*
   of practice, 74, 77–98
   timelines for, 103–6
   women's rights and, 153*f*
intoxication, 100
intrinsic processes, 80–81
intuitive knowledge (*marifa*), 96–97
Iran, 37, 119–20
Iraq, 1
Islam. *See specific topics*
Islamic activism, 15
Islamic frameworks, 95–98
Islamic Group (IG), 83
Islamic jurist (*faqih*), 8
Islamic jurists (*fuqaha*), 91
Islamic justification, 195–96
Islamic knowledge, 7, 8, 9–10, 10n.7, 63, 90
Islamic literature, 64, 96
Islamic mysticism (*tasawwuf*), 143, 144
Islamic piety (*taqwa*), 143, 144
Islamic scholars (*ulama*), 91, 96–97
Islamic scholarship, 29–30, 178
Islamic scripture, 25
Israel, 1
istihsan (juristic preference), 97

Jahanbakhsh, Forough, 38–39
John Paul II (pope), 114
Johnston, David L., 35–36
Journalists and Writer's Foundation, 116–17
Judaism, 86–87, 114, 115, 119
judges (*qadis*), 178
jurisprudence, 37
juristic consensus (*ijma*), 91–92, 91n.14, 100–1, 103, 190
juristic preference (*istihsan*), 97
justice (*adl*), 32–33

Kadivar, Mohsen, 33, 36n.10
Kamali, Mohammad Hashim, 93
Kapoor, Dip, 53–54
Karaca, Cem, 114–15
Keating, Michael, 67–68, 69
Kelman, Herbert C., 82–83

kendini vakfetmek (life dedication), 143–44
King Lear analogy, 40–42, 41*f*, 42*f*, 47–48
knowledge
   context for, 50–51
   conversion, 95–98
   experiential, 68, 183–97, 187*f*, 193*f*
   explicit, 77–78, 89, 95–98
   formalised, 45, 183–97, 187*f*, 193*f*
   human rights, 195
   intuitive, 96–97
   in Islam, 196
   Islamic, 7, 8, 9–10, 10n.7, 63, 90
   knowing, 80, 181, 183–84, 186
   organisational, 55, 55n.22
   personal, 77–78
   pieces of, 85–86
   practice and, 4–5, 44–53, 85
   practice-based knowledge production, 94, 132–33
   pre-reflexive, 51–52, 77–78
   rationality and, 45
   in religion, 4, 183–84
   religious, 40, 43, 47, 63
   reproduction, 63
   social movements and, 53–58
   spiral of, 79n.11
   tacit, 77–84, 89, 95–98
   tacit-to-explicit knowledge conversion, 89, 95–98
knowledge production
   cumulative outcomes and, 164–79
   direct outcomes and, 182
   fiqh and, 129–30
   Gülen and, 180–82
   Hizmet movement and, 58, 59–62, 68, 90, 162–64
   movement practice and, 190–91
   practice and, 162–64
   practice-based, 94, 132–33, 195–96
   process tracing and, 70–71
   symbiotic interplay in, 183–97, 187*f*, 193*f*
Koru, Fehmi, 115, 116
Kurucan, Ahmed, 123–27, 123n.23, 131
Kuwait, 1

Lambek, Michael, 48
language, 18–19, 51–52

laws, 50–51. *See also specific topics*
leader/follower paradigm, 62
legal schools (*madhhabs*), 27–28, 91–92, 96, 101–2, 133–34, 190
life dedication (*kendini vakfetmek*), 143–44
Loefller, Reinhold, 48

madhhabs (legal schools), 27–28, 91–92, 96, 101–2, 133–34, 190
Manji, Irshad, 137
maqasid al-Sharia (objective of the Sharia), 32–33
marifa (intuitive knowledge), 96–97
Marxist/postcolonial critiques, 26
maslahah (public interest), 32–33, 97
Mawdudi, Abul A'la, 1, 29–30
Mayer, Ann Elizabeth, 29–30
media
   education and, 109
   globalization of, 116
   headscarfs in, 2–3
   Hizmet movement in, 144–45
   Islam in, 109–10, 122–27
   Journalists and Writers Foundation, 116–17
   Muslims in, 177–78
   in Turkey, 114, 115
Mernissi, Fatima, 138
meta-theory, 71–72
methodology of *fiqh*. See *usul al-fiqh*
Middle East, 1, 27–28, 102–3, 111–12. *See also specific countries*
migration (*hicret*), 110–13, 184–85
mind/body dichotomy, 62
minimally sufficient explanations, 191–92
modernity
   apostasy doctrine in, 100–3
   bayanlar hizmeti in, 166, 166f, 170–72, 181, 184–85, 192
   ideology in, 6
   Muslims in, 13–14, 34–35
   premodern *fiqh*, 16–17, 33–34
   scholarship in, 102
   in Turkey, 14
motive, 119–22
movement practice, 53–54, 190–91
movements. *See specific movements*

Muhammad (prophet), 112
mujaddid (renewer), 92–93
mujtahid (person engaged in *ijtihad*), 93–95, 96–97
multiple practice, 189–90
multiresolutional methodology, 65–66
mundane practices, 74–75
Müren, Zeki, 114–15
Muslim women
   challenges for, 178–79
   context for, 137–40, 162–64
   dissonance with, 174–76
   education of, 149–53
   externalisation by, 176–79
   Gülen on, 135, 143–47
   headscarfs to, 154–62
   in Hizmet movement, 153–54
   internalisation by, 166–73
   outcomes for, 140–43
   politics of, 158–62
   role of, 148–64
   segregation of, 164–79
   women's rights and, 135–36, 180–82
Muslims
   apostasy doctrine of, 100–3
   beliefs of, 40–42, 41f, 42f, 160–62
   Christianity to, 115
   culture of, 6–7
   cumulative outcomes for, 140–43
   Eid al Adha for, 48–49
   in Europe, 130, 138–39
   excommunication of, 127–28
   ex-Muslims, 5–6, 103
   feminism to, 138
   fiqh to, 7–8
   generalizability of, 193–95
   humanistic tradition to, 25–34, 63
   Judaism to, 114, 115
   in media, 177–78
   in Middle East, 102–3, 111–12
   in modernity, 13–14, 34–35
   Muslim apologists, 26–27, 29–30
   Muslim sensibility, 25, 34
   non-Muslims and, 87f, 114–17
   practice of, 34–43, 41f, 42f
   Prophetic tradition to, 125–26
   religion of, 3–4
   sensibility of, 183

Muslims (*cont.*)
  social interaction with, 86–89, 87*f*, 88*f*
  Sunni, 196–97
  traditions of, 86–87
  in Turkey, 101–2, 122–27
  in Universal Declaration of Human Rights, 1
  in Western Civilization, 2–3
  women's liberation to, 137
  women's rights to, 139, 142*f*
  youth, 148–49

Nasreen, Tasleema, 137
nationalism, 163–64
Nesin, Aziz, 114–15
Niçin Diyalog (Kurucan), 123–27, 123n.23
Nicolini, Davide
  on explanations, 164
  philosophy of, 43–45, 51, 58
  practice theory of, 24
  on reflexivity, 89
  toolkit from, 8–9, 74–76
Nonaka, Ikujiro, 77–81, 79n.11, 83–84, 96–97, 97n.20
non-human rights practice, 9–10
non-Muslims, 87*f*, 114–17
North Africa, 102–3
Nursi, Said, 13–14, 13n.13, 61, 143–44

OIC. *See* Organization of the Islamic Conference
Öktem, Niyazi, 115
Önal, Ayşe, 116
ontology, 64–65, 71, 196–97
organisational knowledge, 55, 55n.22
organisational studies, 78–81
Organization of the Islamic Conference (OIC), 29–30
orthodoxy, 39–40
othering, 110–11
outcomes. *See specific outcomes*

Pantzar, Mika, 57
Park, Bill, 14–15
patriarchy, 176
Pattison, Stephen, 47–48
Pedersen, Rasmus Brun, 69–70, 71–74, 73*f*, 76

performance, in Christianity, 40–42, 41*f*, 42*f*
Perinçek, Doğu,, 122
persecution, 109
personal beliefs, 160–62
personal knowledge, 77–78
philosophy
  of conciliatorist approach, 30–34
  culture and, 1–3
  in grassroots religious activism, 42–43
  meta-theory and, 71–72
  of Nicolini, 43–45, 51, 58
  of orthodoxy, 39–40
  reasoning in, 18
  of rejectionism, 26–30
  of religion, 4–5
  of uncritical appropriation, 27–30
  of Universal Declaration of Human Rights, 9–10
Polanyi, Michael, 77–78
politics
  in coalition governments, 155, 155n.18
  of Hizmet movement, 148–64, 157*f*
  of humanistic tradition, 1–2
  identity, 2–4, 18–24
  of Islamists, 137
  of Muslim women, 158–62
  of religion, 7–8
  in Turkey, 12, 14, 15, 23–24, 114–17
  of women's rights, 31–32, 138–39
positivist-generalisations, 64–65
Pouliot, Vincent, 71–72, 74
Poyraz, Ergün, 122
practical theology, 47–48, 49–50
practice
  competition in, 192–93, 193*f*
  context for, 50–51
  discontent in, 149–53
  discourse and, 60
  elaboration of, 185–86
  empirical studies of, 38
  encouragement of, 120
  epistemic effects of, 76
  epistemic outcomes of, 64, 67–76, 98, 178
  faith and, 91, 96
  in Hizmet movement, 6, 8–9, 20–21, 56–57, 88, 99, 106*f*, 136, 139, 176–79, 184

informal, 12–13
internalisation through, 188
intervening process of, 74, 77–98
knowledge and, 4–5, 44–53, 85
knowledge production and, 162–64
movement, 53–54, 190–91
multiple, 189–90
mundane, 74–75
of Muslims, 34–43, 41f, 42f
non-human rights, 9–10
operationalising, 64–67
production and, 119–20
process tracing and, 70
in religion, 11–12
single, 189–90
social conformity and, 186
social mechanisms of, 74
social movements and, 53–58
unintended internal epistemic outcomes of, 51–53, 80–81, 121
practice-based context, 163–64
practice-based epistemology, 47, 81–86
practice-based externalisation, 89
practice-based internalisation, 81, 89, 122
practice-based knowledge production, 94, 132–33, 195–96
practice-based ontology, 64–65, 71, 196–97
practice-based outcomes, 73–74
practice theory, 24, 43–62
practitioners, 126–27
pre-emptive outcomes, 178–79
premodern *fiqh*, 16–17, 33–34
pre-reflexive knowledge, 51–52, 77–78
process tracing methodology (PTM)
  causal mechanisms of, 64, 66–67, 69–74, 73f, 75
  knowledge production and, 70–71
  practice and, 70
  scholarship on, 69
  variants of, 70
  zooming with, 74–76, 148–49
processual methodology, 65–66
professional religious associations, 138
Prophetic tradition, 125–26
PTM. *See* process tracing methodology
public interest (*maslahah*), 32–33, 97

qadis (judges), 178
Al Qaida, 27
Qaradawi, Yusuf, 29–30
qiyas (analogical reasoning), 91–92, 92n.15
Qur'an. *See also specific topics*
  Gülen on, 106–10
  hadith and, 37
  ijtihad and, 130
  interpretations of, 86–87
  Islamic literature and, 96
  law in, 100–1
  scholarship on, 61
  Sharia and, 37–38
  Sunna and, 27–28

Ramadan, Tariq, 33
rationality, 45
Rausch, Margaret J., 59
readers, texts and, 34–43
rebellion, 100
reconciliation, 30–34
reflexivity, 19–20, 23–24, 89, 132–33
reform, in Iran, 37
rehberlik (religious mentoring), 12–13, 170
reinterpretation, 40–42, 127–32. *See also ijtihad*
rejectionism, 26–30
religion
  bölgecilik in, 12–13
  categorical rejection of, 27–30
  fiqh and, 32
  hegemony in, 42
  interpretations of, 40–42, 41f, 42f, 60
  knowledge in, 4, 183–84
  leader/follower paradigm in, 62
  legitimacy in, 173
  of Muslims, 3–4
  philosophy of, 4–5
  politics of, 7–8
  popular, 36, 40
  practice in, 11–12
  proper, 36, 40
  rehberlik in, 12–13
  religiosity, 26–27
  religious absolutism, 30
  religious epistemology, 133–34
  religious knowledge, 40, 43, 47, 63

religion (cont.)
    Sunni Hanafi Maturidi orthodoxy, 13–14
    theology, 7
    in Turkey, 5, 106–10, 139
    in Western Civilization, 36
    women's rights in, 31–32
religious mentoring (rehberlik), 170
religious reinterpretation. See ijtihad
religious texts, 34–36
renewer (mujaddid), 92–93
researcher positionality, 18–24
research limitations, 191–92
riddah, 100
rights, 158–59
Risale-i Nur (Nursi), 13–14

Sachedina, Abdulaziz, 35–36, 102
saying, 66–67, 105f, 135–36, 140–43, 142f
Schatzki, Theodore R., 57
Schillinger, Jamie, 35–36
Schwedler, Jillian, 22–24, 38
SECI model. See socialisation, externalisation, combination, internalisation model
secularism, 26–27, 28, 110–11, 120–21, 137
segregation
    bayanlar hizmeti, 166f, 166, 170–72, 181, 184–85, 192
    gender-based, 145–47, 157f, 174–76, 184–85
    Gülen on, 176–79
    of Muslim women, 164–79
Sener, Omer, 117
sequencing, motive and, 119–22
Shabestari, Mohammad Mojtahed, 33, 36n.10
Shah, Niaz, 26
Sharia. See fiqh
Sharia objective (maqasid al-Sharia), 32–33
Shove, Elizabeth, 57
Sleap, Frances, 117
social conformity, 82, 186
social interaction, 86–89, 87f, 88f
socialisation, externalisation, combination, internalisation (SECI) model, 78–81

social learning theory, 54–55
social mechanisms, 74
social movement outcome theory, 76, 79–80
social movements, 53–58
social psychology
    cognitive compromise, 82–84, 86–90, 194–95
    cognitive dissonance, 84–90, 194–95
    of conflict, 188
    emerging dissonance, 122–27
    of externalisation, 176
    of gender-based segregation, 157f
    of internalisation, 78–79
South Asia, 102–3
spiral of knowledge, 79n.11
sub-Saharan Africa, 102–3
Suh, Doowon, 52–53
Sultan, Wafa, 137
Sunna, 27–28, 27n.2
Sunnatullah (divine behavior), 196–97
Sunni Hanafi Maturidi orthodoxy, 13–14, 143
Sunni Muslims, 196–97
symbiotic interplay, 183–97, 187f, 193f

tacit knowledge, 77–84, 89, 95–98
tacit-to-explicit knowledge conversion, 89, 95–98
takfeer (excommunication), 127–28
taqwa (Islamic piety), 143, 144
tasawwuf (Islamic mysticism), 143, 144
Tawheed (Unity of God), 197
Taylor, Charles, 43–44
texts, readers and, 34–43
theft, 100
theology, 7, 37, 47–48, 49–50, 91, 99, 196–97
theoretical expositions, 30–34
theoretical-methodological frameworks, 20–21
thick textual renditions, of mundane practices, 74–75
Tittensor, David, 14–15
türbans. See headscarfs
Turkey
    culture of, 10–11, 15–16, 21
    dershanes in, 149, 149n.14
    education in, 111–13, 154–62

exile from, 127–32
gender-based segregation in, 174–75
in globalisation, 176
government of, 67n.1
Gülen and, 149–50
Iran and, 119–20
Journalists and Writers Foundation in, 116–17
media in, 114, 115
modernity in, 14
Muslims in, 101–2, 122–27
nationalism in, 163–64
politics in, 12, 14, 15, 23–24, 114–17
religion in, 5, 106–10, 139
secularism in, 120–21
United Kingdom and, 19–20

ulama (Islamic scholars), 91, 96–97
Uluengin, Hadi, 115
uncritical appropriation, 27–30
unenforced laws, 50–51
unintended internal epistemic outcomes, 51–53, 80–81, 121
unintentionality, 121, 185
United Kingdom, 19–20, 23–24, 29–30, 117, 175–76
United Nations Universal Declaration of Human Rights, 1, 9–10, 29–30, 31–32
United States, 117, 175–76
Unity of God (*Tawheed*), 197
Universal Declaration of Human Rights, UN, 1, 9–10, 29–30, 31–32
university preparatory centres. See *dershanes*
Ünlü, Ahmet Mahmut, 122
usul al-fiqh (methodology of *fiqh*), 7–8, 32–33, 91–92

Vennesson, Pascal, 69, 74
Verzelloni, Luca, 57
violence, 27
Voll, John O., 14

Wadud, Amina, 138
Watson, Matt, 57
Weller, Paul, 59n.26
Western Civilization
  Christianity in, 33–34
  Coca-Cola in, 17–18, 18n.16, 109–10
  conciliatorist approach in, 34–35
  cultural imperialism by, 122
  education in, 30
  European Union and, 12
  globalisation of, 17–18
  to Gülen, 14
  hegemony of, 29
  Middle East and, 1, 27–28
  Muslims in, 2–3
  religion in, 36
  secularism in, 28
women in Islam. See Muslim women
women's hizmet (*bayanlar hizmeti*), 166, 166f, 170–72, 181, 184–85, 192
women's liberation, 137
women's rights
  bayanlar hizmeti and, 166, 166f, 170–72, 181, 184–85, 192
  doing and, 142f
  gender-based segregation and, 145–47
  to Gülen, 143–47
  headscarfs and, 147
  intervening process and, 153f
  Muslim women and, 135–36, 180–82
  to Muslims, 139, 142f
  politics of, 31–32, 138–39
  sayings and, 142f
  scholarship on, 140
Woodhard, James, 47–48

Yamanlar Koleji (school), 111, 149–50, 151
Yankelovich, Daniel, 118
Yanow, Dvora, 89
yaqeen (certainty), 96–97
Yavuz, M. Hakan, 14, 117, 118
Yilmaz, Ihsan, 60–61

Zigler, Ronald, 96–97, 97n.20
Zijderveld, Anton, 82
zooming, with process tracing, 74–76, 148–49